FORKING SEATTLE

for

TALES OF LOCAL FOOD & DRINK
FROM FARM TO TABLE TO LANDFILL

May the forks be with you!

Ronald

ISBN-10 1537324985
ISBN-13 978-1537324982

Designed by Darlin Gray, Darlin Gray Worldwide

Printed by CreateSpace

Available from Amazon.com and other retail outlets
Also available on Kindle and other devices

Updates online at www.forkingseattle.com

To contact the author directly: inyourglass.com@gmail.com

FORKING SEATTLE

FORKING SEATTLE is more than a book about Seattle restaurants; it's a guide to Washington's sprawling and complex food ecosystem (oceans and streams, farms and vineyards, cafes and restaurants, chefs and bakers.) They all feed Seattle's appetite, and these are their stories.

FORKING SEATTLE stands in the tradition of important books about the city's history (Murray Morgan's Skid Road, *Roger Sale's* Seattle Past to Present, *Knute Berger's* Pugetopolis, *Tim Egan's The Good Rain) and tells the tales, one fork at a time, behind Seattle's evolution as one of America's most inspired food cities.*

Praise for
HOME GROWN SEATTLE

"A romp through Seattle restaurant history. The author anoints heroes, describes memorable and now-gone eateries, and pokes wicked fun at the pretensions of Starbucks CEO Howard Schultz."--Joel Connelly, Seattle Pl.com

FEEDING A MODERN AMERICAN CITY

INTRODUCTION · 7

FROM LAND & SEA · 9
1. Fish from the Sea 11
2. Bivalves 18
3. Fruit of the Land 22

TO MARKET, TO MARKET · 35
4. Hallowed Ground 37
5. Supply Chain 40
6. The Supers 47
7. Farmers Markets 51
8. Corner Delis 53

FOOD ARTISANS · 55
9. Specialty Purveyors 57
10. Big Salamis 67
11. Big Cheeses 70
12. Big Sweeties 75
13. Tinkers 82

LET'S EAT · 87

14. The Big Three 89
15. Big Nights Out 91
16. Today's Big Toques 99
17. Top Indy Chefs 113
18. "Big Pho" 126
19. Pizza, Pizza 138
20. Fish Are Jumping 143
21. The Steaks are High 148
22. Picture Windows 157
23. Excursions 162
24. Forking It Over 168
25. Comic Relief 172
26. Phoning It In 174

I'LL DRINK TO THAT · 177

27. Big Grapes 179
28. Craft Beer 197
29. The Spirit World 204
30. Coffee & Tea 213
31. It's the Waters 222
32. Mother's Milk 224

CLEARING THE TABLE · 225

33. Deliverance 227
34. Graveyard 232

FEEDING BACK · 235

35. The Big Picture 237
36. Will Write for Food 243
37. Stroke My Keyboard 255
38. Show & Tell 260
39. Applause Lines 266
40. Pitchforks 273

CONCLUSION · 283

Index 284
Credits 292
About the Author 293

INTRODUCTION

What makes a city great? Specifically, what made the city of Seattle great? It started, we admit, as a fishing village on an obscure body of water on the Northwest coast of the American continent. To the north, Vancouver, British Columbia, became the Canadian equivalent of San Francisco and Los Angeles, attracting wealthy refugees from the far-flung British empire, and Hollywood film makers who cherished the long daylight of summer evenings. To the immediate south, Tacoma was supposed to be the City of Destiny, western terminus of the great Transcontinental Railroad; alas, it collapsed in bankruptcy and Seattle –marginally closer to Alaska–took over as the jumping-off point once gold was discovered in the Yukon. Side note: the potatoes grown in the Yakima Valley were so enormous that they eventually became a prized feature of the Northern Pacific's dining cars.

It's almost always some geographic accident that supports a settlement, encouraging economic development, and, eventually a concentrated population. Then the logistics. To feed a community of several million, a modern city needs ready access to great food. Natural products that provide more than mere sustenance will inspire creative cooks and, in turn, attract adventurous eaters. The upward spiral is self-reinforcing.

It takes a colossal ecosystem–the agricultural and social equivalent of a permanent military-industrial complex–to feed a city. The numbers are staggering: a supply chain that can generate and distribute billions of meals a year to all corners of an urban area. To do it sustainably with locally sourced ingredients (and not just trucked-in boxes of processed industrial sludge), you need nearby oceans and streams; fields and farms, forests and vineyards; a network of processors, distributors and markets; platoons of skilled professionals to cook and serve the ravenous denizens who turn up daily with their appetites and their forks.

Such a system doesn't come about by chance. The process in Seattle was sometimes messy and non-linear. It took vision and determination, creativity and foresight. It took people willing to risk everything and steer their lives toward an unknown shore; it took people who dug in the dirt to plant gardens, or dug in the sand to harvest oysters from tidewater beaches. It took longtime ranchers sending grass-land cattle to market, first-generation foragers plucking mushrooms from the forest floor, recent immigrants serving organ meats, scientists testing experimental seeds. It took artists and butchers, dreamers and bankers.

One could be tempted to equate Western Washington's natural bounty and economic vitality with moral superiority. That would be a mistake. There is more to Seattle than meets the eye; for many, today's prosperity is built on years of struggle.

This book celebrates the enterprise of those whose talents contribute to the region's vigor: fishers, farmers, and ranchers; grape growers and wine makers; chefs, line cooks, and bakers; servers and dishwashers; foragers and purveyors, indeed all whose products and efforts feed the souls of those who call Seattle home.

Here then are their stories, organized in seven broad categories:

- **FROM SEA & LAND**: Farms, fields, forests, lakes, streams, oceans, fish
- **TO MARKET, TO MARKET!**: How our food reaches us
- **FOOD ARTISANS**: Specialty purveyors, bakers, cheeses, chocolates
- **LET'S EAT !**: Chain restaurants, indy restaurants, great views, great pizza.
- **I'LL DRINK TO THAT**: Coffee, tea, beer, wine, spirits, waters
- **CLEARING THE TABLE**: Getting rid of the waste
- **FEEDING BACK**: Consultants, pundits, food community websites

Let's be clear: *Forking Seattle* is not a guidebook to the hundreds, nay thousands, of restaurants in the metropolitan area.

Instead, it's a historical handbook, a reference, a who's who. Used to be, a reviewer (restaurants, books, theater) was someone who'd been around long enough to know where the bodies were buried, who'd been fired by whom, who'd slept with whom. In an age of smart phones, the notion of institutional memory has been discarded in favor of the latest tweet. In fact, in the age of Daily Deals and "What's Trending (Hot) Right Now," an encyclopedic knowledge of local history is actually a burden. Fresh young faces prowling for a place to eat (and untethered from a houseful of kiddies) rely on the spontaneous, untrained, and unedited voices of fellow foodies (rather than food journalists) to tell them the who-what-where-when-why and how of what's for dinner.

Nationally, the story is Big Food (Big Pharma); here the story is the artisanal trifecta of Farms (vegetables, meat, cheese), Fish (and not just salmon and sushi) and Pho (Vietnamese beef noodle soup, the leading dish in Seattle's Asian food firmament). Our preference in Seattle is for slow and steady over fast and flashy. Oyster-farming doesn't lend itself to Big Bivalve; you have to shuck them one by one. Grapes may be grown by the acre, harvested by the ton, fermented by the gallon, and sold by the case, but wine is still consumed one glass and one bottle at a time

Nor is *Forking Seattle* a substitute for Yelp: no inflated praise, no false accusations, no blatant misinformation, no petulance over water glasses not refilled or gluten not removed. You want Yelp, go read Yelp. Or Twitter or Facebook or Eater. You want daily dispatches, weekly updates, or monthly summaries of what to order in which trendy establishment, they're just a click or two away.

What you'll find in these pages is the road map: the tales that explain how we got here, and the story of where we're going.

From Sea & Land

Where Our Food Comes From

Chapter 1 · FISH FROM THE SEA

We're surrounded in Seattle by the saltwater of Puget Sound, with pockets of fresh water lakes and steams punctuating the land, all inhabited by edible aquatic creatures. Some thousand miles further along the Pacific Coast, the waters of Alaska provide a home to millions of King salmon and tons of King crab, most of which passes through Seattle en route to their final markets.

SALMON Poached or Grilled, Always Sainted

The concept of Redemption by Salmon is central to our civic religion, our Northwest Faith. We celebrate the Salmon: it dies for us, we eat it and are saved. In gratitude, we expend a fair measure of our riches to assure its immortality. In the wild, salmon are carnivores. Unlike, say, vegetarian cattle, they eat smaller fish on the road to our dinner plate. So here's the conundrum: should we buy a fish that's literally eating up the ocean's resources? What's the alternative? Farmed fish raised on an inexhaustible supply of soy pellets, a burger from a feedlot steer, an industrial chicken?

We Americans are a devout lot. We remember our nation's dead in May, venerate fireworks in July, celebrate the arrival of a boatload of European settlers in November. What we don't honor, strangely, is the first demonstration of nature's annual generosity: the salmon run. Helpless mankind, sacrificial fish. They've taken care of us for centuries, now it's our turn to take care of them.

JON ROWLEY Seafood Guru

In addition to being our go-to guy for peaches, Jon Rowley is Seattle's seafood guru, the man who brought us Copper River salmon and Puget Sound oysters. He may not be a household name, but he's known to fishermen, farmers, chefs and food writers across the country. Without Rowley, a Reed College dropout who spent a decade fishing in Alaska, Seattle wouldn't know what a fresh oyster even tastes like.

The least ostentatious of Seattle's food stars, Rowley is probably the most influential. He's the oyster guru, the peach guru, and above all the salmon guru. No one in town has done more to change the way we eat, or the way our farmers and fishers think about the food they grow or catch. The writer Georgia Pellegrini (no relation to Angelo Pellegrini, p.23) calls him a "Food Hero." *Saveur* put his name on its "Top 100" list, most of which were foods, not people. His 500-word biographical sketch is titled Disciple of Flavor. "We admire the passion that's sustained him in his pursuits, which, in hindsight, more closely resemble a quest than a career."

There's much more about Rowley in our entries about oysters (just ahead) and peaches.

PAUL GREENBERG Big Salmon, Little Artemia

Paul Greenberg began his career teaching journalism in post-Soviet Russia, a country that had no tradition of a free press. When he returned to the US and began researching and writing in earnest, he did a piece for the Boston *Globe* about fish, which led to another piece for the New York *Times*, which earned an award from the International Association of Culinary Professionals. Then a book that challenged the way we consume the ocean's resources, "Four Fish: the Future of the Last Wild Food."

The four are salmon, cod, bass, and tuna. All pretty big, as fish go. And they dominate the American fish market.

"Imagine hunting big wild animals," he postulates, tracking them down across field and through forest to kill and eat them. How long did the continent's herds of wild buffalo last? Turkeys?

We stupidly squander resources, as if eating sirloin strip were a birthright. Yet we're squeamish about songbirds, and each generation has a different notion of what "nature's bounty" means. Big fish, like the bluefin tuna, for instance, are disappearing.

Are we, is the planet, running out of fish? Hardly. The annual catch is on the order of 90 million tons, the human weight of China. (Is that a lot? Yeah.) But the abundance is decreasing, not increasing.

Which brings us to the conundrum. Tuna and salmon are the more fashionable red or pink fish; cod, tilapia and pollock are white. But farmed Atlantic salmon--our most "domesticated" seafood--is white. To make it marketable, growers literally add color. (Many species of white fish are also farmed these days; branzino, loup de mer, sea bass, daurade, sea bream, orata.) Israel has been in the vanguard, farming fully half its fish since the 1950s. And why should farming be all that bad? We farm game, don't we?

Fine, we'll farm fish, but how do we feed them? What will the live bass eat? The answer (drumroll, please) is *artemia*, a teensy organism that grows only in (wait for it) the Great Salt Lake. You remember those comic book ads for Sea Monkeys? Yup, *artemia.*

Greenberg's personal favorite: arctic char. They look like trout or salmon, sleek and silvery with pink flesh. They survive in crowded conditions; in the wild, they feed on abundant shrimp and krill; in closed systems, they simply squeeze together.

PAUL ALLEN Smart Catch

Does your house cat like fish? The average American kitty *loves* fish. Thirty pounds a year, in fact. Twice as much as *you* eat, if you're an average consumer. Fish they catch off the coast of Thailand. (Sadly, the men who work those boats, whose job it is to feed your Fluffy, labor in conditions far worse than medieval servitude.) It's not that Americans don't like fish, don't go fishing, don't catch fish and don't eat fish. They do, but that last part, *eating* fish, they do most of that in restaurants. And restaurants serve mainly four fish: tuna, salmon, bass, and cod. Four fish whose popularity puts their very survival at risk.

All pretty big, as fish go. And they dominate the American fish market.

We humans have developed a preference for big animals (cows, pigs). American humans, at least, prefer beef to bunnies, even though rabbits, easy to raise and a fine source of protein, are devoured by families across the globe.

Paul Greenberg's book, "Four Fish" (previous entry) called attention to this paradox; he recommends eating smaller species like herring, mackerel and butterfish. Restaurant chefs might think they can't sell "trash" fish, but now there's a new impetus to change the Americans consume the world's resources of shellfish and fin-fish by appealing to the chefs themselves.

Paul Allen, the Seattle mogul who co-founded Microsoft, who owns the Seahawks, and whose real estate company, Vulcan, has developed South Lake Union, has a keen interest in environmental stewardship, specifically sustainable seafood. Vulcan's philanthropic arm even created a program called Smart Catch to encourage restaurants to serve more sustainable seafood.

Not a question of large of small, wild or farmed so much as pinpointing species that can maintain or increase production without jeopardizing the health of the marine ecosystem. The Monterey Bay Aquarium has been in the forefront of this effort for some time with a campaign to raise consumer awareness of endangered species through its Seafood Watch recommendations (avoid farmed Atlantic salmon and bluefin tuna, for example, in favor of arctic char or Pacific albacore).

Yet it's not always clear, from a restaurant menu, where that dish of "seared tuna" comes from, and it's not always a sure thing that the server or even the chef know, either. Hence the Smart Catch program, which was designed to train chefs and restaurant staffs. Decals at the door and symbols on the menu will alert consumers to restaurants and specific dishes that meet the Smart Catch goals.

Allen's group signed up some heavyweight chefs prior to launching. Along with several dozen other high-profile restaurants, both the Tom Douglas and Ethan Stowell restaurant groups went through through the certification process.

Says Stowell: "We see Smart Catch as a great opportunity to keep diners engaged, simplify their decisions around seafood, and recognize restaurants that are leading the way in supporting environmentally responsible fisheries."

"Since the launch of SmartCatch last year, we have more than 80 Seattle restaurants participating and making a difference in the sustainability supply chain," the PR people write. "More importantly, we are working on a great plan to make expand the program both in Seattle and elsewhere that will create an even greater positive impact."

BRUCE GORE LongLine Fisherman

Like so many things we take for granted today, it wasn't obvious at first sight. But the notion of "long line" fishing combined with at-sea bleeding and freezing the fish you catch on those long lines, well, no one had ever done that until Bruce Gore came along. Fishermen have long sought out salmon for their taste as well as their appearance, but salmon and tuna both used to reach American supermarkets and dinner tables in cans. (There's a terrific cannery museum in Richmond, BC, that shows the process.) The best *fresh* salmon was flown directly to restaurants in Chicago and New York.

Then, after Bruce Gore developed his process and began licensing it to the owners of fishing boats, you could buy frozen-at-sea salmon that was even better than a lot of the bruised and aging fish you'd find at the store.

Gore was all of eight years old when he hooked his first big one, a 44-pounder on the Columbia. He grew up in Longview, spent summers on purse seiners in Alaska, bought his own boat, but never lost sight of the essential nobility of the salmon. "They need to be treated with reverence," was his motto.

Back on land. Gore took his long-line, frozen-at-sea salmon to Ray's Boathouse. It was 1978, and most people in the restaurant business thought of frozen food as inferior. But Wayne Ludvigsen (Ray's chef) and Jon Rowley (the seafood consultant) understood the quality of the product that Gore was bringing in. Before long, the rest of the city did, too.

As it turns out, the frozen-at-sea fishery has been a remarkable boon to the entire run of Alaska salmon. When Gore started, the state was harvesting 20 million fish a year. Today, the number is well over 200 million, and, says Gore, "that's on a sustainable basis. It's a huge success story." Gore's business has gone from one boat to 30, and his fish is sold (via Triad Fisheries) on three continents: North America for the traditional fish in the round, Japan for sashimi, and Scotland for smoked salmon.

MOVE OVER COPPER, THERE'S A NEW FISH IN TOWN

 Better believe it, the 25-year reign of the Copper River salmon is over. The new king comes from the mighty Yukon River, and the architect of its ascendancy is (no real surprise) the same power-behind-the-throne, Jon Rowley.

Nothing personal, Copper, we want you to know. You've had a remarkable run, leading Seattle diners into new realms of taste. But the new guy, well, he's everything you were (and still are) only more so.

Technically, the more intense flavor comes from additional fat: up to 50 percent more of those nutritious Omega 3 oils. The Yukon River is 2,000 miles long and the salmon have to swim for up to two months without eating before they reach their spawning grounds. (The Copper is much shorter, though more rugged.)

Until last year, most Yukons were frozen and shipped to Japan; very few fresh fish ever made it out of Alaska. It's a long, tough slog from the village of Emmonak, pop. 767, so remote that a dozen eggs cost $5.50 past-pull-date milk is $10 a gallon, and an airplane ticket to Anchorage, 1,000 miles across the tundra, is $800. What's made the difference in this remote location is a five-year-old cooperative established by the local Yup'ik Eskimo community called Kwikpak Fisheries, which hooked up with Rowley to work out logistics and marketing. The season is a short one, maybe three weeks, 30,000 to 60,000 fish max.

Down on the Copper, the fishery is sophisticated: big boats with communications gear and power winches to reel in the gill nets. The mouth of the Yukon is broader and shallower, so boats are open skiffs; it's not unusual to find an entire family aboard to haul the nets in by hand. The natives have been fishing like this for the past 10,000 years.

What's different for the Yukon fishery these days is simple: ice. Kwikpak, buying only from boats that keep their catch iced, ships them by bush plane to Anchorage, then by regular airfreight to Seattle.

Rowley reminds us that the oilier the fish, the denser the flesh, and the more important to cook it properly. No rare, pink-in-the-middle preparation here; it needs to reach an internal temp of 115 degrees. A bit of salt is all it needs for seasoning. Sear it quickly, then let it absorb the heat of a 250-275-degree oven for ten minutes or so. It will ooze that nutritious Omega 3 oil all over the plate, spreading its rich, deep flavors to a few simply grilled summer vegetables.

The fish will taste like velvet.

KETA SALMON Don't Get No Respect

They've been out there for three to six years, those poor fish. Undervalued, underused, under-appreciated, and misnamed to boot. Once known as "chum," they really are underdogs. And by the time they make it to market, they're the last salmon run of the season. In fact, the keta are also the last intact, sustainable salmon run left in Puget Sound, according to their champion, John Foss of Eelgrassroots, a PR firm. Says Foss: "Our local fishing fleets are out daily working to bring these beautiful fish to market, and put some dollars in their pockets after a tough season fishing up north in Alaska."

Foss calls the keta the zeitgeist salmon of our tough economic times. Mild of flavor, a great friend of all sauces, and a smokers dream. And affordable. Keta retail for $8 or less for filets. Tens and tens of thousands of pounds are getting shipped out weekly to the Midwest and East Coast, but relatively few keta are consumed in locally. More's the pity. The cool smoke of a backyard barbecue is ideal to preserve its high Omega 3 content.

SKUNA BAY Happy Salmon From Happy Farms

Seattle, we may have a problem. The fish that defines us, the fish to whom many of us owe our lives and that most of us worship as a deity, the wild-caught Alaska King Salmon, turns out, may not be a unique, invulnerable resource after all.

Vulnerable to environmental vagaries, vulnerable to spontaneous genetic mutations, vulnerable to human predation: the sought-after Alaska King may also be vulnerable to near-perfect impostors. Still of noble birth, to be sure, but no longer wild-caught.

Ironic, isn't it? In order to save and protect the Alaska King, we're being offered a near-perfect, "craft-raised" replica. Still the same fish, but no longer wild. Not quite "farm-raised" in the sense of pen-raised Atlantic salmon fed chicken meal laced with Red Dye No. 2, harvested at two pounds because they've too expensive to feed any longer.

No, these fish are raised by artisan farmers in the icy waters off Vancouver Island, happy fish swimming in the mineral-rich estuary of Gold River, well-fed and raised for over three years, until they weigh ten pounds. The "farmers" live on houseboats surrounded by penned fish (8 days on, 6 days off), and scoop out the fish to order. They're transported to Quadra Island, where another artisan family guts and grades the salmon and packs them in recyclable shipping containers (no styrofoam! no ice!) before sending them off, by truck (eaiser to control the "cold chain," no airplanes!) to customers across the US Mainland.

Skuna Bay, the enterprise behind this painstaking methodology, is a subsidiary of a vast Norwegian holding company, Grieg Seafood, that operates around the world, harvesting some 80,000 tons of seafood a year. The operation in British Columbia is small part of that, but an important one, since it's also a model for the future of sustainable salmon farming.

Skuna Bay employs some 90 people on Vancouver Island and ships two million pounds of Kings to 35 states. In Washington, the company distributes through Ocean Beauty Seafood (itself an enormous outfit that's half-owned by the Bristol Bay Economic Development Corp.). Ocean Beauty doesn't publish its wholesale price list, but folks in the know say the Skuna Bay product is in the $12 per pound range, which means it's going to be a $40 item on the menu, right up there with halibut.

Their first restaurant customer was none other than John Howie, hardly a man to compromise quality. "Skuna Bay salmon takes pressure off wild stocks, and deserves a place on our menu," he says. "We love the fish." If it's not on the menu this month, it's because there's wild salmon available.

SIDEBAR: Salmon in the Trees

Amy Gulick is a nationally known conservation writer and nature photographer who lives in the Cascade foothills but journeys far to capture astonishing images. Her most recent book, "Salmon in the Trees: Life in Alaska's Tongass Rain Forest," shows millions of wild fish under the dense canopy of an unimaginably lush wilderness. As the salmon spawn and die, they feed a steady parade of wildlife (bears, wolves) and, as the fish decompose, their bodies are absorbed by the vegetation. Hence the notion that the salmon really are "in the trees."

SIDEBAR: Saving Sharks

One more Paul Allen initiative is worth mentioning in this context: he wants to save sharks. Yes, sharks, the most feared predators of the ocean. Movies like "Jaws" aside, sharks pose considerably less danger to humans (10 victims a year) than jellyfish (100), water buffalo (200), lions (200), hippos (300), elephants (500), crocs (2,000), scorpions (5,000), snakes (50,000), and mosquitoes (500,000). But hunting sharks (for sport, for their fins, for their skin) creates havoc with life the ocean. As a top-level predator, sharks are needed to maintain a balanced marine ecosystem; the research funded by Allen, under the umbrella of a nonprofit called FinPrint.org, is sending teams of scientists into the water to gather more data.

Chapter 2 · THE BIVALVES

Oysters–beloved by some, avoided by others–have been consumed by humans for millennia. In the 19th century, the oyster beds of New York harbor were the largest on the planet. Puget Sound is home to some of the world's best oyster beds, thanks to cold, clean water and nutrient-rich runoff from the Cascades and the Olympics. Originally scorned as simple food for working-class people, they are considered sophisticated delicacies today.

BILL TAYLOR Oysterman

Among Seattle's quirky notes of here-and-only-here culinary expertise (shade-grown coffee, artisanal breweries, craft cocktails, Copper River salmon, and so on), one could argue that none is more local than the humble oyster.

In 1895, meeting in the new state capital of Olympia, the Washington State Legislature reaffirmed a unique provision of state law that had been enacted by the Territorial Legislature. Known as the Bush and Callow Land Acts, it allowed private parties to lease coastal tidelands for commercial purposes. Bush-Callow upheld the validity and value of private investment – even on public land– in cultivating and propagating clams and other shellfish. The argument was that shellfish farming should enjoy the same status as "other agricultural activities, programs, and development within the state."

Thus was born Washington's $150-million shellfish industry. (In Oregon, on the other hand, all tidelands have always been considered public, with no commercial use allowed. In second place for shellfish production comes Virginia, followed by Connecticut.) Bush-Callow and various follow-up legislation ensured that shellfish cultivation and aquaculture became protected activities on nearly 50,000 acres of tidelands, which the state leases out at rates from $100 to $2,000 depending on location and harvest.

One company in particular has grown exponentially, not just because of land it owned, but because of the other tidelands that it leased. Taylor Shellfish, with 650 employees, annual sales of $75 million, and operations around the world, is the biggest American provider of bivalves. The company farms 11,000 acres of Puget Sound and coastal tidelands for oysters, mussels, clams and geoduck. It sells oysters and clams to restaurants across the country. For many years it also sponsored a West Coast Oyster Wine Competition. It currently operates three retail outlets in Seattle (on Capitol Hill,

Lower Queen Anne, and Pioneer Square) and has plans for at least one more outlet.

Bill Taylor is the fifth generation of his family to head the company, and he takes his stewardship seriously. His company produces 50 million half-shell oysters and four million pounds of clams a year, among other shellfish. And 700,000 pounds of geoduck, a very high-value crop.

BILL DEWEY Ghost Shrimp

Bill Dewey runs his own clam farm near Shelton, but it's as Public Affairs director for Taylor Shellfish that his name is most often in the news. So when the company announced in May, 2015, that it would spray its Willapa Bay oyster beds with a pesticide called imidacloprid to control an infestation of burrowing shrimp in the intertidal sands, it had the blessing of the Department of Ecology (which had banned the previous treatment, with carbaryl). But Taylor did not reckon on the public outrage its decision would unleash.

Imidacloprid is an insecticide widely used in land-based agriculture (you can buy it at the hardware store), but it's not recommended for aquaculture. It's a neurotoxin with a warning right on the label that it shouldn't be applied directly to water. The U.S. Fish & Wildlife Service and the National Oceanic & Atmospheric Administration have also warned about unintended consequences.

Taylor argued that the state's scientists, along with the Environmental Protection Agency, supported his company's efforts, which he claimed were necessary in order to save Willapa Bay's shellfish beds. But the public protests were too loud. After several days of social media outrage, Taylor decided to abandon the spraying idea. "We have chosen to respect the concerns of our customers," according to a company statement.

Still, the decision was not an easy one. It "weighs heavily on us knowing it will affect other growers in Willapa Bay and Grays Harbor," Taylor said. "Without an effective control for burrowing shrimp, many multi-generational family businesses may not survive."

This year the smaller growers on Willapa Bay submitted a new proposal, promising to apply the pesticide directly to the infested zones rather than attempt a program of aerial spraying. Whether the safeguards are adequate is still to be determined.

JON ROWLEY (Again) Oysters and Hemingway

The same Jon Rowley we met in the previous chapter as the champion of Copper and Yukon River salmon, and in the next chapter as the guru of sweet, juicy peaches, is also the guiding spirit of Seattle's love for oysters. Through regular travels to Paris, he had become a huge fan of bivalves on the half shell. His epiphany came when he discovered this passage by Ernest Hemingway: "As I ate the oysters with their strong taste of the sea and their faint metallic taste that the cold white wine washed away, leaving only the sea taste and the succulent texture, and as I drank their cold liquid  from each shell and washed it down with the crisp taste of the wine, I lost the empty feeling and began to be happy and to make plans." In 1983, the same year that he brought the first Copper River kings to Seattle, Rowley also introduced Olympia oysters on the half shell to a gathering of journalists at Ray's Boathouse. Re-introduced them, to be specific, since they had all but died out, and no restaurant save Canlis was serving live oysters on the half shell.

The quest is never-ending. "Rowley is acutely curious about what makes a particular food taste good. Environmental factors are crucial, he's discovered: whether it's the unique blend of local algae and minerals that allows the Virginica oysters of Totten Inlet, in Washington's Puget Sound, to grow incomparably plump and sweet." wrote *Saveur*.

Soon, on assignment for Taylor Shellfish, Rowley began organizing the West Coast Oyster Wine championships. (His Twitter handle is @oysterwine.) Refreshing white wines with bracing acidity and full flavor, sauvignon blanc and pinot gris, occasionally a chenin blanc; rarely a chardonnay. The concept of "oyster wine" is now part of our local restaurant vocabulary. Alas, Taylor no longer sponsors the event, and doesn't mention the concept of oyster wines at its three retail outlets. Pity.

BILL WHITBECK Oysters for Your Table

How can you not love this guy? Ruddy, bearded, jovial, with an insatiable appetite for bivalves, "Oyster Bill" Whitbeck is the brand ambassador for Taylor Shellfish Farms, and the company's most recognizable presence at oyster events across the region. Trained as a photo-journalist, he's also a musician (drums) who has performed at Carnegie Hall; he made the acquaintance of oysters while operating a photography studio in what turned out to be an old oyster house on Long Island Sound. He's also a licensed lobster boat captain.

Selling oysters wasn't Whitbeck's first line of work, but, after he rode his motorcycle across the country from Connecticut and resettled himself on the west coast, he hooked up with the Taylor family.

For several years he ran the farmers market program for Taylor Shellfish, then moved to the restaurant side of the business. He found time to write a book, in 2001, titled, what else? "The Joy Of Oysters," co-authored with Lori McKean. The subtitle is "A cookbook and guidebook for shucking, slurping, and savoring nature's most perfect food."

In an business filled with show-offs and self-promoters, Whitbeck's modesty and good humor are refreshing. But there's another image of Oyster Bill that will stay with you for a good while. Picture this: in his days as a young musician, he played drums in the on-stage band for a season of summer stock in Stamford, Conn. The show was *Cabaret*, where, in the words of the leering Emcee, "All ze girls are beautiful. Even ze orchestra is beautiful." And one of the "women" in the orchestra was long-haired Oyster Bill, playing a woman (padded chest, beard made up to look fake) pretending to be a man, banging away on his drum kit. Shades of *Victor Victoria!* But then, oysters are hermaphrodites, right?

Chapter 3 · FRUIT OF THE LAND

The notion that city-dwellers might, could, nay should grow at least some of their own food seems counter-intuitive. After all, people who live in cities might putter in the garden but they don't farm. Gardening is a pleasant pastime that lets you pick a few flowers or a couple of tomatoes from time to time, but farming is altogether different. Farming is work. Hard, sweaty, often unrewarding work. We live in cities, don't we, so that we can avoid farming. Farming is something other people do, in other parts of the country and faraway parts of the world. Turns out that's the wrong thinking.

URBAN FARMING Feeding a Modern American City

Consider that something like 40 million acres of land in the US–an area the size of Washington State–is devoted to lawns, to grass surrounding private homes, to golf courses, to parks and playfields. We owe our agriculture, it's said, to six inches of topsoil and regular rainfall.) Yet even with encroaching development (housing, roads, shopping centers, offices), there are still 1,800 farms in King County, covering 50,000 acres in Seattle's home county alone. Many are close-in: Vashon Island, the Kent Valley, and along the Green, Snoqualmie and Sammamish rivers. It was 25 years ago that county voters authorized a Farmland Preservation Program that currently protects 13,000 acres of dairies, cattle and horse farms, row crops, flowers, even Christmas trees nurseries.

Lest we feel smug (or threatened) about the proximity of barns and fields, we should note that there are over *four dozen farms within the city limits* of our neighbor to the north, Victoria suburb Richmond, BC. Richmond--one third Seattle's size in terms of population, roughly similar density--devotes a third of a magnificent, 100-acre city park, Terra Nova, to urban agriculture. The city employs environmental educators and restaurant chefs to teach schoolchildren the virtues of growing food. "Those aren't weeds," the park director told a group of grade-schoolers harvesting edible wild greens, "just another form of money."

And there is a beacon of hope on Seattle's Beacon Hill: a new, seven-acre **FOOD FOREST**, which operates under the umbrella of the Department of Neighborhoods P-Patch program. The same planners had earlier led efforts to establish the Seattle Tilth garden at the Good Shepard Center. Only a cynic would point out that the average neighborhood supermarket covers an acre or more under a single roof; back-to-the-land in South Seattle seems more like back-to-the-parking lot.

ANGELO PELLEGRINI Grow Your Own

© Bob Peterson

We continue our stories of local food & drink with the tale of an immigrant, a peasant boy from Italy who ended up making Seattle his home. You know Angelo Pellegrini's name because he's the author of *The Unprejudiced Palate, Lean Years, Happy Years,* and *The Food-Lover's Garden;* he is noting less than the spiritual godfather of Seattle food as we know it today.

A Professor of Classics at the UW, Pellegrini was devoted to the pleasures of a convivial table. But you would not have imagined this career for him had you met him in his boyhood home in rural Tuscany, where he and a gaggle of farmyard urchins would gather up roadside cow pies and sell them for fuel to earn a few coins. He followed his family to western Washington, where his father had found work in Grays Harbor County, then put himself through school. It's hardly the boyhood one expects for a revered professor of literature at the University of Washington, an astonishing story of intellectual achievement in the face of incredible odds. (A cow pie is a terrible thing to waste.)

By the time Angelo Pellegrini died, in 1991, at the age of 88, his books–his life, in fact–had inspired a generation of foodies. Not just in his adopted home of Seattle, but throughout the entire country. Though many of his books (except for *The Unprejudiced Palate*) are now out of print, we remember Pellegrini as the sage of Seattle's culinary revolution in the 1960s, the subject of an admiring profile in the *New York Times* in 1989, and blurbs from colleagues like "A rare intelligence about food."

"As an immigrant," Pellegrini writes, "the discovery of *abundance* has been the most palpable and impressive of my discoveries in America." And he is made furious by the wasteful ways of his new-found countrymen: "the consequences of having used with reckless imprudence the precious yield of the good earth."

Remember, in the first half of the 20th century, southern Europe was racked by unimaginable poverty. Millions fled toward land they hoped could feed them; those left behind boiled and ate whatever they could find. We cannot imagine today the level of deprivation they faced, so we celebrate, instead, the bounty they helped create. Pellegrini's own words describe his efforts to become a regular American kid (he misspells "sizzers" and finishes second in a spelling bee); he plants a garden; his prejudices evolve: he's fond of the cornmeal staple of northern Italy, polenta, but disdains the salted sardines of the south.

"Grow your own, cook your own, make your own wine," he implores his readers. "You must build a garden." he mandates, "with a pick and shovel, dig up a portion of your lawn." In growing your own food, "there will be joy in the harvest, and the greatest pleasure in eating the fruit of your labor."

Mario Batali writes, "*The Unprejudiced Palate* is about nourishing the soul with the food we eat." Alice Waters admires "his unwavering vision of how to live a beautiful and delicious life." We really should remember Pellegrini every time we say grace.

KURT TIMMERMEISTER Kurtwood Farms

On Vashon Island we have the embodiment of the genuine, back-to-the-land movement, a man named Kurt Timmermeister. A restaurant owner in Belltown and Capitol Hill (Café Septième) who bought a few acres on the island two decades ago, Timmermeister became a farmer and cheese maker incrementally. His book-length accounts of the process (*Growing a Farmer* and *Growing a Feast*) give helpful advice ("don't go into debt") without sugarcoating the hard work, from morning chores to evening chores.

One of his role models was a 95-year-old dairyman who had spent the first half of his life a practicing accountant. He admired the people he met at farmers markets: youthful if not young, healthy, happy. "I wanted to be like them." So he sold the restaurant and became a farmer.

Craigslist was a huge help (for used tractor parts, for baby pig "weaners"). Two-day-old chicks came in a box, by mail. When it was time for the chickens to be dispatched, the wings got fed to the pigs, "smart, attentive, aggressive, stubborn and charming." Before Timmermeister brought himself to the painful business of killing a pig, he took his reader through the agony and the joy of buying a gun. The dairy especially prospered, and Kurtwood Farm, as it's now known, began to produce a highly regarded, creamy cows milk cheese called Dinah's.

Timmermeister used to open his kitchen table to a dozen visitors for weekly farmhouse dinners, a multi-course feast produced almost entirely from his own land (less so, lately, especially as production of Dinah's cheese has taken off). "I want there to be more small farms, more ways to connect to our food, more links to our cultural past of food raising, preparation and preservation," he writes. So, back to the garden!

Now he has Kurt Farm Shop on Capitol Hill's Chophouse Row, selling Dinah's cheese, curds, and farmstead ice cream. A happy man indeed.

DAVID BURGER Stewardship Partners

Let's say you happen to own a stand of trees a few miles east of Seattle, or some farmland in suburban King County. Do you sell it to a developer? Do you rent it out to a farmer? David Butler wants to talk to you. He's the executive director of Stewardship Partners, a local non-profit that helps landowners preserve the environment, and he has a fervent message about sustainability, about the importance of connections between urban chefs and suburban farmers. About keeping beef cattle (and their contaminated feces) out  of the streams and forests. About the paramount importance of preserving forest habitat and biodiversity.

There's a good reason that the urbanized western part of Washington State is so fertile. The cool hillside forests and moist valleys are so valuable because of their rivers and streams, the Snoqualmie and Skagit especially. Those lazy, crazy ribbons of snow-pack runoff carrying mountain minerals down to the valley? Nope. It's because of salmon going upstream. Salmon runs provide the region's built-in, natural fertilizer. Their carcasses, dense with nutrients, are carried into the woods by bears and eagles; the entire forest ecosystem is built on on this interdependence of wildlife and salmon.

Dangers! Erosion and silt can easily wash into streams, covering the pebbles where salmon eggs hatch; runoff from fields treated with chemicals gets into the gravel and decreases the survival of hatchlings. Without trees to shade riverbanks, the water temperature rises, further threatening both juvenile and adult salmon.

So agriculture can be the scourge of local rivers, but it can also be their salvation. Salmon-Safe, an Oregon non-profit, has been working with farmers for two decades now and offers a certificate of compliance with best practices; Stewardship Partners administers the program in Washington.

JEFF MILLER Easy Rider

In 1985 a 23-year-old Pittsburgh city kid named Jeff Miller, a CIA-trained chef and veteran of Jeremiah Tower's Stars in San Francisco, strapped on a backpack filled with seeds (seeds!), climbed on his Honda Hurricane 600, and headed from the Bay Area to Washington State. He'd never farmed, but he found land to rent near Monroe. Backbreaking work, 90 hours a week, but by 1997, he'd done well enough to buy a farm of his own, which he named Willie Green's Organic Farm, Willie being his middle name.

He started selling organic produce to farmers markets in Seattle, to a network of 100 CSAs, to produce wholesalers like Charlie's and Rosella's, to Whole Foods. When he bought the property, it was nothing but grass. Today, he's growing 60 to 70 different vegetables, pays a big staff: 30 field hands to work the 60-plus acres, half a dozen people to work eight markets, plus admin, marketing, social media updates.

Now the next step. The Fields at Willie Greens, turning about 10 newly manicured acres into an event venue for weddings and the like. The flip side of farm-to-table, if you will, bringing people from the city out to learn about organic farming, people who've never been on a farm. You can get here on freeways and divided ribbons of asphalt, or you can take the back roads, over Novelty Hill and along the Snohomish River, past stately barns and horses grazing in fields of clover, Mt. Pilchuck to the north, Rainier to the south. Ironically, the meandering scenic route is faster.

FULL CIRCLE FARMS

Full Circle is more than just another CSA; it's a delivery service for organic, artisan grocery items. It has more than 15,000 subscribers, who get boxes of farm-fresh goodies every week. Full Circle started, as so many of these ventures do, in casual conversations among college friends. The business was originally called Earthworm, based out of a five-acre property near North Bend, but in 2003 the company bought 53 acres of farmland (they now own and lease an additional 350 acres) and does half a million deliveries a year. Boxes go to Alaska as well. Says Andrew Stout, one of Full Circle's co-founders and the captain of the ship, "We grow it, we select it, we pack it, we box it, we ship it, and *you* eat it." That's the essence of farm-to-table.

P-PATCHES

P-Patches have nothing to do with peas. The P actually stands for Picardo Farms, a parcel of agricultural parkland of about two acres in north Seattle's Wedgwood neighborhood that 45 years ago became the city's first community garden. Today, the P-Patch program involves nearly 3,000 households, who "farm" a total of 31 acres. The average plot is about 100 square feet, which doesn't sound like a lot of land, and it's not; that's the point, that you don't need acres and acres to feed one family, just a few rows of dirt to grow whatever you feel like (corn, cuckes, zooks, carrots.) The city's Department of Neighborhoods runs the program, which encompasses 90 sites around town. Not surprisingly, there's a long waiting list; no charge for the plots but gardeners are expected to volunteer their time on community projects.

WSU Extension Programs

"Extension" programs are at the heart of land-grant colleges around the country; in Washington State they provide a bridge between the rural, Ag-dependent eastern half of the state, and the populous, urban western half. One of two dozen programs is the Small Farms Team, with offices in virtually every county to help foster a profitable farming system, to promote land and water stewardship, and to ensure that Washington citizens have unrestricted access to healthy food. In King County, this means supporting Master Gardner programs, 4-H programs, nutrition education..

The team provides information and educational programs for farmers, consumers, decision-makers, and others involved in local food systems. It's a statewide affiliation of professionals from WSU, state agencies, and an assortment of non-governmental organizations. The primary goal is obviously to build public support for agriculture in the broadest sense. This translates to preserving Washington farmland for food production, and to help farmers with sustainable practices that will also allow them to make money.

AUDRA MULKERN Female Farmer Project

Audra Mulkern did not grow up in the Snoqualmie Valley, surrounded as she is now by farms; she was in business development and moved to Duvall with her husband 25 years ago. She always knew that farming is hard work. But the people doing the work? Not Hollywood's mythic tough guys in flannel shirts and bluejeans but *women*. (Women in flannel shirts and bluejeans, true, but females.) A self-trained photographer, Mulkern has made their stories the focus of her life: The Female Farmer Project. Around the globe, women run 570 million farms, according to the United Nations, and Mulkern tells their stories on Twitter (@ModFarm, @ILookLikeaFarmer) and in a series of spectacular photos on Instagram (#femalefarmerproject). Says one of her subjects: "I think the biggest benefit to having women in farming is that women are used to multitasking and making quick decisions. Women have a different way of thinking that is very practical."

HOW YA LIKE THEM APPLES?

The United States is home to some 7,500 apple producers who grow nearly 100 varieties of apples on approximately 363,000 acres; half of that acreage is in Washington State. Total U.S. apple production is around 250 million bushels with an estimated farm-gate value of almost $2.4 billion. The average yield was over 600 bushels per acre. Apples are grown commercially in 32 states; Washington is by far the leader, with New York and Michigan in second and third place. Washington state grows 125 million boxes of apples per year. At 40 lbs per box, that's 2.5 million tons of apples.

Thing is, you may not *like* the shiny Red Delicious, that staple of the lunch box. Or the mealy Golden Delicious. Apples built for shape and color, not taste. The tart Granny Smiths compete with Fujis, Galas, Braeburns, Pinks, Pacific Rose, Pinova or Pinata. Subtly different, intriguing, the less familiar varieties share a name:club apples.

Turns out, you can breed and patent apples. Tedious stuff, but profitable. That's what agricultural research programs at big land grant universities do, they patent a fruit, then license the technology. The royalties can be substantial, and help fund other programs at the schools. One example: Stemilt of Wenatchee has the rights to the Pinova, developed in Germany, and sells it in North America as Pinata.

What happens to all those apples, you ask? Two thirds are eaten "fresh," directly from the hand. The rest are processed (Fruit cups! Apple juice! Applesauce!)

The United States is the world's second largest producer of apples, behind the People's Republic of China. Third, fourth and fifth: Poland, Turkey, and Italy. A quarter of the crop is exported, with Mexico and Canada being the biggest buyers.

The US also imports fresh apples, predominately from the Southern Hemisphere, to keep grocery store shelves stocked from March to July. Not a lot though, between five and ten percent, mostly from Chile and New Zealand. Most of the bottled apple juice is from concentrate, a lot of which is imported. Oh, and there really was a Johnny Appleseed. His name was John Chapman, born in Massachusetts on September 26, 1774.

JON ROWLEY (Yet Again) Guru of Juicy Peaches

Nothing is more subjective than the phenomenon, the experience we call "taste." Identifying good taste isn't as easy as picking one sample (of wine, of hot dogs, of ice cream) over another. (Side-by-side comparisons are easy; try picking two identical samples out of a group of five, for example.) Chemists and psychologists in white lab coats have this down to a science; the result, alas, is that everything tastes like nothing but "Salt Sugar Fat" (the title of a book by Michael Moss). But out here on the edge of the North

American shelf, we're better than that. We've got a secret weapon: Jon Rowley.

Rowley is the man behind the campaign to bring Copper River Salmon to Seattle. He is the man to whom Taylor Shellfish turned to popularize "oyster wines." He is the man hired by Metropolitan Markets to run the annual Peach-O-Rama promotion.

For over 20 years now, Metropolitan has been seeking out peaches that are "measurably" sweeter. Measured with a refractometer, the same gadget that wine makers use in the vineyards to determine sugar levels in the grapes so they know when to harvest. It's a simple, hand-held device that checks density. Grapes get riper than any other fruit, between 22 and 26 Brix (percentage of sugar); peaches are next, nudging close to 15.

Two growers specifically: Pence Orchards in Washington's Yakima Valley, outside of Wapato; and Frog Hollow Farms, an organic grower in Brentwood, Calif. "Just like the peaches of yesteryear, the juice runs down the chin and off the elbow," said Metropoltan's former CEO Terry Halverson.

Determined to improve the quality of the peaches they were selling in their stores, Metropolitan commissioned Rowley to find the best peaches on the west coast. It took him two years and countless miles to find what he was looking for: not just great peaches but growers willing to pack directly into a single-layer box and to refrain from holding the fruit in refrigerated storage facilities. Straight to market, in other words.

Everywhere he went, Rowley would squeeze a few drops of nectar onto his refractometer (which he still carries, the way a sommelier carries a corkscrew everywhere, the way we all now carry cellphones). The level of sweetness is immediately apparent. Other stores are content to sell peaches with 11 Brix; Metropolitan's, at 14 to 18 Brix, are also plumper, averaging almost half a pound each. Fair to say that Seattle is a sweeter place because of Rowley's refractometer.

CHERRIES, CHERRIES

Washington, it's worth repeating, grows two-thirds of the nation's sweet cherries on 35,000 acres of orchards, on the sunny hillsides of the Yakima Valley and overlooking the Columbia in the Wenatchee basin. The cherry season generates enormous demand, especially in Asian countries. Freshly picked Washington cherries--airlifted to Japan and China--can sell for up to $40 a pound, and Washington cherry exports to China alone have tripled. The Port of Seattle recently paid $23 million to update two  cargo terminals at SEATAC so that larger planes can load even more cargo.

Acknowledged by his peers to be one of the best--most careful, meticulous, successful--of the 2,500 cherry growers in the state, Marcus Griggs is a fourth-generation farmer. A decade ago, in an orchard of Rainier cherry trees overlooking the Columbia River at Orondo, Griggs noticed that the fruit of one tree had more color that the others, a scarlet, red-blushed skin. The yellow flesh tasted sweeter than Rainiers, too. Now, most growers would have shrugged it off as a random variation; not Griggs. He had the tree tested by Washington State University scientists, and it turned out that its DNA was, in fact, unique. Twenty percent more sugar, twenty percent more acidity. Griggs filed for a patent, named it the Orondo Ruby, and began propagating seedlings. By 2010, he was ready to take it to market.

Rather than sell cuttings and licensing the fruit (the usual route for patent-holders like university research stations), Griggs and his brother-in-law Bart Clennon decided to retain exclusive rights to the Orondo Ruby. But they needed what you might call "critical mass." Enough product on the supply side to satisfy the demands of the fickle, time-sensitive fruit industry. If consumers pay attention to cherry varieties at all, they remember two names: Rainiers (yellow) and Bings (dark red), but there are several more: Lapin, Chelan, Skeena, Tieton.

The brothers-in-law had owned a fruit-packing company called Orondo Fruit, which they sold to a packing house so they could concentrate on their own orchards. They recruited their family: Griggs's son, John, and daughter, Char, both work in the business, as do Bart's son, Cameron, and daughter, Cory. ((She calls them "Ka-Pow!" cherries.) They hired a market-research outfit in Chicago called The Perishable Group to run taste tests nationwide, with positive results. Locally, QFC and Fred Meyer became customers, Kroger and Sam's Club nationally.

The traditional cherry business requires lots of land and lots of patience. You can plant maybe 250 trees to the acre, and your yield per tree is less than 100 pounds. Most growers are at the mercy of the weather; cool spring weather just delays the harvest but early summer rains are disastrous. (Griggs and Clennon have helicopters standing by to blow rainwater off the fruit before the skin splits.) They have planted their Rubies along a V-shaped trellis, a system that allows for almost a thousand trees to the acre. Smaller trees, sure, but fairly similar yields. By now, their company has propagated over 100,000 trees; their field crews will pick 60,000 boxes by the middle of July.

One box holds fifteen pounds of cherries, so the Ruby harvest this year will be close to a million pounds, double that within five years. Even after paying the packing house about 20 cents a pound to process the fruit, that's a pretty good payoff. Ka-Pow!

GROWING THE STAFF OF LIFE

Once the most populous region of the northwest states, the **Palouse** is a fortunate corner of the globe. From Walla Walla to Spokane, from Coeur d'Alene back down to Lewiston, the rolling hills of the Palouse grow the nation's richest crops of wheat and barley, lentils and chick peas.

Wheat grown on the Palouse yields up to 100 bushels an acre, twice the national average. Some 125 million bushels a year, worth $10 or so a bushel, harvested by lifelong farmers driving combines along the steeply contoured landscape with self-leveling, air-conditioned cabs (the world's most awesome riding mowers).

But crops are worth next to nothing unless they can find a market. And here's where the Palouse trumps the Midwest: by taking advantage of the deep-water channels of the Snake and Columbia Rivers. From an altitude of 700 feet above sea level in Lewiston (the furthest-inland ocean-going port on the Pacific coast), giant barges (holding twice the payload of barges on the Mississippi) float the wheat 360 miles downriver, through a system of eight dams and locks (the Lower Granite, the Little Goose, the Lower Monumental, Ice Harbor, McNary, John Day, The Dalles and Bonneville), to Cargill's complex of grain elevators in Portland and Vancouver. From Portland, it's another 100 miles downriver to the Pacific, then open water as far as China and Japan.

Ironically, this engine of private enterprise--wheat is worth a billion dollars a year in Washington, half that in Idaho--is driven by an agent of Big Government, **the US Army Corps of Engineers,** which has the responsibility to keep the channels dredged and the dams maintained.

Where will all this grain go? The vast majority, low-gluten, low-protein, soft white wheat, heads to Asia, where it gets milled and converted into noodles and dumplings. (American mills prefer wheat grown in Montana and the Dakotas, with higher gluten content, for baked goods like bread.) But some of the Palouse's wheat stays close to home, finding its way into the products of an innovative regional food cooperative.

Washington State University in Pullman and the University of Idaho in Moscow are twin land grant institutions located just five miles apart. WSU has added a high-tech incubator in a business park adjacent to its campus. It's the headquarters of Schweitzer Electrric Labs, started 30 years ago by a WSU grad, a supplier of advanced equipment to the power industry; it provides thousands of local jobs. In the same complex is Merry Winery, operated by a computer Ph.D. turned enologist, Patrick Merry, who supervises WSU's student winemaking programs.

Back to the wheat. It may not have the cachet of cabernet sauvignon, but wheat from the Palouse is too valuable to graze the beasts of Wazzu's Large Animal program. In fact, with yields of 100 bushels (at 60 pounds per bushel), the production is three tons per acre, worth up to $1,000.

Just to compare: an acre of wine grapes produces between two and five tons, worth up to $10,000 in Washington. Wine grapes require irrigation and constant care, but the payoff explains why so many wheat, carrot and potato farmers have also planted vineyards.

One problem with farming commodity crops, however valuable, is that the producer is at the mercy of market forces. That, and he never gets to know his customers. So Palouse farmers Karl Kupers and Fred Fleming co-founded a thriving cooperative called Shepherd's Grain that does something virtually unthinkable: they not only market their own wheat, they demand that coop members (several dozen families) change their farming practices to a more environmentally friendly model known as no-till direct seeding to avoid erosion on the steep slopes of the Palouse.

Says Kupers, "Our farmers use no-till cultivation methods, which plant a crop directly in the stubble of the previous season's crop rather than till the field first."

Just as important is the closer relationship that the farmers have with their customers. Bakers learn more about the way the flour is produced; farmers see how their product is used.

Growing grain for local markets, Fleming said, also puts control of pricing in the hands of the farmers rather than distant commodity brokers or Wall Street speculators.

"Karl and I both thought that we needed to be that price-setter rather than a price-taker and de-commodify our product," Fleming said. To that end, milling is done close to the Palouse, in Spokane. The miller, ADM (Archer Daniels Midland), is a global behemoth, but its Spokane milling team recognizes the value of sustainably produced wheat and treats Shepherd's Grain with unusual care.

For their part, bakeries can identify the grower of each bag of Shepherd's Grain flour using a code on the bag, and can print out a color poster of the family that grew the wheat. Now, that's a connection you can't get with Gold Medal or Pillsbury.

JANELLE MAIOCCO From Farm & Barn to Door

Janelle VanderGriend grew up in Lynden, on Washington's Canadian border, where the Dutch Village Inn on Front Street features a real windmill. Her family, like many others, had a berry farm in Whatcom County's dairy country. She worked in restaurants (for Schwartz Brothers), went to culinary school (Art Institutes), earned an MBA (from Seattle Pacific) and put it to use in the food industry (Pasta & Co.). Then Janelle and her husband, James Maiocco, took off for Europe, and in the course of a year in Florence came to appreciate the "clean, humble food" they found in Florence. Maiocco (here with her son, Anthony) returned to Seattle determined to recreate that connection. She joined direct buying groups and bulk buying groups, but soon realized that she was seeing only the "demand" side of the business: consumers who wanted fresh food grown without pesticides; on the other were farmers (and bakers and ranchers, and fishers) with products to sell.

Gee, you might ask, isn't that what markets are all about? A place for buyers and sellers to meet? Isn't that what the farmers markets in two dozen Seattle neighborhoods are all about, organic carrots for yuppie householders? Not to mention the grand-daddy Pike Place Market, or the "local, fresh" aisles of enlightened supermarkets.

All well and good, but it's worth noting that *there aren't enough farmers to go around.* Too many markets! Every neighborhood wants one! And a farmer can only be in one place at a time. So if there's more than one market on a given day, the farmer has to pay an employee to staff the booth (not to mention pay a percentage of the day's take to the market master), which kind of takes the edge off the whole exercise. But what if you didn't have to depend on physical markets, on parking lots and canopies and market masters and health inspectors? What if you could use (wait for it) this thing everyone uses every day to watch cat videos? The internet, right! C'mon, this isn't brain surgery, it's nothing less than Amazon's business model. No need for book stores. In fact, Amazon did try shipping groceries (as if they were books), without great success. Maiocco's motive was different: connecting farmers directly with shoppers.

Farmers have a tough enough time dealing with agriculture; even if they weren't already working 18-hour days in their barns and fields, they're not particularly skilled at business development. So Maiocco created a website to facilitate their outreach to consumers. She named it Farmstr.com, and it eventually connected about 80 producers (farms, ranches, dairies) with about 500 buyers. The producers would list whatever they wanted to sell (from a dozen eggs or a bucket of organic honey to half a hog); the items would be added to the buyer's cart, and click! Just look at what you can buy: goat bones, kidney and heart; a share of pasture-raised Red Angus beef; grass-fed alpaca as braising steaks or hamburger. The farmers were located as close to Seattle as Auburn and Monroe, as far afield as central Washington and eastern Oregon. Pickup points vary; that's the bottleneck, obviously, so expansion of the Farmstr.com concept depended on adding more "partner drop sites," as they were known. Several are close to downtown Seattle. The hope was that Farmstr would mean better margins for local producers and lower cost for local consumers. "It's like the airbnb for local food," Janelle Maiocco says. "It's a big deal for us to see small farmers succeed."

Trouble is, Maiocco soon recognized that the business model wasn't working after all. Her competition (Instacart, AmazonFresh) was far better funded, far better versed in the logistics of delivery. Rather than go back to her investors for another round of financing, she shut Farmstr down. "Managing logistics, distribution, aggregation and drop-sites was cost-prohibitive." But within a month she was back, this time with a tweaked concept, Barn2Door, that let the farmers handle their own supply chain. Different business model but same mission.

Maiocco and her company aren't out of the woods by any means. Farmigo, a similar outfit based in Brooklyn, shut down its retail operations in July, 2016, and will concentrate on providing software to farmers instead.

AGRICULTURAL FOOTNOTE: Demise of the Moldboard Plow

What do city kids know about farming? Pictures of ancient farms, an ox pulling a stick through the dirt. Not until the 13th century was agriculture revolutionized by what we now consider emblematic of "modern" agriculture, the moldboard plow that dug down and turned the earth, aerating the soil and allowing for the more secure germination of seeds. With more food, the population of western Europe doubled.

Today, though, the moldboard plow is dying out. "Turning the soil" is no longer needed. The plow turns up *too much* soil, which encourages erosion (not enough plant material on the surface to stop wind and rainwater from carrying off topsoil. Not to mention the fuel required to run the tractors, plus the fact that plowing the soil releases carbon dioxide into the atmosphere.

Except for smaller farms that can't afford new machinery (yet), most American cropland is now minimum-till or even no-till. Herbicides, perhaps (Monsanto, gahhh!), but space-age equipment like these giant seed drills at Dewald Farms in eastern Washington's wheat fields that plant seeds directly and consistently at precisely the right depth

To Market, To Market!

Leaving the Farm

Chapter 4 · HALLOWED GROUND
SEATTLE'S PIKE PLACE MARKET

The Market is Seattle's preeminent tourist attraction, and why not: it's ground zero for everything that the city considers central to its identity. Even though the number of locals who do their everyday grocery shopping at the Pike Place Market is relatively low, it offers incredible views of the Olympics across Elliott Bay, it features the guys who throw the fish, the Hmong women selling flowers, the artists and artisans whose stalls line the western side of Pike Place, the restaurants and shops tucked into corners, the curiosity seekers lined up outside what they think is the "first" Starbucks (it's not, but the original building has been torn down).

Other cities (Baltimore, Boston, Philadelphia) have old farmers markets, too. Other cities (Portland, San Francisco) have built similar markets to revitalize their downtowns. But how did Seattle's come about? And how did it avoid the fate of urban development (Les Halles in Paris, Crescent Market in New Orleans)?

JOE DESIMONE Market Man

An immigrant truck farmer from southern Italy was responsible for keeping Boeing in Seattle. You might have heard this story, but you probably know only half of it.

The end of the 19th century brought hard times to Italy. Peasant farmers paid high taxes, industrialization was almost non-existent, and eight years of military service were compulsory. Little wonder that over four million Italians simply picked up and left, most of them emigrating to the United States. Among them was one Giuseppe Desimone, a strapping lad over six feet tall, over 300 lbs., who arrived from the Naples area in 1898.

When he reached Seattle he rented (and later bought) some land south of town and became a truck farmer, selling his produce directly to householders in Seattle. By 1907, there arose a new farmers market on the bluff at the western end of Pike Street. (The wholesale market was on the waterfront, at the foot of Madison.) The real estate belonged to an architect named Frank Goodwin, who had designed and put up a couple of buildings inside which farmers rented their stalls. Before long, Joe Desimone bought his own stall from the landlord, and then another, until he literally owned the entire Market. The Desimone family would continue to retain ownership until the 1970s, when it was taken over by a public agency, the Pike Place Market Preservation and Development Authority.

Meantime, Bill Boeing's flying boat company, which had started at the old Heath Shipyard on the Duwamish River, had built airplanes that helped win World War One. Boeing himself was a timber guy, and kept his company around after the war so it could have access to the spruce trees used to build planes. But Seattle didn't have a "real airport," and Boeing was stuck using waterfront along Lake Washington, first at Madison Park, later in Renton.

Now, even if you know the name Desimone from the tributes inside the Market itself, here's what you may not know. Because he was an important landlord in Seattle, people told Desimone things. One rumor he heard, for instance, was that Bill Boeing wanted to move his airplane company to a city with a "real" airport. As a civic-minded guy, Desimone offered Boeing a deal he couldn't refuse: he would cede a big chunk of his farmland along the Duwamish, the 28-acre tract at the heart of what's known today as Boeing Field, in exchange for one dollar. One dollar, plus Bill Boeing's promise not to move the company. Deal.

The Boeing Company straightened the river bed, built new runways, and kept its headquarters at the new airport until 2001, when it decamped for Chicago.

VICTOR STEINBRUECK Savior of the Market

© Bob Peterson

Not many people find themselves, in the course of a career in urban planning, responsible for the design of a city's icon. Victor Steinbrueck did, though. It was his squiggle that created the Space Needle, and it was his love for the quirky, rundown, yet vibrant Pike Place Market that prompted him to save it.

There was a time, and it wasn't terribly long ago, that "developers" wanted to take over the Market and, in the name of what was ironically called "urban renewal," destroy it. True, many of its buildings were crumbling. True, many of its

38

denizens were scruffy. But the Market had its defenders, chief among them an architect named Victor Steinbrueck, and to save the Market Steinbrueck did something extraordinary: he wandered through its alleyways and stalls, recording what he saw in a series of pen & ink sketches, drawn with a Mont Blanc pen. All the lettering in the book was done by hand as well. A few photographs from 1906 were included, but the charm of the book is its simultaneously detailed yet wide-angle perspectives on the market's daily life. Far from being a Chamber of Commerce poster or Visitor Bureau whitewash, Steinbrueck's *Market Sketchbook* showed the Market in all its disorder and vitality. In fact, neither the Chamber nor the Visitor Bureau were paying much attention to the Market as a tourist attraction back then.

Steinbrueck did not represent the lunatic fringe of Seattle public life. Quite the contrary. He was a respected professor of architecture at the University of Washington. He was also one of the designers (the principal designer, if truth be told) of the structure that symbolized the city's commitment to forward thinking for the 1962 World's Fair: the Seattle Space Needle.

In the late 1960s, Steinbrueck organized a group called Friends of the Market to stand in opposition to the developers (who claimed they wanted to "save" it. To be successful in a special election held in the fall of 1971, Steinbrueck had to convince the voters that the existing Market could be salvaged without wholesale demolition. Even though most Seattle residents didn't shop there (except, perhaps, when accompanying out-of-town guests), they nonetheless considered the Market a local treasure. The *Market Sketchbook* was a perfect representation: unglamorous, to be sure, but innocent, lively, unsentimental, and *charming*. As Elizabeth Tanner, executive secretary of Friends of the Market writes, it is "a fragile kaleidoscope of merchants, mostly foreign born and fiercely independent." The painter Mark Tobey (still alive at the time, and widely considered the greatest American artist of his day) called it "the soul of Seattle." Farmers would register ($3 a year) and certify that they had grown or made the goods they were selling; a stall with water cost 85 cents a day.

Steinbrueck's *Market Sketchbook* was published in 1968, and by the summer of 1970 it was the chief campaign medium for the citizens initiative to save the Market. Come election day, it wasn't even close: the margin for passage was 23,000 votes. The newly formed Historic District and the public agency formed to oversee it, the Pike Place Market Preservation & Development Authority, took over from the Desimone family and has run it ever since.

In the 1980s, the owners of the Space Needle decided to add additional dining and meeting space at a new, 100-foot-level. Leading the opposition was none other than Victor Steinbrueck, who had designed the Needle's original shape. Steinbrueck lost that battle. But the vantage point he so much admired, overlooking Elliott Bay from the intersection of Western and Virginia, was named Victor Steinbrueck Park in his honor.

Chapter 5 · SUPPLY CHAIN

Very few restaurant owners and executive chefs actually go out every morning to see what's fresh at the market. Most sit at their desks and examine spreadsheets, catalogs, newsletters. They answer phone calls from job applicants, vendors of wine, providers of table linens, suppliers of toilet paper. Sure, they'd love to be out there, squeezing the tomatoes and smelling the peaches, but it's just not practical. So how do those fresh oysters arrive at the back door? Those organic mixed greens? The biggest food network of all is the one that delivers the goods.

WAYNE LUDVIGSEN A Chef's Chef

 Summer of 1975 and Wayne Ludvigsen, with one more year of high school to go, found a summer job packing herring on the dock at Ray's Boathouse. The following year he moved inside, washing dishes and busing tables. Ray's, with fishermen lined up to supply their prize catch, was Seattle's premier seafood restaurant, and Ludvigsen proved a natural in the kitchen. Within three years he was in charge. When Jon Rowley brought in the first-ever Copper River Kings to Seattle, he took one to show Ludvigsen. "It was fat, not slender, and had a unique color, persimmon," he recalls. "We'd never seen anything like it.. Our hands would be covered with orange fish oil." The fashion was to poach salmon, or to barbecue it, or to bake it; Ludvigsen's approach was minimalist: grill it with a bit of herb butter until it just lost its transluscency, then serve. Ideally, according to wine steward Jeff Prather, with one of them newfangled wines called pinot noir.

Salmon wasn't the only thing, though. There was also black cod, also called Alaskan sablefish. Shiro Kashiba was marinating it in lees from the sake-brewing process at his restaurant, Nikko, in the International District; Ludvigsen tweaked the recipe to American tastes (by making it less alcoholic), curing it in lees and sugar for at least 24 hours, then broiling it to caramelize the sugar. Not all that complicated, but easy to screw up.

In 1997, Ludvigsen left Ray's but stayed in the industry as director of national accounts for Charlie's Produce. A chef selling to chefs, in other words. Charlie's, which provides produce to restaurants, groceries, the maritime industry, institutions, and even other wholesalers, is owned by Ray Bowen, Charlie Billow and Terry Bagley under the corporate umbrella Triple-B Corp. It's the largest grocery wholesaler on the west coast, with four distribution centers. In Seattle alone, there's a sprawling warehouse complex in the Sodo district and a fleet of over 200 trucks that deliver everything from kale to carnations. From the outset, over 30 years ago, Charlie's has worked directly with a network of local and regional farmers to help them plan their crops and guarantee them a market; in turn, their customers (independent groceries and restaurants) have a reliable supply of locally produced items.

Back to the black cod for a moment. It's actually a very traditional Japanese dish, *kasu* being the lees of sake. And *zuke* meaning "to apply." Sablefish is also prized for its high fat content, and in New York delis it's very popular smoked, like salmon. These days, it's the most famous dish on the menu at Nobu, in Manhattan, but it was Wayne Ludvigsen, in the wilds of Ballard, who gave it life in America

ANGELO MERLINO Not Costco

The way Angelo Merlino saw it, Seattle in 1900 was a city full of opportunity. Arriving from southern Italy's mountainous Abruzzo region, Angelo started a business importing olive oil, which would be expanded into a full-service restaurant supply company by his sons, Ubaldo and Attilo. The following generation included a bright youngster named Armandino Batali, who had a straightforward career as an engineer at Boeing and didn't get into food (specifically, meat) until after he'd retired. *His* son, of course, is Mario Batali. As Bethany-Jean Clement pointed out in a *Seattle Times* story in 2015, "Seattle's most famous export when it comes to Italian food is the great-grandson of its first Italian food importer."

The business is owned today by the Biesold family, who bought it from Attilo Merlino in 1976. (Phyllis Biesold's sister, Dorene Centioli McTigue, founded Pagliacci Pizza in 1979.) Merlino's has expanded dramatically over the decades; the warehouse on Fourth Avenue South is as big as the Costco across the street.

GEOFF LATHAM Nicky USA

He's technically more of a farmer, not a chef, but he's at home in dozens of restaurant kitchens and has been a guest of honor at the Movable Feast TV show. Geoff Latham fills a key role in the region's food chain by supplying what the big purveyors like Cisco and Food Services of America can't (or won't): specialty items like veal sweetbreads, water buffalo, and alligator.

At heart, Latham is a butcher, and the company he founded 20 years ago, Nicky USA, is a specialty meat distributor. Now, having purchased a 30-acre, certified organic farm outside Aurora, near Portland, Latham plans to raise his own products (rabbits, game birds, and other unique animals) for top chefs across the Northwest.

Before he got into the butcher's trade, before he started the food distribution business, Latham was a farmer himself. The newly-acquired property, dubbed Nicky Farm, is located on the meandering Pudding River half an hour south of Portland. The landscape is home to flocks of geese and quail, among other wildlife, and features both a century-old farmhouse and a barn similar to one that already appears on the Nicky Farms logo.

The first animals Latham will raise on the farm will be rabbits ("our keystone protein," Latham says), which the company began selling in 1991. But success didn't come overnight. The Nicky Farms brand didn't start until 2009; Latham expanded to Seattle a couple of years ago.

"I am lucky to have established my business in a place with some of the nation's best chefs and locavores who are excited about locally grown high quality protein. Because of them I am now able to fulfill my life-long dream of growing my own meat on my own farm," says Latham.

In addition to acting as a working farm, Nicky USA will host chefs and interested eaters for farm dinners, hunting trips, boating on the river and tours of the property, with the goal of deepening the connection between the farm and tables across the Northwest. His most recent product is game from Hawaii, small wild deer native to the island that are culled in legal hunts. Definitely does not taste like chicken.

JAMES BROOKE Corfini Gourmet

Jim Brooke's path to his own food-service venture started with a business degree from Gonzaga and a stint in Silicon Valley, but his heart was always in the kitchen. The connections between land and dinner table just required some tweaking, that's all. He moved from San Francisco to Seattle to launch Corfini Gourmet a decade ago, starting with nothing more than his mother's maiden name painted on the side of a refrigerated trailer and a beat-up Subaru for deliveries. But he had the right kind of clients, celebrity chefs with high standards like William Belickis and Scott Carsberg, and his business grew quickly. Today Corfini has two dozen vans on the road delivering to clients, and a staff of 70. The company occupies a converted space in SoDo (the old Johnson Wax building) that's been outfitted with a gourmet kitchen and a USDA-certified meat cutting and dry-age facility.

Brooke doesn't see Latham as a competitor so much as as a colleague. His own line runs to beef, lamb, pork, poultry and game; he leaves the more exotic stuff, like water buffalo, to Nicky USA. That said, Corfini does seem to have a lock on one Italian specialty, *cinghiale,* wild boar, which it sources in the scrub lands of West Texas. And hard-to-find oils, vinegars, cheeses, and truffles.

JUSTIN MARX Marx Foods

On a very different level is Justin Marx of Marx Foods, a longtime (five generations) specialty supplier to the very top restaurants on the East Coast and, more recently, an online business as well. For the past couple of years, Marx has also operated a retail outlet at his company's test kitchen in Lower Queen Anne. Delicate pasta bearing the Filotea brand, from Ancona in Italy's Le Marche region. Many products come from the Pacific Northwest, to be sure, but most from wherever in the world the best examples might be grown or packaged.

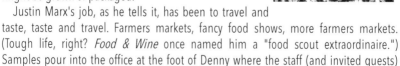

Justin Marx's job, as he tells it, has been to travel and taste, taste and travel. Farmers markets, fancy food shows, more farmers markets. (Tough life, right? *Food & Wine* once named him a "food scout extraordinaire.") Samples pour into the office at the foot of Denny where the staff (and invited guests)

blind-taste and vote. Online, Marx Foods offers well over 1,000 items; in the shop, only 300 to 400. (The overage supermarket, which must appeal to a wide range of customer needs and tastes, has 20,000 to 30,000 items.) Online, too, the producers take care of shipping (airfreight, usually), which means that the point of difference for Marx is customer service: an unusually rich assortment of "how to" information: recipes, background, history, stories.

With a physical store, Marx goes head-to-head, (jar-to-jar? box to box?) with established retail importers like Big John's PFI (in SoDo) and ChefShop (up the road on Elliott Avenue). But Marx has more than a few tricks up his sleeve, starting with a unique array of "specialty" meats not previously available to home cooks (elk, venison, bison, boar, kangaroo, poussin, poulet rouge, squab, quail, pheasant). Yes, it's all cryovac'd and frozen, because, let's remember, Marx isn't repackaging anything. Sure to be popular: the "woolly" Manganitsa pork, which virtually vanished from the Seattle market when Heath Putnam's inventory was shipped to New Jersey.

Who's the market? Is anyone really going to buy kangaroo? Maybe not your average family dinner, but chefs, caterers, and food service companies in the market for something unusual. Or just to drop in and pick up some edible flowers or exotic produce. One potential drawback, a lack of on-site parking, doesn't faze Justin. "We're interested in building relationships with serious customers. There's actually plenty of street parking on Lower Queen Anne."

TOMIO MORIGUCHI Uwajimaya

Humble beginnings: Fujimatsu Moriguchi, who came to Seattle from a Japanese fishing village called Uwajima, sold fish cakes from the back of his truck to Japanese immigrant laborers in railroad, seafood, farming and lumber camps throughout the area. Then came Pearl Harbor; like every Japanese family in the region, the Moriguchis were deported to California's Tule Lake Internment Camp.

Despite harsh racism after the war, Fujimatsu was able to buy a tiny building in Chinatown for $400, where he opened a little grocery store that he called Uwajimaya. He and his wife Sadako also operated a successful gift shop at the World's Fair in 1962. After Fujimatsu passed away, Sadako and the seven Moriguchi children kept the business going. Tomio Moriguchi, a mechanical engineer at Boeing, quit his job when his father died and became CEO shortly thereafter, a position he held for over 40 years. Though she never held a formal position in the company, Sadako worked at the store every day, making lunch for the employees. Footnote: Sadako's brother is George Tsutakawa, the artist and sculptor whose iconic fountains adorn many of Seattle's public plazas.

One of the first things you notice at Uwajimaya: the wall of mushrooms, names and shapes more or less familiar, trompète royale, hedgehog, wood-ear, shiitake, maitake, shimoiji, nameko, eryuni. Further afield: goat tripe. Big market for goats in many Asian and Latino communities; stands to reason there would be customers for goat offal as well. Over in the fish department, Seattle's most varied selection of seafood in all its guises. Live oysters, crab and lobsters. Sea urchins. Whole fish too numerous to count. Fish fillets, steaks, roasts. Fish sliced for sushi and sashimi. Steamed octopus, fish heads for stock. A crew of 19 works two shifts, cutting everything in-house: snapper, salmon, tilapia, yellow fin, yellow tail, sockeye, cod for kasuzuke marinade, mahi-mahi, Chilean sea bass, whole mackerel ... to say nothing of the shellfish and squid. When Salumi wants branzino for its Sunday dinners, they call Uwajimaya. Lampreia would call. So would Shiro. There's even a separate set of knives, cutting boards and sinks for kosher. A rabbi from Seattle's Va'ad HaRabinim inspects regularly; the Kashruth certificate is posted on the wall.

The clientele is changing. No longer a market exclusively targeted to Asians, Uwajimaya serves Seattle's growing eastern European communities as well as the traditional Scandinavian families, in addition to a growing foodie community that demands freshness at moderate prices. Next up: a smaller-footprint Uwajimaya in South Lake Union, on the ground level of the 400 Fairview Building.

LAM'S SEAFOOD MARKET

 The shelves are stocked with cans of coconut milk, bottles of fish sauce, jars of grass jelly, boxes of mogu lemon drink, cellophane bags of vermicelli, and burlap sacks of brown rice. The freezer bins contain headless shrimp, giant prawns, baby squid, and fish balls, The meat counter features ox tail, duck tongue, and pork uterus; there are bins of durian and rambutan out front. Dozens of green vegetables labeled only in Vietnamese. On the edge of the International District, Lam's Seafood Market is the most cosmopolitan shopping experience in town.

"In white-people grocery stores, the aisles are wide, the floors gleam, and the labels are in English–but the produce is mediocre, the meat is pale, and everything is expensive. This is not true in Little Saigon, up the hill from Chinatown, where grocery stores are hard to identify, distinguished outside by boxes of fruit under tarp awnings and inside by imperfect linoleum floors. But there you will discover prices so low, you'll think you've died and gone to 1954." So began *The Stranger's* review of Lam's Seafood Market penned by none other than my son, Dominic Holden, back in 2010. Five years earlier the original owner (Mr. Lam) returned to Vietnam and left the property to his son and daughter, Yen Lam-Steward. She soon bought out her brother's share and now runs the place on her own. Not yet 40, she embarked on a campaign to improve the store inside and out. She upgraded the merchandise and equipped the checkout lanes with computerized cash registers; outside, she repaved the parking lot, doubled the number of spaces, and posted a yellow-vested traffic monitor. The result? Sales per square foot that exceed Costco's.

The heart of the place remains the seafood counter at the back of the store, accessible only by jostling your way along narrow aisles filled shopping carts pushed by people speaking Vietnamese, Chinese, Laotian, Cambodian, Spanish, and Hindi. What's back there? Live oysters, live crab, lobsters, tilapia; fresh and farm-raised whole fish from waters near and far: Pacific, Atlantic, Indian Ocean. Whole branzino at half the price charged at the Pike Place Market., cleaned for you (or not) by a disciplined crew of fishmongers. Tip: if you want the skin to come off in one piece, tell them not to scrape the scales. "No scrape!"

PETERSON More than Cheese

The Peterson Company may have started as a cheese outfit but the current catalog has nearly 10,000 non-cheese products, almost anything a restaurant would need. Bags, boxes, cleaning supplies. Canned fruit, fresh fruit, grab-n-go chimchangas, gluten-free cheesecake, food coloring. If your cooks are too clumsy to make sweet potato gnocchi, the Peterson rep can have a case of them delivered, first thing tomorrow morning. More about the origins of Peterson's George Lyden in Chapter 11, "Big Cheeses."

BIG JOHN, BIG MARIO, ROSELLA

The big guy was John Croce, an importer of Italian foods who set up shop in SoDo back in 1976. Even today, the sprawling warehouse filled with hard-to-find Italian foods, is open to the public as **PACIFIC FOOD IMPORTERS**. Or Big John's PFI to family and friends.

Ron **ROSELLA'S** family, on the other hand, sold out a decade ago to a much larger food distributorship, Pacific Fruit, based in Portland. Ron's daughter, Sumitra, was the original owner of Sostanza, the restaurant at the foot of East Madison now occupied by BeachHouse Bar & Grill.

VELLOTTI FINE FOODS is a well-respected one-man operation headed by the indefatigable Mario Vellotti. One of his early restaurant accounts, Via Tribunali, made him an offer he couldn't refuse: his own pizzeria (Big Mario's). More in Chapter 10 (Chain Restaurants) and in Chapter 13 (Pizza

Chapter 6 · THE SUPERS

Local grocers and supermarkets have shuttered before, most memorably the widely admired Larry's Markets. Brothers Mark and Dave McKinney bought the six-unit business from their father, Larry, in 2003. But Mark's lavish wine-buying habits (it was said) caused the company to became over-extended. Forced to declare bankruptcy, Larry's sold off its stores in Bellevue and Kirkland; Bellevue is currently a Total Wine outpost. The Lower Queen Anne store was taken over and revitalized by Met Market.

METROPOLITAN MARKET Fresh Northwest

Sometimes, all you want from a grocery store is stuff you can throw together for dinner, a steak or piece of fish. Sometimes, though, you want more, much more. Even here, in laid-back Seattle, we want to do all our shopping in one stop, soup to nuts, flowers to toilet paper. Obsessive scurrying isn't needed to find just the right brie, the perfect cupcake, the loveliest teapot; ideally, they're all under the same, 50,000-square-foot roof, all with validated parking.

In this bleeping economy, restaurants are bleeding (and bleeping) themselves with price cuts, but grocery stores, by and large, are doing well. In fact, they're able to spend money on significant upgrades to attract and keep shoppers who might otherwise scurry to specialty stores. It's not a slam-dunk, but the analysts preach that "tuning in to consumer data and retailer partners' needs" leads to success. Gobbledy-gook, better interpreted on a local level, which leads directly to the region's sole remaining player, Food Market Northwest, formerly Thriftway, now dba Metropolitan Market.

Terry Halverson, whose company, Fresh Markets Northwest, owned Metropolitan Market, started his career at the age of 14 (it's said), bagging groceries at the Queen Anne Thriftway. Before long, he bought the place from its owner, Dick Rhodes, and eventually acquired or built several other neighborhood groceries around town: Admiral, Proctor, and others, ending up with six stores. In 2004 he turned the Admiral Thriftway into the flagship of the newly named Metropolitan Market chain. After competitor Larry's Markets imploded, Halverson bought the Larry's on Lower Queen Anne and completely transformed it.

Halverson was an innovator, who moved flowers and fresh produce to the front of the store, hired Jon Rowley to promote a better selection of fresh fish, including Copper

River salmon (Julia Child was impressed), bought a bakery (Boulangerie) to provide fresh bread, brought in a B&O Espresso bar, and added a mini-kitchen for in-store demonstrations and author signings. This is ho-hum today, but was cutting edge when introduced.

All good things don't have to end, but they do have to evolve. Especially businesses like supermarkets with high operating costs, ultra-thin margins, tens of thousands of individual products (called SKUs stock-keeping units) to keep track of, lots of traffic but customers who don't want to spend either time or money in your store. The old-fashioned way was for grocers to beat suppliers down to the lowest possible price, then send fliers offering weekly deals or brand-name bargains to the neighborhood. The newer way, which found its way to Seattle in the 1970s, was to build customer loyalty through higher quality items (meat, produce, imported wine and beer) and in-store experiences like fresh flowers, cooking demos, and tastings.

For Met Markets, some of that valuable advice came from Jacques Boiroux, a Frenchman who had seen the move toward upscale shopping work at stores like the food hall inside Selfridge's in London, the upscale Peck shops in Milan, the giant KDW superstore in Berlin, and La Grande Épicerie inside the Bon Marché in Paris. He led site inspection tours of European markets for Metropolitan managers, persuaded them to include mobile chef's kitchens in their remodeling plans. It all paid off, and Boiroux even took an ownership stake in the company.

You have to ask yourself why anyone would stay in the supermarket business these days. If you own the real estate (at least a city block in residential neighborhoods, so the 60-foot semis making deliveries can back into your loading dock without using side streets), that's great, but there's enormous pressure from developers to build housing or office parks in the best locations. And if you don't own the real estate, you're afraid the owners will jack up the rent beyond what you can reasonably pay. You need a large workforce, not particularly skilled (and therefore more transient); you have huge issues every day with logistics, with stock-keeping, with spoilage (perishable meat, fish, produce). You need sophisticated software to determine if customers are buying the items you're selling. Weekly advertising circulars inserted into daily newspapers are relics of the past; today's shoppers expect to read notifications of daily (even hourly) specials on their smart phones. And the margins are terrible. At the end of the day, 10,000 customers may have spent half a million dollars in your store, but you (the owner) are lucky to clear one percent of the gross. Who'd want t take over a business like that? Only a giant national company (like Walmart, like Kroger) is structured to run that sort of enterprise for decades at a stretch, so it's no wonder that family-owned supermarkets are a thing of the past. But how to unload your precious baby? Who's going to keep your special vision alive? Surely not your biggest competitor.

Well, Met Market seems to have found an exit strategy, selling to a private equity fund. It's a homegrown fund at that, Seattle-based Endeavour, with controlling investments in over 50 "mid-market" companies from Columbia Distributing (booze, wine, beer) and Columbus (deli meats) to Lone Star (construction materials for the housing market). They also have a similarly upscale, 12-unit chain in southern California called Bristol Farms. One hopes, one hopes, that they avoid another catastrophe like Haggen's.

HAGGEN Overreach & Fall

You really can't get much further into the northwest corner of the US than Bellingham, a town of under 100,000 on the Canadian border. A surprisingly good chain of supermarkets called Haggen was launched there, with innovative practices (like presenting fresh seafood on ice, a floral department, an in-store Starbucks) that helped draw local shoppers as well as Canadian day-trippers. The family-owned chain grew to a baker's dozen stores, including not counting those on the Seattle periphery branded as Top Foods. (The Seattle market already had Larry's, Metropolitan, Albertsons, Safeway, QFC, and Fred Meyer stores.) In 2009, to run the growing empire, they hired Jim Donald, former CEO of Starbucks, no less. Then, in 2011, the Haggen family (led by brothers Don and Rick) decide the time had come to sell. From the ranks of suitors they picked a private equity outfit from Miami called Comvest. But what should have been the family's proudest moment–a clean exit from the dog-eat-dog grocery business–turned out to be the beginning of a nightmare.

Comvest installed its own CEO, C.J. Gabriel, a retail exec a year away from retirement, who started things off by dumping the Top Foods concept. Haggen then cashed in its real estate holdings, spinning off the sites occupied by 15 of its stores to a California outfit, Merlone Geier Partners in return for almost $200 million. Still, at this point, it looked like a pretty good payday for the Haggen family. But then Gabriel retired and was replaced by a troika of Comvest executives, who proceed to close or sell off one store after another, until, whoa! In a huge shakeup of the supermarket business, Safeway made an offer to buy Albertsons.

Not so fast, said the Federal Trade Commission, always on the lookout for mergers that might reduce competition and raise prices. The FTC required that nearly 150 west coast stores (mostly Albertsons) be excluded from the merger and go back on the market. And here's where Comvest got in way over its head. Sure, they say, we'll take 'em and turn 'em into Haggen stores. To go from a small chain with a dozen units to a regional powerhouse with 150? Definition of hubris, of overreach. But private equity, like the honey badger, don't care. It's not their circus, it's not their money. In fact, to make the deal work, most of the proceeds from the real estate sale were committed to taking over the new stores.

It all proved such a boneheaded move that it didn't take long for the whole venture to go south. Haggen lawyers (well, Comvest lawyers) went to court to claim that Albertsons sabotaged the deal (with mispriced inventory, rigged invoices, poisoned supplier relationships); it asked for more than $1 billion in damages. As if to prove its point, Haggen filed for bankruptcy protection a week later. As it happened a vulture-buyer was waiting in the wings: none other than arch rival Albertsons, itself now part of another private equity firm, Cerberus Capital Management.

Whatever paltry percentage of equity the Haggens retained in their family company has probably evaporated (hope they kept some of that real estate cash, right?) because Comvest certainly got taken to the cleaners in this deal. Who got screwed the most? Well, the thousands of hourly workers (checkers, clerks, warehouse staff) who had no idea what was going on, and had no one to look out for them. Their union, the United Food & Commercial Workers was no help at all. The Federal Trade Commission did put out a statement after the dust settled saying, essentially, "We're sorry things didn't work out the way we hoped." American capitalism at work, a Wagnerian opera called "The Death of Haggen."

Chapter 7 · FARMERS MARKETS

Identifying good taste isn't as easy as picking one sample (of wine, of hot dogs, of ice cream) over another. And nothing is more subjective than the phenomenon, the experience we call "taste." Chemists and psychologists in white lab coats have this down to a science; the result, alas, is that everything tastes like nothing but "Salt Sugar Fat" (the title of a book by Michael Moss). But out here on the edge of the North American shelf, we're better than that.

It's simplistic, here on the wet side, to think of our state's economy as Boeing for manufacturing, Microsoft for software, and Amazon for everything else. The state's number two export, after airplanes, is agricultural products: potatoes, wheat, cherries, apples. Grain harvested in the Palouse gets loaded onto barges and floated down the Columbia, where it's loaded onto ships that sail across the Pacific to make noodles in China. Apples keep pretty well if stored properly, and many uses: eating , baking, sauce, juice. Spuds go to processors in Idaho. Cherries, with a short shelf life, go out by air to markets in Europe as well as Asia. (There's talk of building a major new airport in Moses Lake, by the way.) Ag exports to the TPP nations came to $2.5 billion last year.

Agriculture is at the heart of eastern Washington's economy. Some 40,000 farms throughout Washington employ 200,000 workers and generate $40 billion in revenue. The state's four leading agricultural counties (Yakima, Grant, Benton and Franklin), responsible for $3.5 billion worth of crops, actually adjoin the Hanford Nuclear Reservation, with Walla Walla, in fifth position, only 20 miles downstream. Is that a problem? Should it be?

One reason the plutonium is stored at Hanford in the first place is the dry climate; it's assumed there will be no torrential rains leaching through the contaminated soils. The slightest leak, however remote the possibility, would compromise the state's image and stature as an agricultural breadbasket. Washington leads the nation as a producer of apples, sweet cherries, and hops; it ranks second in potatoes and wine grapes. But while apples and cherries are sold as fresh fruit, and potatoes are ground up and smooshed into french fries, the grapes are more valuable in their processed form: premium wine, a product that carries the Washington State brand far beyond the state's borders.

CHRIS CURTIS Market Maven

For all of our self-satisfied, navel-gazing smugness about being such a livable city, Seattle didn't have any farmers markets, beyond the "main" one at Pike Place, until 20 years ago. No Whole Foods, either, come to think of it. But Farmers Markets, which allow city dwellers to buy produce directly from farmers, have become an emblem of modern urban life. The first one was in the University District, the second in Columbia City, then West Seattle. Eventually, an organization called Neighborhood Farmers Markets Association took hold, all of this spearheaded by a woman named Chris Curtis.

"We only allow farmers who grow and produce everything they sell. They must grow and produce in Washington state. We conduct farm visits and often send a third-party inspector in our stead…It's not the easiest model to manage, but since the beginning we've stuck to these principles."

Today the NFMA oversees two dozen neighborhood markets, which are patrolled by a swarm of young families pushing strollers or trailing dogs (sometimes both at once). It's a social outing, classier than ducking into Starbucks for a Frappuccino. Healthier, too.

But here's the problem: there aren't enough farmers markets to go around.

Think about it: up at 4 AM to load the truck and hit the road, unload, stand around all day talking to a stream of urbanites who can barely tell a carrot from a parsnip, load up the truck again and head back to the barn. For what? A few hundred bucks (if you're lucky) and the pleasure of meeting your customers. But if you're not the actual farmer, you're paying someone (a farmhand who's already around, if you're lucky), buying gas, providing lunch. There are easier ways to make a living. The biggest problem, though is not the lack of market opportunities but the lack of farmers. Sure, there are almost 2,000 "farms" in King County, but most have nothing to sell and no way to get their products to market even if they wanted to.

And yet. Even with encroaching development (housing, roads, shopping centers, offices), there are still 1,800 farms in King County, covering 50,000 acres. Many are close-in: Vashon Island, the Kent Valley, and along the Green, Snoqualmie and Sammamish rivers. It was 25 years ago that county voters authorized a Farmland Preservation Program that currently protects 13,000 acres of dairies, cattle and horse farms, row crops, flowers, even Christmas trees nurseries.

Lest we feel smug (or threatened) about the proximity of barns and fields, we should note that there are over four dozen farms within the city limits of our "Neighbour to the North," Richmond, BC. Richmond--one third Seattle's size in terms of population, roughly similar density--devotes a third of a magnificent, 100-acre city park, Terra Nova, to urban agriculture, and employs environmental educators and restaurant chefs to teach schoolchildren the virtues of growing food.

"Those aren't weeds," the park director told a group of grade-schoolers harvesting edible wild greens, "just another form of money."

Chapter 8 · THE CORNER DELI

The big guys, the Safeways and Met Markets, they're the ones who move most of the food from farm to market. But specialty retailers like Sur La Table, and delicatessens like De Laurenti also play an important role.

ITALIAN CONNECTIONS Verdi, DeLaurenti, Centioli, Merlino

© Bob Peterson

Pasqualina Verdi, matriarch of a truck-farming family, symbolized the Pike Place Market to a generation of Seattle residents. Her son, Mike, still operates Whistling Train Farm in the Kent Valley, providing piglets to specialty butcher shops and restaurants, and selling produce at farmers markets around town. Her grandson Cosmo runs the farm stand at the end of the driveway.

Gill Centioli's name has passed from modern vocabulary, but he deserves wider memory, not so much for the restaurant called Gill's Beachhead that he operated at 2nd and Virginia but for opening Seattle's first 19-cent hamburger shop, Gil's Drive In on Rainier Avenue in 1950, three years before the first Dick's started slinging burgers in Wallingford. Legend has it that they dropped the second "L" in the neon sign to save money. Centioli, whose parents were immigrants from southern Italy, went on to fortune, if not fame, by opening over 40 Kentucky Fried Chicken franchises in western Washington.

In 1979, one of his daughters, Dorene Centioli-McTigue (along with a brother and a cousin) started the Pagliacci chain of pizzerias on "The Ave" in Seattle's University District. It grew to encompass two dozen pizzerias around town plus three on the UW campus. She eventually sold Pagliacci to the folks who would also take over DeLaurenti's. Another daughter, Phyllis, along with her husband, Bruce Biesold, purchased Merlino Fine Foods in 1976 and became one of the leading purveyors of Italian products to the Seattle restaurant community.

Speaking of DeLaurenti's, the original immigrants, Pete and Mae DeLaurenti, opened it as Pete's Italian Grocery in 1946 on one of the lower levels of the Pike Place Market. Their son Louie DeLaurenti moved it to the "front door" of the Market (at First & Pike) in the 1970s, and he (gulp!) sold it in 2001 to outside investors. But not just any investors. Pat McDonald's father had started Torrefazzione Italia (a specialty coffee company swallowed up by Starbucks); McDonald's grandfather had started Gai's Bakery, and McDonald himself had taken over Pagliacci Pizza. Got that?

SHIRLEY COLLINS, RENEE BEHNKE Sur La Table

In 1972, the best-known chef in America was Julia Child (who had displaced Chef Boyardee), and the American public's appetite for better food was quickly followed by an appetite for better cooking equipment, specifically the Cuisinart. You could buy one at a store in the Pike Place Market called Sur La Table. (They cost $150 apiece, over $1,000 in today's money.) The owner, Shirley Collins, told an interviewer that she would sell several at a time to wealthy customers in chauffeured limousines. She ran the store until 1995, when she sold to the Behnke family, longtime supporters of the local arts community, who added new locations as well as cooking classes, and expanded into online catalog sales. Though it is still headquartered in Seattle, Sur La Table was taken over by Investcorp in 2011. Who dat? It's an offshore holding company, originally based in Bahrain, that describes itself as "a leading provider and manager of alternative investment products." Price was about $200 million. Kinda makes your head spin.

Food Artisans

Butchers, Bakers, Candlestick Makers

Chapter 9 · SPECIALTY PURVEYORS

Whether buzzing overhead or crackling underfoot, the independent artisans who season our food provide an indispensable taste of Seattle. But beware. Several superstars have lost their way and sold their souls.

STEPHEN BROWN Eltana Bagels

The Canadian cities of Montreal and Toronto have an old-fashioned rivalry unlike anything we see in the US, more intense than Noo Yawk v. Beantown, more nuanced than Tinseltown v. Frisco. Stephen Brown grew up in Toronto but attended McGill in Montreal, which introduced him to Montreal's surpassing gift to North American cuisine: the bagel. Hand-rolled, dense, chewy. An entrepreneur at heart, Brown does nothing by accident. By the time he graduated, he had decided that one day, when the time was right, he would open a bagel bakery and deli.

What most startups lack, Brown posits, isn't customers but a mechanism for customer *engagement.* So he gave his bakery an offbeat name, Eltana. It sounds vaguely Hebrew (not a bad thing, given the product's ethnic background), but it's not a real Hebrew word. The point of the name, the only point, is that customers will *ask what it means.* And what the question creates is an opportunity for the staff to engage with the customers. (There's no sign pointing to the restrooms, either.) Brown and his managers hire new employees based on their candor and generosity of spirit in addition to standard abilities to deal efficiently with a diversity of job duties. Answering the same question a dozen times a day? Shouldn't be a problem. "If it were a real word, it would mean something like 'God's Bread Basket.'"

Lots of stores offer what Brown calls BSOs, bagel-shaped objects, but they're not bagels. "A hole and a soul" is Eltana's bagel. Seven varieties, from plain to salted to "everything." In Montreal, you used to buy a bagel for 50 cents; in Seattle, it'll set you back a buck and change.

Eltana opened on Capitol Hill, and has opened three more stores (Seattle Center, South Lake Union, Wallingford). The existing wood-fired oven at 12th & Pine cranks out 900 dozen bagels a day, with plans for a commissary near Seattle Center. There's technology in place to flash-freeze par-baked bagels with liquid nitrogen when they're 75 percent baked, then finish them onsite in convection ovens, a new batch every 15 minutes.

Ironically, customers want to buy hot, fresh bagels even though they really need to cool for an hour to set the crust. Waiting! Now, *that's* a hard sell. But—more opportunity for engagement—you can do a crossword puzzle while you wait. A new one every week. "What many of us wish we could say we'd done more of this year"? "GOTSOMEEXERCISE."

Bagels are one of those products that seem unnecessarily complicated. First you mix the dough, which you roll into thickish ribbons. Then you pinch a length of dough, form it into a circle, and boil it in water with a bit of honey. Only then do you roll the bagels in a generous amount of "toppings" (salt, garlic, sesame seeds, etc.) and send them into the low-ceiling wood-fired oven. And they're not giant bagels, either, not truck tires. Vegetarians love the spreads: red pepper & walnut, eggplant & pomegranate, and a spicy garlic cream called za'atar. A terrific mashup of Mediterranean street food and Jewish comfort fare.

RILEY STARKS Blue Chicken

Back in the day, turn-of-the-century, a commercial fisherman named Riley Starks took over a rustic lodge on Lummi, a little island tucked under the Canadian border off the coast of Bellingham at the northeastern tip of the San Juan archipelago. That was the original Willows Inn. Then, shortly after he had hired a dazzling 24-year-old line cook named Blaine Wetzel to run the kitchen, and just as the resort was on the cusp of becoming world-famous, Starks sold the property to a group of local investors.

The new owners would quickly remodel the accommodations, reconfigure the dining rooms, and rebrand Willows Inn as a luxury resort with a world-class chef.

Not one to dwell on opportunities lost or roads not taken, Starks retreated to his own place, Nettles Farm, a 15-minute stroll from the beach on land he'd cleared himself, and set about turning it into a European-style *agriturismo*, a working farmhouse bed & breakfast. Fussy, thread-count-obsessed tourists should stay away, they won't find turn-down service with imported chocolates on the pillows. Starks sells the farm's produce at a farmstand near the ferry terminal, and offers his guests the novelty (for city-slickers) of real farm experiences like classes in chicken slaughtering ($50 per person plus the cost of the bird, which you then eat for dinner).

Starks, you see, is on a mission: he intends to restore the reputation of the noble chicken. Not, he's quick to say, those plastic "broilers" from an industrial facility that go from hatchling to supermarket styrofoam in under six weeks. Nope, these are more like the most famous of all French chickens, the proud *Poulet de Bresse.*

The Bresse itself is rich farmland on the left bank of the Saône river that lies between Burgundy and Lyon, and it's here that the local birds reach the height of chickendom. Part of it, sure, is what they eat. But it's mostly their genetic makeup. And herein lies the story of Starks's quest.

Bresse poultry (says the official French statute) has a "melting" flesh impregnated with fat right into its smallest fibers. To ensure that the Bresse Poultry conserves these qualities, it must be "cooked inside itself" In this way, the greater part of the intramuscular fat and even the water it contains will remain inside and the chemical reactions caused by heat, which give the delicate taste, will impregnate the whole bird.

For security reasons, actual Poulet de Bresse birds aren't allowed out of France, but a poultryman across the bordre in Canada has been breeding chickens developed from French stock since the 1980s. The animals, known as Poulet Bleu for their blue feet, are worth $10 a pound, 20 times the value of a supermarket bird.

Says Starks, "This is a chicken we are proud to grow, restaurants can be proud to serve, and you can be proud to eat."

GRANT JONES Kukuruza Popcorn

 America's love affair with exotic foodstuffs is fickle. Need we remind you that Starbucks, 40 years ago, was considered exotic? Turns out, the operative word may be fashion. Pizza continues to reign supreme, with barbecue and burgers close behind. Slurpee machines draw big crowds at the 7-Eleven every summer, and cotton candy gizmos whirr like crazy at fair grounds across the land. Cupcakes and doughnuts have become stand-alone snack categories. Even good old popcorn, that staple of movie theaters, has survived an onslaught from the pleasure police (fake butter, too much salt) and is coming into its own. In fact, gourmet popcorn, with a relatively low barrier to entry, is poised to be the next big thing. And one of its leading practitioners–KuKuRuZa, headquartered in the International District, with a thriving store in the heart of downtown–is having its greatest success in Japan, of all places.

Fashion is part of the explanation; novelty is another. The Japanese have long been impressed by American (and French) consumer trends, but popcorn? Well, why not? It's reasonably exotic, it's portable, doesn't require expensive equipment, and it tastes good. And the name, KuKuRuZa, even sounds Japanese (though it's not).

The word kukuruza is actually Russian for "maize." *Kukuruznik* is a nickname for crop-dusting airplanes, or a jibe at Nikita Kruschchev, who was wont to order random plantings of corn in the former Soviet Union.

KuKuRuZa's corn comes from Nebraska, a "mushroom" variety that looks like kernel corn candies; it puffs up beautifully when air-popped at the company commissary. There's also that "movie-theater" version, which requires an all-white "butterfly" strain that breaks open when it pops to better absorb the melted butter.

Behind the surge of popularity for gourmet popcorn is a boyish Magnolia resident named Grant Jones. A philosophy major at UW, Jones (and his wife, Ashley) had opened Popcorn Pavillion at Bellevue Square and run it for three years when a downtown competitor, Robert Hicks, approached him with the offer to sell *his* store, called KuKuRuZa. (Hicks's wife, Laura, had come up with the name.) For a time, Jones ran two separate, stand-alone popcorn outfits before deciding that KuKuRuZa had better potential. And with the enthusiasm of a puppy Jones began expanding and franchising his concept.

"It was a challenge when we started," Jones recalls. "We were all inexperienced, but we were young and scrappy."

First locally (Ballard), then by franchising internationally (Saudi Arabia, Egypt, Japan), Jones began expanding. When the company's franchisee for Japan opened its second store in a Tokyo suburb, the demand was so high that the average wait just to get into the new store was over two hours." In hot weather, KuKuRuZa hands out fans to patrons standing in line, and also offers tickets with a specific time to return. Once customers get into the store (two at a time), they will often buy for a larger group.

The small team at headquarters tries to develop a new flavor every month. Right now, it's lavender lemonade, but the backlist (to use a publishing term) has some 75 titles. Pumpkin Spice Pecan turns up, as you might expect, once a year. The most popular flavor, around the world, is Hawaiian Sea Salt.

Jones's franchise partners often have food-service experience. In Japan, it's actually an advertising company that also runs a donut franchise and a chain of ten stores that sell "Seattle-themed" soups and chowders.

Providing his franchisees with the precise Hawaiian pink rock salt is one of the few items that Jones exports from the US. In return, the Japanese have come up with a one-gallon fabric bag that's quite popular, reducing the need to ship or store bulky tins.

The only wholesaling KuKuRuZa does is through Made In Washington stores, and then just one flavor (a chocolate-and-vanilla drizzle called Tuxedo), sold in a one-quart container. On its own web site, you can order pretty much anything: some 20 flavors, half sweet, half salty, from an espresso-dusted "Seattle" to that chocolate-drizzled "Tuxedo" to a "Maple Bacon" and a "Buffalo Bleu Cheese." The "Brown Butter & Sea Salt" tastes like old-fashioned "movie theater" popcorn.

You may scoff, but in Japan, let me remind you, they stand in line for two hours just to get in the door. And remember, they laughed at Gordon Bowker, too, when he talked about espresso. Not even Howard Schultz believed him at first.

CORKY LUSTER Ballard Beekeeper

It's the little things. Ten thousand little worker bees, as it happens, plus one queen, inside a three-pound, $75 "box" of bees. Transfer contents into a 10-frame Langstroth hive and you're ready to take on the world. Save the world, actually.

Five years ago Corky Luster was a contractor installing Koehler fixtures. When the construction market softened, Luster looked for other ideas. He'd gone to WSU to become a vet and had done some beekeeping, so he started Ballard Bees with a couple of boxes in his back yard. Today the company has over 100 hives, most of them in backyard gardens around town, and the homeowners--happy to have the advantages of bees (flowers, birds, seeing nature-at-work) pay him.

Ballard's Bastille Restaurant and Kathy Casey Studios use his honey, but would beekeeping fly in downtown Seattle? Gavin Stephenson, executive chef at the Fairmont Olympic, came to Seattle with a mandate to expand the hotel's "lifestyle cuisine." Serving honey from the hotel's own hives was an attractive alternative to pasteurized commercial alternatives. He called Luster and they worked out a deal. Five brightly painted boxes went onto the roof, and, at the beginning of May, the hives were populated. By the end of the year, each hive will grow from 10,000 to 50,000 bees and eventually produce over 150 pounds of honey.

"A bee can forage in a six-mile radius," Luster says. "We don't know exactly where they go, but they're already coming back with pollen on their legs." Once bees find a particularly attractive site, they do a waggle dance inside the hive to tell the others how to get there. The first thing they do is dive straight down from the roof, then they make (you should pardon the expression) a beeline for their feeding grounds. Trees, gardens, parks, p-patches, anything that blooms is a target. It's a short season in Puget Sound; the weather has to be above 55 degrees for these particular species (the Italian and Carniolian western European honey bees) to leave the hive. "But just wait until blackberry season!" Luster exclaims.

Seattle's a good place for urban beekeeping. Backyard chickens are everywhere. Goats? Well, not so much. But bees, not a problem. Luster has a two-year waiting list of households.

HOWARD LEV A Tradition of Peppers

And speaking of goats, specifically of Hungarian goathorn peppers, let's talk for a moment of Mama Lil's and her son, Howard Lev. There really was a Mama Lil, an immigrant from Romania, who settled in Youngstown, Ohio. She got a recipe for pickling the peppers from a Serbian neighbor, who in turn based it on the Italian tradition of pickling peppers in oil. Lots of Italians from Abruzzo in Youngstown, not so many in the Northwest. But the Yakima Valley was home to Krueger Farms, which had a fine crop of Hungarian goathorn peppers. Done deal. Lev started selling the peppers at farmers markets, and eventually started wholesaling as well.

PICKLES, PICKLES, PICKLES

FIREFLY KITCHENS: Julie O'Brien and Richard Climenhage built their business, Firefly Kitchens, around fermented foods. Originally, of course, before the advent of reliable refrigeration, you would salt or pickle or ferment vegetables in order to preserve them. Fermented foods have more beneficial properties; they're "probiotic" by virtue of the living organisms created during fermentation, helpful to digestion. Grocery store shelves have plenty of probotic supplements. But even cheese and yogurt are fermented. And then there's sauerkraut, a "gateway" food, as far as O'Brien and Climenhage are concerned.

BRITT'S: There's only one location (so far), in the Pike Place Market, but this pickle outfit is worth mentioning. Pickles, kraut, kim chi, all handmade and fermented in wooden barrels.

BOAT STREET PICKLES: For over 20 years Renee Erickson has produced a variety of pickled fruits and vegetables as a way to preserve fresh, Northwest produce at the height of ripeness and flavor. This compulsion to pickle nearly everything became an integral part the Provençal-inspired cuisine of her first restaurant, the Boat Street Café. Now the pickles have become an essential pantry element.

MARK ZOSKE & NAOMI NOVOTNY Salts of the Earth

Mark Zoske and Naomi Novotny founded Salt Works 15 years ago because no one else was distributing gourmet salt. Salts from the sea, salts from volcanic hillsides, salts that smell like truffles, salts that flake, salts that crumble. Blue salt, pink salt, black salt, gray salt. Fleur de sel from the marshy coast of France. Salt for the table, salt for the cocktail glass, salt for the bathtub. There's a modest retail shop at the warehouse in Woodinville, but they ship nationwide to gourmet shops and to restaurants. It wouldn't have occurred to me to question their marketing materials, but Zoske and Novotny want to assure the public that their products are "the most trusted name in gourmet salt."

DALE & BETSY SHERROW Fishy Eggs

There's a shop on Eastlake, in one of the newer apartment complexes, whose website bears one of the most prestigious brand names in the world of fine food: Caviar.com. Seattle Caviar Company is the full name of the business, founded in 1990 by Dale and Betsy Sherrow; the internet was just cranking up, but Sherrow already then didn't want to be constrained with the word "Seattle." It's been a rocky quarter-century, though. Illegally harvested sturgeon roe was a big issue. Most of the Russian caviar on the market these days is black market except for Iran's production, under the control of a central, authoritarian government, which makes it less vulnerable to poaching. The Caviar.com website offers an excellent primer on caviar in general. And there's an occasional happy hour where you can educate your palate with a range of caviars, from legitimately sourced Iranian osetra to increasingly plentiful caviar from farm-raised domestic species of sturgeon. Sign up for the Caviar.com newsletter for a schedule.

GERARD PARRAT & DOMINIQUE PLACE Smoke that Salmon!

Seattle in the late 1960s and early 1970s had the good fortune to welcome some fine French chefs. Gérard Parrat held forth at Gérard's Relais de Lyon on the northern shores of Lake Washington, while Dominic Place, who'd run the kitchen at Annie Agostini's Crèpe de Paris in the Rainier Tower downtown, moved to Madison Park and opened Dominique's. Then they both walked away; the Relais de Lyon became Preservation Kitchen, and Dominique's became Sostanza, then Madison

Park Conservatory, and now Beach House. The two Frenchmen went into business together, a modest venture (it seemed at the time): Gérard & Dominique's smoked salmon. It was a traditional Nova-style salmon (a cool smoke that retains the moisture of the fish), and proved quite successful. Since 2008, they have partnered with SeaBear, an Anacortes firm that specializes in the "Northwest" style, a hot-smoke salmon.

Long ago, a Ballard outfit called Portlock was the lone supplier of the east-coast style; they sold to Port Chatham, which became part of Trident Seafoods. But there's an excellent retail outlet near the Ballard Locks, and they carry lox as well. Depending on the season, they also furnish lox to Trader Joe's and to Costco.

JOSH SCHROETER & EDMOND SANCTIS Sahale Snackers

Over a decade ago, two friends were climbing Mount Rainier. They would usually load up with gourmet food, but they'd packed for efficiency on this climb so all they had to sustain themselves was ordinary trail mix. Yuk! When they got off the mountain, they headed straight for the kitchen, determined to create something better. No less nutritious, but tastier.

By this time, the two pals, Josh Schroeter and Edmond Sanctis, had known one another for 25 years, ever since attending Columbia School of Journalism and working at the same company, NBC. Josh had already run digital media ventures for NBC and launched his own internet company, Blockbuy.com; Edmond had become president of NBC Internet as well as Acclaim Entertainment, a video game business. Their kitchen experiments eventually produced several combinations of nuts and fruit glazings (cashews with pomegranate, almonds with cranberries among others) that would form the basis for their company, which they named for Sahale Peak, one of their favorite climbs.

Then came the hard part for the two entrepreneurs: producing their recipes in commercial quantities, and recruiting executives who knew how to manage a food company. Well, we wouldn't be writing this if they hadn't succeeded. Erik Eddings and Erika Cottrell had both worked at Tully's Coffee and Monterey Gourmet Foods, and knew their way around branding and food production; they signed on as CEO and VP Marketing, respectively. And as testimony to their savvy, Sahale Snacks was named Food Processor of the Year by *Seattle Business Magazine* in April, 2014. The Sahale Snacks line has expanded with "to-go" packaging; the pouches are distributed to 10,000 Starbucks stores, hundreds of Whole Foods and Costco locations.

Even though their creations are sold around the world, success hasn't gone to the founders' heads. Edmond and Josh still live in Seattle with their families; they still climb mountains together. Sahale Snacks has grown into a $50 million company with 150 employees; it's now owned (not surprisingly) by a private equity fund, Palladium Partners. (Private equity is often maligned, but it's a godsend to closely-held companies whose owners want to cash out their shares.) Then it was announced that food giant JM Smucker (annual revenues about $5.5 billion) was buying Sahale Snacks as part of an expansion into "lifestyle brands." Their current lineup is pretty impressive: in addition to Smuckers and Dickinson's jams, there's Pillsbury flour and Crisco shortening, a line of coffee brands (Folger's, Dunkin' Donuts, Medaglio d'Oro) and a couple of peanut butters (Jif and Adams). A happy, crunchy ending, right?

MARK PIGOTT It's no Croc!

That's Croc as in croccantini, a made-up word from the Italian croccante, crispy-crunchy. Not potato chips but baked. They're the latest Seattle entry in the "healthy snack" aisle, the lucky offshoot of a commercial bakery on Capitol Hill, La Panzanella. Mark Pigott, whose family controls PACCAR Inc (truck manufacturing) bought the bakery from founder Ciro Pasciuto in 2003 when crackers were still a sideline. Before long, they took over. When the Cap Hill corner changed hands, Pigott moved the company to Tukwilla and added a line of cookies. (They're Kosher and Halal, though not gluten-free). He's got 150 people working for him, turning out snacks. Hey, 300 million crackers a year. Even Canlis serves them. Seriously.

Today its croccantini are distributed throughout the US, and show up in snack-loving countries around the world (Japan, Australia, Hong Kong, Shanghai). There's a second bakery in Charlotte, NC; payroll is approaching 200. The company has just introduced new flavors and sizes. La Panzanella, Pigott says, is the nation's number three specialty cracker in the grocery channel, but the number one cracker in the Specialty category. (Nabisco and its ilk go into the regular cracker aisle, a space so crowded and competitive that supermarkets charge manufacturers a slotting fee just to display their products.) La Panzanella is sold at Whole Foods and at Publix, almost always in the higher-priced deli section, because the price is relatively high: $6 or so for a box of the original La Panzanella crackers, roughly four times the price of a box of Ritz crackers.

MARIAN HARRIS Snack Partners

Can't help but love a company whose best-selling product is called Wise Crackers. They've got a granola, as well as a line of gluten-free snacks. Partners, now based in Kent, has been around for 25 years. Marian Harris was working as a bookkeeper in downtown Seattle when she opened her first restaurant, called Partners; it was an unusual luncheonette, an unheard-of combination deli and bakery. These days, Partners has 85 people on the payroll, and Harris has been inducted into the Specialty Food Association Hall of Fame.

DENISE BREYLEY Whole Foods Forager

Got an idea for a product that ought to be in this list? Here's a woman you should get to know. Say what you will about Whole Foods Markets (starting with Whole Paycheck), we've already heard it. Insufferably self-absorbed, stroller-pushing supermoms who turn even the simplest purchase, from a can of beans to a tuna steak into a deadly serious project more complicated than a PhD thesis. Staff that coddles the cucumbers with loving kindness. Unbearably cheerful courtesy clerks. An entire section of the store that smells like vanilla. The frustrating lack of national brands. And yet, in the produce section, a sign for a vendor called Willie's Greens. Hey, we've got him, too! And another for Denise Breyley, an employee with the title Whole Foods Forager.

Breyley's job is to hit the road and look for local suppliers, from cheese to cider to bagels. She goes out to find and meet farmers, ranchers, and producers in Oregon, Washington, and British Columbia. When she finds the right combination of product and producer (a mint grower in Clatskanie, Oregon, for example) she brings them into the store. Not enough capital? There's even a loan program. CB Nuts, for example, needed to upgrade their processing equipment, so Whole Foods came through with a $55,000 loan.

Chapter 10 · BIG SALAMIS

Pity the pig, reviled as a filthy glutton in our language and our literature. Cooks know better. They praise the pig, revere it as the embodiment of everything delicious.

If you eat meat, you most likely eat sausage as well. Ground meat, spiced and stuffed into a casing of some sort. The noblest of all is the giant loaf called Mortadella, made in Bologna, and defiled by the American manufacturer Oscar Mayer (and by the English language) as "baloney." Thank goodness that artisan butchers abound these days.

ARMANDINO BATALI Conquering the Pig

Fresh pork spoils quickly. It needs to be cooked and eaten before it decomposes, breaks down under the assault of micro-enzymes, or else preserved by some means. Refrigeration slows decay, freezing kills unwanted bacteria. Man has long preserved his food in other ways as well: smoking, air drying, sweetening and, since ancient times, salting.

Simply put, the harmful bacteria cannot live in a salty environment. But the process of salting has many variables and success takes both a scientist and an artisan.

Armandino Batali is both. After an engineering career at Boeing, he spent the first years of his retirement learning both the craft and science of curing meat. "If at first you succeed, hide your astonishment," he says.

Restaurants always want something new, says Armandino Batali. The worst offender, he says, is his own son, the larger-than-life restaurateur Mario (Iron Chef, Babbo, Eataly, etc.), who relentlessly seeks innovation. Armandino, on the other hand, doesn't want to be trendy. Rigorous process control (the engineering background!) in the service of tradition. And tradition in the service of family. Today, his daughter Gina and son-in-law Brian d'Amato do the heavy lifting for the storefront deli, Salumi, and its online marketplace, SalumiCuredMeats.com.

One hundred pounds of meat can make 50 salamis, for example, but a 20-pound pork leg only yields four or five pieces of coppa. And coppa's (relatively) easy. Chorizo's complex. Finocchioni's complex (when you can even get the fennel pollen that provides the essential seasoning). There's a lot of chemistry (checking pH levels and humidity, to determine stability and edibility). Green and blue molds are no-nos; white mold is okay.

Salumi's pigs are local, many of them raised at Skagit River Ranch in Sedro Woolley, where the livestock are pasture-fed on nuts, grass and grain. But Salumi's mail-order business requires a steady supply of pigs, as many as 100 a week, so the company now taps into a network of farmers who subscribe to the ideals of the Slow Food movement, in particular, Newman Farm in Missouri. Salumi prizes animals with more heavily marbled fat, juicier and richer tasting than most pork. The Berkshire pigs that he buys fit the bill for Salumi's dry curing processes and produce a better texture, flavor and consistency. Praise the pigs, indeed!

MAX HOFSTATTER Bavarian Meats

It was 1933 when 19-year-old Max Hofstatter arrived in Seattle from his native Munich carrying (his family likes to say) a small suitcase and big plans. He'd already apprenticed to a sausage-maker in Germany, so he went right to work. Then, in 1961, on the eve of the World's Fair, Hofstatter pulled his family recipes out of the suitcase and launched Bavarian Meats in the Pike Place Market. Fair goers went nuts for his Wieners–hot dogs.

Authentic German recipes for Wieners and Knackwurst, for Braunschweiger and Leberwurst, for Leberkâse and Blutwurst. Most famous of all is the mildly spicy Bavarian Loaf, made from pork, veal, and chopped eggs. "Luncheon Meat," they call it. It's the best sandwich you can buy at the Market.

And then there are the imported goods. Jams, mustards, pickles, powdered desserts. Jars of sauerkraut and red cabbage. Breads and crackers.

At the end of 2015, the company–now owned by two of Hofstatter's granddaughters –adopted a new logo (a lion named Max), a new website, and a new social media presence. (Max was probably not in the suitcase.) Lyla Ridgeway and her twin sister Lynn Hofstatter are firmly in charge, with solicitous, motherly types like Uta Adamczyk behind the counter. They may no longer speak German ("*Und dazu? Sonst noch was?*") but the meaning is clear: "Would you like anything else? What else can we do for you today?"

ULI LENGENBERG Famous Sausages

What distinguishes Uli's sausages from countless others is that company founder Uli Lengenberg used to live in Asia and developed a deep understanding of Asian spices. His shop at the Pike Place Market sells a variety of flavors; you can also sit down for lunch.

Plenty of others to consider. Pino Rogano, an Italian sausage-maker, produces some of the best sausages in town at his little house in Ravenna; it's also a restaurant called da Pino. Just down the street is Edouardo Jordan's Italian-themed Salare, where he also cures much of his own charcuterie. Delicatus and Rainshadow Meats, both in Pioneer Square, put their home-cured meat into sandwiches. And Miles James has reopened his Dot's Deli at the Pike Place Market.

FRANK ISERNIO, ART OBERTO Italian Salumiere

Frank Isernio's family came to Seattle from Abruzzo, on Italy's Adriatic coast. Everyone contributed to the family feasts; Frank's job was making the sausage. He had no intention of "turning pro" (in fact, he worked as a pipefitter and as a driver for Coca Cola), but continued to make sausage for friends and neighborhood restaurants out of a makeshift kitchen in the basement of a friend's house. By 1982, though, he had turned Isernio's into a real business, with a production facility in Georgetown and a growing reputation for quality. At a time when "sausage" was almost a synonym for garbage, Isernio's stood out: whole cuts of fresh pork (and, later, chicken) with tasty seasonings courtesy of Frank's mother, Angetina, who lived to the age of 102. Today, Isernio's is the nation's leading distributor of bulk sausage, sold in one-pound rolls.

Art Oberto is 30 years removed from the day-to-day operation of the sausage company founded in the Rainier Valley 1918 by his parents, Italian immigrants named Constantin and Antonietta. Its flagship product is a brand of beef jerky known as Oh Boy! Oberto. For years, there was an Oh Boy! Oberto boat in the Lake Washington hydroplane races; for years, Art himself drove a vehicle dubbed the Jerkymobile. The crazy, kitschy self-promotion has paid off: Oberto is the number two company nationally in the crowded field of snack meats.

Chapter 11 · BIG CHEESES

For a lot of people, cheese is replete with mystery. Fake cheese is kind of like bad wine: cheap and artificial. Real cheese is packed with flavor, full of the subtlety of its origins (like the terroir of a fine wine), with the additional complexity of the cheese-making process itself.

KURT BEECHER DAMMEIER His Cheeses, They Pleases

 He's become known first as the owner of Beecher's Handmade Cheese in the Pike Place Market, but keep in mind that Kurt Dammeier is an entrepreneur, a guy who loves doing business deals. Increasingly, those deals revolve around his passion for natural ingredients and pure food; with evangelical fervor, he stages comparative tastings to spread the gospel of artisan cheese.

Dammeier made a fortune when his family's high-tech printing company was acquired by a Canadian rival in 1994; with the proceeds, he started investing. First came Pyramid Breweries, where he served for a time as chairman of the board and opened the popular Alehouse across from Safeco Field. Next he acquired the four Pasta & Co. stores, founded by Marcella Rosene, which had established a reputation for high quality ingredients. Then he launched Bennett's Pure Food Bistro on Mercer Island, because that's where he lives and he wanted a good restaurant nearby. And then came Liam's, in University Village.

For its part, Beecher's occupies a central spot in the Market, long the home of the Seattle Garden Store. To snag the coveted space, Dammeier couldn't just put in another Pasta & Co. shop; the Market watchdogs frown on chain outlets. (Starbucks is exempt because it *started* in the Market.) But an artisan cheese factory? Well, yeah, that was a concept the Development Authority could go for. And Dammeier, a 1982 grad of Washington State, had been aching to produce a cheese of his own ever since he discovered Wazzu's award-winning cheddar-in-a-can, Cougar Gold.

Then, instead of the usual steps (raw materials, manufacturing, distribution), Dammeier put the deal together backwards. He had the sales outlet and the basic concept in hand; now he went looking for a production guy, a cheesemaker. And he found Brad Sinko, whose own family operation on the Oregon coast, Bandon Cheese, had just been snatched up by Tillamook. Together, Sinko and Dammeier went looking for a dairy to supply the operation. They found what they were looking for at Green Acres Farm in Duvall. The herd was originally all-Holstein; now they've added an equal number of Jerseys. Green Acres doesn't actually own the 40 new cows; instead, it leases them from a local entrepreneur, who just happens to be Kurt Dammeier.

France has hundreds of traditional, regional cheeses; not so in the US. Dammeier set out to create a specifically local cheese for Seattle. He and Sinko quickly settled on a cheddar-Gruyère hybrid; they named it Beecher's Flagship—Beecher was Kurt's grandfather—but it would have to age almost a year. While they waited (and the raw milk version was particularly promising), they built up an 80,000-pound inventory...and sold a lot of fresh curds. Dammeier also perfected a pasta recipe, "World's Best Mac & Cheese," that's now shipped nationwide. That's the one he cooks up for guest shots on TV; it's rich, creamy and utterly delicious.

GEORGE LYDEN Imported Cheese Man

When young George Lyden started working at the Peterson brothers' market at 15 W. McGraw atop Queen Anne, stocking shelves and answering the phone, he didn't know how to spell cheddar but he did know how to make himself useful. His own family had a store in Auburn, Lyden's Market, but cheese wasn't part of the inventory. George had a freshly minted degree in marketing from the University of Washington (though construction still paid better, and, for a few months, so did real estate).

George was a likable kid and people trusted him. So did the Petersons, who soon let him take over their store and its niche as Seattle's premium supplier of Scandinavian specialty food. This was at the end of 1968, when the influence of Swedes and Norwegians and Danes was evident in traditional Scandinavian neighborhoods, most notably in Ballard. All of ten cheeses in the beginning: Danish blue and Havarti, Jarlsberg and Gjetost from Norway, Lappi from Sweden.

As George Lyden (assisted by his brother, Chuck) started traveling to find more specialty items, he branched out to French cheeses. Not just Camembert but Soumatrin; not just Brie but Brillat Savarin. A bleating cacophony of goat cheeses: Chaources, Crottin, Cabécou, Chevrot. A cantata of Roquefort variations. From Italy, the creamy buffalo cheeses and the intense Parmigianos. From the British Isles, Gloucesters and Stiltons, Wenslydales and two dozen farmhouse Cheddars.

Today Peterson carries well over 2,000 different cheeses (cow, goat, buffalo) from nearly 20 countries, crumbled, grated, pre-cut; raw, pasteurized; fresh, washed rind, rolled in ash, smoked. Cheddar? Easy. Cheddar from the land-locked central African country of Burundi? No worries, Peterson has you covered there, too. And cheese is only one category. Meat, poultry, seafood, pasta, condiments, baked goods, chocolate.

The company is now based in a 200,000 square-foot facility in Auburn, and operates a second distribution center in New Jersey. That makes it "mid-market" compared to the big national outfits like FSA (Food Services of America) and Sysco (which just called off a merger with US Foods), or even brick & mortar stores like Restaurant Depot (for industry members only) and Cash & Carry (no frills, but open to the public).

Peterson's charcuterie business is booming, too, with its own catalog. So is mail-order and online ordering. A decade ago the French ambassador to the US, his Excellency Jean-David Levitte, decorated Lyden with the medal of *Chevalier de l'Ordre du Mérite Agricole* to honor his decades of support for French agriculture.

The biggest problem George Lyden faces these days is (grumble-grumble) compliance with the plethora of well-meaning regulations, certifications, and liability coverage. Yet his biggest pleasure is traveling the two-lane highways of the country looking for undiscovered, "back road" cheeses. There's one, Tarentaise, deep gold like an Abondance, that comes from a small farm in Vermont. Another, Winnimere, also from Vermont, this one from a farm called Jasper Hill, resembles a Vacherin Mont d'Or, and won Best of Show when the American Cheese Society held its conference in Seattle in 2010. The larger local dairies like Mount Tam and Quillisascut have their own distribution networks, but every once in a while, there's a newcomer, like Amaltheia Organic Dairy out of Montana (organic goat cheese), or Bellwether Farms, a legendary sheep's milk cheese from Petaluma, Calif., and then George gets out of the car and starts the process all over again, helping a producer become a vendor.

SHERI LAVIGNE Cheese Maven

You may have met Sheri LaVigne at Calf & Kid, a wondrous cheese shop in the Melrose Market, or at Culture Club, her short-lived restaurant on Capitol Hill.

Artisanal cheese trumps industrial every time: quirky, changing with the seasons, dependent on weather, on aging conditions, and so on. There are different styles of cheese (fresh, soft rind, hard rind, washed rind, and so on) produced from lactating animals as different as goats and buffalo. Portable protein; cheese is easier to carry than milk.

At Culture Club, there were a few prepared dishes, like mac & cheese and grilled cheese sandwiches, but the stars are the wine & cheese pairings. Three cheeses (goat, cow, sheep) paired with three wines (red, white, or sparkling), alongside crackers and jam. These aren't cheap, and why should they be? They're an extraordinary lesson, a graduate course in both geography and sensory appreciation.

How else would you even discover a cheese called Harbison, a soft-ripened cow's cheese with a "bloomy" rind wrapped in tree bark? Yes, Kurt Farm Shop, sells its magnificent Camembert-style Dinah's Cheese just down the street, and it's as good as you'll find in western Washington. But this creamy Harbison, from Jasper Hill Farm in rural Vermont, was transcendent.

"JERSEY DINAH" Vashon Island Cheese Producer

The original Dinah was a three-year-old Jersey; it took two hours a day to milk her by hand until Kurt Timmermeister could finally afford commercial milking equipment. He's got almost 20 cows now, and produces an amazingly soft and creamy blooming-rind farmstead wheel he calls Dinah's Cheese. (Farmstead cheese, by definition, is made from milk that comes from cows living on the farm, in this case Timmermeister's 20-acre Vashon Island property.) Made by hand, wrapped by hand, sold across the counter at Kurt Farm Shop on Capitol Hill, at a dozen selected retailers and two dozen restaurants. There's also a crumbly cheese called Flora's (think of feta), and an aged tomme-style cheese called LogHouse, aged for four months in a cave on the farm.

NOT-QUITE SO-BIG CHEESES

Cows, goats, sheep: lactating bovines, caprines, and ovines. Washington State alone has almost 75 dairy farms producing cheese. There's an interesting second life for the manure, by the way. Composting dairy cow manure is a sustainable replacement for man-made chemical fertilizers

MONTEILLET FROMAGERIE sounds French, and it is. They're in Dayton, nearly 300 miles southeast of Seattle in the scenic Walla Walla Valley. Pierre-Louis Monteillet and his wife, Joan, operate the 32-acre property, which was the first artisanal farmstead cheese facility in the region. He's from Millau, a town in the mountains of southern France, not that far from Roquefort. She's an artist who grew up in the wheat fields of eastern Washington. They met in Mexico, moved to Walla Walla, and started making cheese with milk from a herd of 50 Alpine goats and 50 sheep (Friesian and Lacaune). The farm offers cheese-making classes and something even more exciting than cheese: vacation farm-stays on the property.

MOUNT TOWNSEND CREAMERY Co-founder Ryan Trail trained as an engineer and learned about the technical side of fermentation at the New Belgium Brewery. But his love of cheese comes from a wheel of Camembert he brought home from France in his backpack one summer. Production (eight or ten styles, depending on the season).is enough to warrant a wholesale operation. The Seastack amd New Moon jack both won best-in-class awards from the American Cheese Society. The Olympic Peninsula's lush landscape and damp microclimate might remind you of the French countryside (Normandy, anyone?) where the tradition of crafting soft-ripened cheeses began.

QUILLISASCUT FARM is located outside of Rice, on the Columbia River near the Canadian border. The owners, Rick and Lora Lea Misterly, have a farm, a cheese shop, and a school that teaches cheese-making as well as basic "day in the country" classes. There's a cookbook as well, "Chefs on the Farm" that Lora Lea wrote with Shannon Borg. Quillisascut comes from the Salish word for "place of scattered bushes." The farm has been producing raw-milk goat cheeses for 30 years now.

Chapter 12 · BIG SWEETIES

Baked goods are back, whether it's for dessert or for breakfast.

JERILYN BRUSSEAU Cinnabaker

 Jerilyn Brusseau, a baker and chef who grew up on a farm in Snohomish County, is happy to share the credit for her greatest creation, the Cinnabon. "It was Rich's idea," she insists, Rich Komen being the founder of Restaurants Unlimited (Clinkerdagger's, Cutter's, Palomino, Palisade among others), who was looking for a new venture in the mid-1980s. Not a full restaurant concept but a sideline. Brusseau used to do catering out of her popular bakery in Edmonds, north of Seattle, using ingredients sourced from local farms (butter, cheese, shellfish) and had done an event for the RUI executive team. "How would you like to make the world's greatest cinnamon roll?: he asked her.

Turns out, Brusseau's grandmother, Maude Delaney Spurgeon had a recipe that she'd taken with her from Buffalo to rural Montana, and it became the starting point for Cinnabon. The key ingredient, not surprisingly, was the cinnamon itself, korintje from Sumatra, which provided both big aroma and big flavors. The rest was trial and error. How many "wraps" (seven and a half), how many minutes bake time (14), and the decision to sell only the latest batch, right out of the oven. (Leftovers, when available, are sold at a discount.) Even so, Brusseau recalls, it was one failure after another until she figured out what was wrong. And no, she's not revealing her secret.

For the launch, they wanted Bellevue Square, but owner Kemper Freeman refused ("too risky") so they opened the first Cinnabon at SeaTac Mall in Federal Way in November 1985. (Bel Square came around eventually for location number six.) Today you can't walk through a mall or airport without encountering the smell of a Cinnabon ; there's no denying that they make a good breakfast and, for some, an addictive nosh at other times of day.

Because she was working on a contract, Cinnabon did not make Brusseau wealthy. She keeps a farm on Bainbridge Island and travels frequently to Asia for the charity she founded two decades ago, PeaceTrees Vietnam, which assists families recovering from the devastation of war. (Brusseau's brother was a helicopter pilot killed in the war.) "Never give up," is her motto.

For its part, RUI is now one of dozens of conglomerate brands owned by Sun Capital, which is based in Florida. (It was at the home of Sun Capital CEO Ron Leber that Mitt Romney delivered his infamous "47 percent" speech during the 2012 presidential campaign.) Meantime, the Cinnabon concept was spun off into a separate corporation 20 years ago, and has been bought and sold several times; it's currently owned by Focus Brands, a private equity outfit based in Atlanta. It has expanded to well over 900 stores; its COO, not yet 40, is a former waitress and VP of training & development at Hooter's.

Did you really want to know? A cinnabon costs $3.50 and contains 880 calories. Want the version topped with caramel? Add 200 calories. The company offered Minibon Delights for a while, with one third the calories, but they flopped.

MARIA COASSIN Gelato & Panettone

Maria Coassin, the owner of Gelatiamo in downtown Seattle, makes about 1,200 panettone every December, essentially by hand, with good cheer and artisanal dedication. Panettone is a traditional Italian Christmas loaf, originally from Milan, not really a fruitcake (like the stubbier, denser German *Stollen*), but airy, bread-y, sweet, yeasty, with plenty of rum-soaked raisins, vanilla from Madagascar, candied orange zest, and lemon bits. You can buy an industrial panettone for under ten bucks, something made in a factory last summer that sat on the warehouse shelf waiting for the holidays, but it will taste like sweetened sawdust. You can try to make your own at home, but it takes 27 hours, start to finish, waiting for the yeast to rise, and rise again. You have to add spendthrift amounts of butter and egg yolks; you have to watch times and temperatures like a hawk, and when it comes out of the oven it's still so delicate that it will collapse like a soufflé unless you hang it upside down on a skewer, like a bat. Then, once it cools, it still has to "mature" for about a week so that its aromatic ingredients (the citrus, the rum, the vanilla) can develop their full flavors and fragrances.

Coassin grew up in a family of bakers in the small town of Maniago, just over 10,000 people, midway between Venice and Trieste in northeastern Italy and known throughout Europe for the local industry: knife-making. The Giulian Alps tower over the flood plains of the Po River. The cows are milked for cheese, and the pigs, fed on the whey, become prosciutto. The mountain streams provide a ready and reliable source of energy to mill grain, stoke forges, and turn lathes. To manufacture highly sophisticated automobiles, for example, you need a work force familiar with precision tools, and most of Italy's racing cars (Maserati, Lamborghini, etc.) are built in the region. But those workers need to eat, too, and the Coassin Bakery has prospered for five generations. With loving parents and five older brothers, Maria was well looked-after, but she realized early-on that the family business was limiting. Pastries and gelato, she knew even then, would be her field. Not yet 20, she married an American airman stationed at the nearby Aviano Air Force Base, moved to California, and took a job with McDonald's so she could learn English and become versed in American business practices. When her husband retired from the military a few years later, she'd climbed the corporate ladder from mopping floors and washing dishes to assistant manager. She was ready to set out on her own, but didn't want to stay in California. They flipped a coin: Seattle or Atlanta.

She signed on with an educational supply company in Seattle while she looked for a spot to open her own business. What she found was "Third & Hell," the then-hardscrabble corner at Third & Union across from Benaroya Hall (announced but not yet under construction) and the neglected Mann building that Rick and Ann Yoder would buy and restore, moving their popular pan-Asian cafe, Wild Ginger, from Western Avenue into the upstairs space, and creating a music venue, the Triple Door, below. Brian Garrity had just opened Procopio, Seattle's first gelateria, in the Pike Street Hillclimb. Dany Mitchell followed with Gepetto in Pioneer Square. By then, Coassin had a name ready to go: a made-up word that's the Italian equivalent of I Love Sushi: "*Gelato Ti Amo*," or Gelatiamo. To an Italian speaker, it sounds as if you're saying "Let's go eat gelato."

Coassin had almost no financing, however, so she cashed out her share of the family bakery business; it came to $200,000. Her father pitched in another $50,000 to help her buy equipment. (Reminder: this was serious money 20 years ago.) In fact, he came to visit the first year, in 1996. "What can I do to help?" he would ask. It was a cold winter, not much demand for that sexy but little-known Italian newcomer, gelato. (Lots of customers thought it was cream cheese.) So Coassin's dad started making panettone.

Brief aside: the confection's name uses the Italian suffix, "-one" (*OH-nay*), which suggests something bigger, grander. So polpetta, a meatball, becomes *polpettone*, meatloaf. Minestra, soup, becomes *minetsrone*, big soup with lots of vegetables. Pane, bread, becomes *panettone*, fancy bread for the holidays.

In addition to the holiday panettone, Coassin added pastries to her repertoire, and Gelatiamo took on the character of an elegant cafe in Vienna or Torino. Gelato is fine for maybe six months of the year in a cool climate like Seattle; cakes, cookies, and coffee are what tide you over. She expanded her workshop in the basement of the Vance Building several times to accommodate high-tech equipment as she increased her gelato production to service wholesale accounts like Pagliacci pizza parlors. That kitchen today includes a food-grade pasteurizing machine to satisfy the Department of Agriculture's byzantine food-safety regulations, several mixing machines, two half-size, Moffat turbo-fan convection ovens, a walk-in fridge, and a couple of freezers. Right now she uses two Italian-made Bravo gelato making machines, automatic models that quickly pasteurize the mixture—a requirement since Coassin makes her gelato from scratch—before batch-freezing it. Unlike the practice of her competitors, she doesn't use commercial mixes. "I don't compromise, though," she told me. "If ingredients cost more, like eggs or hazelnuts, I pay what they cost, but I don't raise my prices."

Over the years she has built up a team of 20. Assisted by longtime employees Gabi Lopez and Elisa Jimenez, Coassin efficiently divides the totes filled with twice-risen panettone dough into 520-gram portions; the women quickly massaged them into smooth balls that they lower into paper molds. It's the only time in the process that the dough is touched by human hands.

In those two small ovens, Coassin can only bake 16 panettones at a time, but she gets a lot of satisfaction from knowing that her brothers in Italy are doing exactly the same thing at the same hour. FaceTime conversations are not unheard of. And after all that effort, 1,200 one-pound loaves of panettone, priced at $20 apiece. (A special treat, Gelatiamo's panettone filled with zabaglione-flavored gelato, is sometimes available by the slice.) Add it up, and it might seem barely worth the effort. But it's a fifth-generation thing in Maniago, and a 20-year Seattle tradition now, and Coassin won't give it up.

GELATO & ITALIAN SWEETS

Denser and more flavorful than American ice cream, gelato has four full-time confectioners in Seattle. In addition to Coassin's Gelatiamo in the Central Business District; there's Bottega Italiana in the Pike Place Market (with two more outposts in California), Procopio, in the Pike Street Hillclimb, named for the Sicilian who invented the gelato-making process. And D'Ambrosio Gelato, a father-and-son operation recently sold, with stores in Ballard, Capitol Hill and Bellevue.

As for bakeries, there's no competing with Remo Borracchini in the heart of Garlic Gulch, as the Rainier Valley neighborhood was known a century ago. The Borracchini sign is an illuminated rotating Italian flag with daily specials announced on the marquee, and you can watch the ladies (almost all Vietnamese and Laotian these days), in hair nets and latex gloves, decorating cakes to order.

CUPCAKE ROYALE

If you're turned on by a phrase like Blueberry Balsamic Goat Cheese ice cream, this is your spot. When Jody Hall launched the company in 2003, there were no cupcake bakeries anywhere outside New York; there are now six Cupcake Royale cafes around town. Best part: field trips to the farms and dairies!

DEBRA MUSIC Theo Chocolate

Things to get out of the way: the name Theo, for starters. Not Teddy, not Vincent's brother, nothing to do with the Deity, nope. It's a small tree, *Theobroma cacao*, native to the deep tropics of Central and South America, whose seeds (called cacao beans) are used to make chocolate. Moving on. Ten years ago, a novel food company based in Fremont burst onto the scene, promising something unheard of and thought to be unattainable: the nation's first bean-to-bar chocolate. The company was called Theo. Its founders were Joe Whinney and Debra Music, and the early press enthusiasm for their products pushed their personal stories aside. Now, with the publication of a handsome Theo Chocolate cookbook, their remarkable tale is being told again.

Over the years, we've heard regularly about Joe Whinney, the environmentalist and activist for sustainable agriculture whose sympathy for the plight of the cacao farmers turned from idealism to advocacy to commercial success. Less about his co-founder, Debra Music, the marketing maven who created Theo as a consumer brand. But we're getting ahead of the story. Whinney and Music married, set up house in Massachusetts, had a son, divorced, but–despite their separate careers–remained close, as their son, Henry, grew up. Henry was ten when Whinney convinced a Seattle-based investor to underwrite his dream of creating a sustainable chocolate business; he asked Music to join him in the move to Seattle.

Theo Chocolate opened a year later in an old trolley barn in Fremont. Originally viewed as a novelty, the chocolate bars, in a variety of unusual flavors, caught on, helped by a logo from a local design firm called Kittenchops.com. Food Network named Theo one of the hottest chocolate companies in the US; WebMD named it the nation's outstanding dark chocolate; Oprah declared her love on TV. Integral to the concept are the free public tours which explain every step of the chocolate process, literally from bean to bar.

And now there's the book, filled with 75 recipes along with innumerable articles about the bean's transition to chocolate. A procession of A-list chefs contribute recipes (Tom Douglas: roast chicken and wild mushroom bread salad with cocoa nibs; Maria Hines: lamb sugo over tagliatelle infused with cocoa nibs). Cocoa's not just for breakfast anymore.

KATE McDERMOTT The Omigod Peach Pie

There are three kinds of people in the world, Kate McDermott will tell you: pie-makers, pie-eaters, and pie-seekers. There's another argument: there are pie people and there are cake people, a distinction that eluded me completely, since I didn't consider myself either one, or didn't until I watched McDermott bake her peach pie. After all, people have been making pie since the dawn of civilization (or since the advent of milled grain, at any rate), and McDermott's mission these days (she used to be a musician) is to teach the mechanics as well as the art of pie-making to whoever comes through the door.

Begin, she insists, with King Arthur unbleached all-purpose flour. "I want wheat growers to take this class," she says, "so they can see what a difference the right flour makes." Irish butter, foil-wrapped Kerrygold, with high fat content. Leaf lard; she gets hers shipped from Pennsylvania. Regular supermarket sugar, a touch of seasoning (salt, nutmeg), some thickener so you don't get fruit soup.

For the fruit, at the end of August, McDermott was using Frog Hollow Cal-Red peaches, shipped in single-layer boxes that cuddle a dozen peaches from the farm in Brentwood, Calif. Her ex, Jon Rowley, started the Peach-O-Rama promotion for Metropolitan Markets with these peaches, using a refractometer to measure the sugar content: at least 13 brix (percent sugar). For a demonstration at Diane's Market Kitchen in downtown Seattle, she used peaches that measured 20 brix, off the charts. "The omigod peach," McDermott called it.

The details of the pie-making process are not complicated as long as you keep everything ice-cold, and won't be repeated here. They're at McDermott's website, theartofthepie.com. She also teaches pie-making classes in Seattle and at her cabin in Port Angeles ("Pie Camp") and, occasionally, in other cities ("Pie on the Road"). Trust me that when you taste the pie, with its flaky crust and luscious filling, you will become a believer. The very act of pie-eating will turn you a pie-seeker. You are a disciple now and you recite the mantra: "Be happy. Eat pie."

SEATTLE CHOCOLATE

Jean Thompson believes in licking the spoon. She started Seattle Chocolate with a store at the airport and a production facility near Southcenter, in 2002 but there are sales outlets throughout the Seattle area in spots like gift shops and delis. Oh, and Frangos. You remember Frangos, right? The Frederick & Nelson chocolates? The box looks different these days but the chocolates are still around, sold by former arch-rival Macy's.

DILETTANTE

Dana Davenport, whose family had made candies in Hungary, founded Dilettante as a high-end chocolatier in 1976, added retail Mocha Café locations, and sold the company to Seattle Gourmet Foods 30 years later. (SGF is an under-the-radar umbrella for a dozen local specialty producers.) The Mocha Cafés even include Martini Bars these days.

FRAN'S

Fran Bigelow started her company in 1982, well before "fine chocolate" was a thing. Even today, she's better known for her salted caramels than anything else. Okay, truffles and bon bons as well. Prestigious locations (the Four Seasons Hotel, for example.) Her kids are taking over, which is just fine with Fran.

JESSIE OLESON The Cake Spy

Well aware that there's a serious lack in this book: not enough cupcakes. But aren't there dozens (it would seem) of cupcake dispensaries on Capitol Hill alone? Sure. But none as innocent and downright cute as Cakespy. That's Jessie Oleson, a talented illustrator and quirky thinker who (in the Internet's infancy, not that long ago) created a sweet-natured character called Cuppy that was really nothing more than a leftover blob of dough. Well, Cuppy, you may remember, became a national phenomenon. A retail shop didn't work out, but Oleson's Cakespy blog lives on.

Chapter 13 · INVENTORS & TINKERS

How many things would we not have today if a few eccentrics hadn't been willing to fuss over something. A bathroom faucet, a way to keep bubbles in the bottle, a coffee machine. Projects that required perseverance with little apparent reward. Edison at his work bench, the conviction that there has to be a way. Because of one Seattle man with a tinker's spirit and determination, Starbucks was able to serve espresso in its first stores.

KENT BAKKE Tinkering with the Marzocco

The *marzocco* is a heraldic lion, the medieval symbol of Florence. Not the fearsome bronze *cinghiale* (wild boar) that the tourists gawk at in the medieval city's central market, but a grey sandstone lion sculpted in 1420 by Donatello, no less, for the papal suite of the Medici palace. (The weathered statue in the central square of Florence, the Piazza della Signoria, is a copy.) The "Marzocchesi" were the Florentines, in honor of their lion, even though there's no etymology connecting them. Mars, god of war, maybe.

Which brings us to La Marzocco, a brand of espresso machines, among Italy's finest. They're produced at a factory in the hills northeast of Florence, in a community called Scarperia that was long known for its knives. In 1927, production of espresso machines began there as well. Bear in mind: the north of Italy, with its abundant streams of running water to power mills, grinding wheels and presses, has always been a hotbed (as it were) of precision metal-working. There's also a 5-km race track, the Mugello Circuit, owned by Ferrari, on the outskirts of town; it's used as a test track and for auto and motorcycle races. Not far away are the Ferrari, Lamborghini, Maserati, and Ducati factories.

Fast-forward to the 1970s in Seattle and a sandwich shop in Pioneer Square called Hibble & Hyde. The owner was a tinker named Kent Bakke, completely captivated by the winged, copper-clad Victoria Arduino coffee-making machine in the back. Needless to say, there was no internet; there were no instruction manuals, either. Bakke was on his own, but he managed to crank it up and make it work, and on a good day he would turned out half a dozen espressos. His business partner suggested a visit to Italy, so

Bakke took himself to Scarperia and returned with a contract as La Marzocco's US importer. One of the first machines he sold went to a six-store chain, just starting to serve espresso by the name of Starbucks.

Before long, thanks in large measure to Starbucks' buying La Marzocco machines for all its coffee shops, Bakke's company became La Marzocco's largest distributor outside of Italy, with offices in the UK, Australia, Korea, and so on. Then, 20 years ago, Starbucks needed 150 machines a month for its new stores. La Marzocco was less than thrilled by the challenge of meeting an order of this magnitude, so Bakke and a small group of investors bought 90 percent of the parent company. They promptly opened a second factory in Ballard to meet the demand from Starbucks.

For a long time, there was at least one La Marzocco machine in every Starbucks store, but in 2004 the Mermaid switched to push-button devices that required less skill on the part of the barista. Bakke closed the factory in Ballard and sold the distribution business to a Swiss company, even though, five years ago, he bought back the distribution rights. It was almost too late: in the interim, several former Bakke employees had opened competing businesses. Machines for home use, machines that allow baristas to control water flow and temperature. Still, says Bakke, "Our biggest competition is complacency."

Bakke's not the only player. Michael Myers has a thriving company called Michaelo Espresso that also sells and services several machines, including a brand called La San Marco. No relation to La Marzocco, though they're also made in the north of Italy.

Most of the big coffee wholesalers also have their own technicians, and plenty of one-man repair companies have set up shop as well. But the news this season is that KEXP, the experimental radio station, is getting a new home at Seattle Center, and part of that space is a La Marzocco coffee shop and showroom. Bakke himself remains CEO of the company, the one that started decades ago with that one abandoned Victoria Arduino.

EVAN WALLACE Keeping the Bubbles Alive

Evan Wallace, ex-physicist and former software exec, lives in a condo at the Market and spends a lot time in his "living room" downstairs, the Zig Zag Café. He's a tinker and inventor with a fondness for bubbles and abhorrence of flat Champagne.

How to keep the sparkle in a sparkling wine? Icy cold temperature helps; an airtight stopper helps, but really, once the bottle has been opened, the only way to keep the contents perfectly fresh is to exactly recreate the conditions in the bottle *before* the cork was popped. Wallace's solution, patented as the Perlage system, is to encase the entire bottle in a clear safety enclosure, and then re-pressurize the head space of the bottle to its original state. For the first three years, Perlage was licensed to a single customer (Dom Perignon), but it's now available for home use.

There's another product from Wallace's company, Applied Fizzics, that will add sparkle to your bar: it's called Perlini, a $200 kit (in a Mafia-style metal attaché case) that includes a shaker, a pressurizer, and a dozen CO_2 cartridges. Starbucks was looking at Perlini to carbonate its Tazo iced tea. Barkeeps around the country are using large-scale Perlini devices to add fizz to their cocktails. (Canon, on Capitol Hill, serves a sparkling Negroni, among others.)

And wait, yes, there's more. It's a device called Fizz-Iq that will carbonate anything. It's the size of a giant microwave and connects via tubes, hoses, gas canisters and mixing valves to kegs of premixed cocktails.

Wallace doesn't outsource the manufacturing, he does it himself, at a workbench in a space he rents from a friend who happens to own the condo unit across the hall from his own. Yes, circuit boards and all. "I had to learn how to do this," he points out. Sometimes he has people come in and help him with the assembly. Production of the Fizz-Iq: about one unit a month. Sales price: between five and ten grand, which Wallace sometimes takes in trade.

Two more things. Wallace is a terrific dancer and for years taught tango. Second, though he almost always drinks bubbles, he has his own list of classic cocktails:.In addition to the Martini, the Negroni, the Manhattan, and the Margarita, there's something called the Seelbach (Bourbon, Cointreau, bitters, and Champagne, named for the hotel in Louisville where it was created in 1917).

DAVID HOLCOMB Choppin' Away

The founder and chief executive of Chef'n, David Holcomb, exhibits the endearing goofiness of Gene Wilder playing Willy Wonka overlaid with the elegant British manners of Gordon Ramsay at his most charming. A fan of the Grateful Dead, he says he came up with the name for his company while listening to their iconic song, Truck'n.

Peelers, hullers, strainers, colanders, steamers, juicers, zesters, baking sheets, spatulas, spoons, devices to measure, bake, shake, grind, dice, and chop: that's the inventory for Holcomb's workshop and showroom close to Seattle's stadiums.

As for the inventions themselves, they vary considerably. The plain silicone spatulas are standard stuff in pretty colors. Things get wacky when you contemplate the deadly efficiency of the Chef'n Garlic Zoom, a ruthless chopping device that makes short shrift of half a dozen peeled garlic cloves. Once the cloves are loaded, the Zoom is rolled vigorously across the kitchen counter; precisely calibrated gears spin a phalanx of lethal scimitars on an interior axle making mincemeat of the garlic. Now you up-end the device and shake out the perfectly chopped garlic. (Don't insert your finger to scoop out the bits that adhere to the inside walls unless you have Medic One standing by for a quick trip to the ER.) A couple of flips and the device disassembles and goes into the dishwasher.

Now, if you have any skills as a home cook, you know that mincing garlic takes no time at all, even half a dozen cloves can be dispatched in less time than it takes to read these lines. So what, pray tell, is the attraction of all these fancy gadgets by Chef'n? "We want to make better tools so you can make better food," Holcomb states, with a perfectly straight face.

Since 2010 his company has been part of Taylor, the folks who make precision scales. The parent company also own Rabbit, which produces corkscrews. Willie Wonka indeed.

ALBERT MOEN In Hot Water

Hot! Yikes, that water's *hot!* If this has never happened to you, you can thank Albert Moen, Seattle kid who graduated from Franklin High School in 1934. He was a mechanical engineering student at the University of Washington when he turned on the faucet–the old, two-handled kind–and, surprise, got his hands burned. Hmm, you can just imagine his inventor's brain clicking.

Moen never graduated from U-Dub, but in the run-up to World War II he easily found work as a tool designer in military shipyards. His personal project–to build a single-handled faucet–had to wait until after the war. Eventually he found Kemp Hiatt at Ravenna Metal Products to work up a prototype, just in time for the post-war boom in housing. Once he conquered the kitchen sink, Moen developed a "cartridge" faucet for home showers that prevented scalding when a toilet was flushed. By the time he retired in 1982, Al Moen had 75 patents to his name; one of the last, ironically, was for a washerless two-handle faucet. Today Moen Faucets is owned by a holding company for a variety of consumer products called Fortune Brands.

NELLA Keeping it Sharp

Italians have a thing for knives, and with good reason. Arrotini, they call them, or moletas, knife-sharpeners and scissors-grinders. They are descendants of early tradesmen in the remote Val Rendena in the northern Dolomites. By what accident of history did its practitioners venture forth at the end of the 19th century for the big cities of North America? Yet come they did, honing the knives of earlier immigrants (German butchers, English cooks, French chefs). Eventually, they brought their families over, too, and set out across the continent: Binellis in Detroit and Chicago; Maganzinis in Boston; and the Nella family to Toronto, Vancouver BC, and Seattle. These days, from its facility in SoDo, Nella services scores of local restaurants with knives, slicers and grinders. The knives they supply to restaurant kitchens in Seattle are utilitarian, with plastic handles, not the elegantly tooled French and German blades you'd see at Sur la Table.

CHEFSTEPS Better Cooks, Better Humans

There are plenty of serious uses for technology in the kitchen, and some good people like Michael Natkin (whom we'll meet again in the Cookbook section, page 243) who know their software and their egg yolks. Turns out, uncertainty over one's egg yolk performance is a very big deal for some home cooks, so much that there's a mini-industry devoted to restoring confidence in just the right intensity of yellow, just the right firmness in the white. (Where else could so much effort be expended in not ending up too hard?) Chefsteps, located in the Pike Place Market, teaches classes (coffee, salmon, knife sharpening) for beginners, and an ambitious premium-level series as well ($24 one-time fee), often involving the process known as *sous-vide*. Drop the item you're cooking in a water bath whose temperature is set to cook your food slowly and evenly; come back hours later to a perfectly cooked steak or salmon. The gadget that makes this possible is a $200 immersion circulator called a Joule; so popular it's hard to keep in stock.

"Cooking smarter makes us better humans," the Chefsteps folks say. And the more you know about cooking, the better you get.

Let's Eat!

Restaurants Then & Now

Chapter 14 · THE THREE BIGGEST FORKS

Three enterprises founded within the past 30 years play an outsize role in what America eats and drinks: Amazon, Costco, and Starbucks. And all three are Seattle institutions. We could probably add Allrecipes.com, and append the phrase "how America cooks," but let's focus on the big three businesses, online, wholesale, retail.

- **Amazon**: $107 billion revenue, 230,000 employees, online retailer
- **Costco**: $117 billion revenue, 117,000 employees, 700 locations
- **Starbucks**: $23 billion revenue, 200,000 employees, 24,000 locations

While we're at it, let's look at the net worth of their corporate leaders. And, for reference, a couple other local billionaires:

- Bill Gates, $76 billion
- **Jeff Bezos, $47 billion and counting, as Amazon's stock skyrockets**
- Steve Ballmer, $22 billion
- Paul Allen, $17 billion
- **Howard Schultz, $2.1 billion**
- **Jeff Brotman / Jim Sinegal $2 billion** each (estimated)

Now, you're going to say that **AMAZON** isn't in the food business. You'd be wrong. Maybe not at the same level as Walmart, which sells over $250 billion worth of groceries a year, half its revenue. But Amazon sees those numbers and drools. Amazon is already bigger (barely) than Kroger (QFC, Fred Meyer), and Amazon's Jeff Bezos knows that to catch Walmart Amazon is going to have to sell more food and more clothing. Won't be easy; lots of consumers still want to smell the peaches and squeeze the Charmin. Which is why there are small steps in the direction of food, like AmazonFresh. Unfazed by the failure of HomeGrocer, Peapod, and Webvan, Amazon is forging ahead. Its trucks have been cruising Seattle neighborhoods for years now, and are moving up and down the North American coasts as well as in the major cities of Merry Olde England. The only downside: a $299 per year membership fee.

Ah, but won't Amazon kill off neighborhood grocery stores? One of their ideas is private label products, like milk, coffee, vitamins, diapers, and laundry detergent. So AmazonFresh seems to be a bigger threat to convenience stores than to supermarkets, at least for now. Except this: the old Louie's Chinese spot on 15th Avenue NW in Ballard is set to become a pickup point for Amazon grocery shoppers. Order online, then zip over to the parking lot , run in and grab your stuff. Great if you're on your way home (to

Ballard, to Crown Hill), but a drag if you live in Laurelhurst. Then again, it's Amazon, so you've got to assume they know what they're doing.

And what about **COSTCO**, a "warehouse club" like Walmart but without the ignominious reputation as a destroyer of small-town retailers. You can buy a good assortment of produce at Costco these days, not to mention fresh meat, poultry, and seafood at wholesale prices, along with brand-name canned goods and dairy items. And if you venture into the private label arena ("Kirkland"), prices are even lower. In produce alone, Costco does $6 billion a year, same in meat. Add in dairy, canned goods, and dry goods, and you can see why Costco's new COO, Richard Galanti, thinks "food is the future."

Costco was one of the financial backers of the initiative to private liquor sales in Washington State, and the result, not unexpectedly, is that Costco is a great place to shop for spirits, too, especially private-label vodka. But the best part might be the rock-bottom pricing for fine wine. When Costco got into the wine business, a generation ago, they hired a professional sommelier to set up the program. Costco has since become the 800-pound gorilla of wine retailing, and employs a dozen wine buyers under the direction of a manager, Anne Alvarez-Peters, whose previous experience was in auto parts. Perhaps that's just as well. Wine snobs can still hold hands with their neighborhood wine merchants; wine drinkers will appreciate the prices.

And a pair of former Costco executives (bankrolled by Costco co-founder Jim Sinegal) are planning to bring their new chain of organic, fast-food chicken restaurants to Seattle. The name? Organic Coup. "Novel and compelling," is how Costco's CFO Richard Galanti described it.

To my way of thinking, **STARBUCKS** is a chain of dysfunctional candy stores. In any event, Starbucks is so much more than a coffee company. It is one of the most-frequented retailers on the planet; tens of millions of customers visit every month, every week, every day. They buy coffee, they buy tea, they buy chai soy lattes and caramel cocoa cluster frappuccinos (one of more than two dozen flavors). And they buy snacks, pastries, sandwiches, salads in see-through clamshell containers. Barbecued beef brisket on sourdough, veggie & brown rice salad bowls, blueberries and Greek yogurt parfaits, egg salad sandwiches and ham & Swiss panini. We're devoting a chapter to Howard Schultz's stewardship of Starbucks later on. For now, there's little doubt that a significant portion of the company's $23 billion in revenue comes from solid food.

Cliff Burrows, who had been leading Starbucks' Americas business unit, will now become head of a new retail group called "Siren Retail," after the retailer's logo and mascot. The division will oversee the Roastery and Reserve stores and build out the new Princi bakery stores and Teavana retail operations.

But the biggest news of all is that Uncle Howard says he's taking a step back from micro-managing day-to-day operations. Instead he will concentrate on the high-end stuff and store design.

Chapter 15 · BIG NIGHTS OUT

Tradition is all well and good, but appetites are renewed every day. And when we get hungry again, we make our way once more to the neighborhood café or diner and stand outside the door, hopeful, awaiting our supper.

Today, once you get past Canlis, you step into a broader, shallower pond. Two longtime mainstays of elegant dining, Rovers and The Georgian Room, have closed. Circadia, which has announced similar high ambitions, is not yet open. Yes, there are fine steakhouses (with their own chapter); yes there are out-of-town destination restaurants in Woodinville (The Herbfarm) and on Lummi Island (Willows Inn, a three-hour trip); yes Il Terrazzo Carmine maintains high standards of elegance in Pioneer Square. But none of Ethan Stowell's restaurants, none of Tom Douglas's places, none of Josh Henderson's or Renee Erickson's many establishments, not a single one uses white tablecloths. Seattle is too casual, too egalitarian. Pity.

BIG NIGHTS OUT The Early Days of Fine Dining

In the early days, when Seattle was less populated with restaurants, we'd stand at the top of the stairs, hungry; or at the bottom of the stairs, skeptical. Then the double-doors would open and our senses would be flooded with the prospect of sensory pleasures within. A sizzling steak, an ice-cold martini. Fresh oysters, chilled Champagne. Red wine, cheese. Chocolate.

Ah, but sensory memory is elusive; we crave specific details. We need the anchor of historic names: Brasserie Pittsbourg. The Other Place. Labuznik. Many in the Pantheon of Seattle's storied restaurants, including the Brasserie Pittsboug, and the legendary Rosellini establishments (the 410 and The Other Place) are long gone, victims of urban development.

But look what else is gone. In recent years, the Frontier Room in Belltown and the Alki Tavern in West Seattle. The Funhouse, Manray, the Sit & Spin, Ernie Steele's, the Fenix Underground, the Dog House. Three grand hotel restaurants (the Cloud Room at the Camlin, Trader Vic's at the Westin, the Golden Lion at the Olympic). Sorry Charlie's in

Lower Queen Anne didn't survive the death of its piano player, Howard Bulson. The Beeliner Diner and the Mannings in Wallingford and Ballard respectively, gone. Labuznik on First Avenue, Trattoria Mitchelli in Pioneer Square, the Buckaroo in Fremont.

Manca's, a downtown mainstay, is gone, yes, but its iconic invention, the Dutch Baby, survives as the star of the breakfast menu of a hugely successful chain out of Portland, the Original House of Pancakes. Two more beloved survivors on Capitol Hill: Vito's, venerable hangout for cops and pols, lost none of its Prohibition charm in a recent renovation; and The DeLuxe Bar & Grill, home of burgers, inexpensive steaks, and craft beer, celebrated its 50th anniversary last summer. There's hope for the world.

FRANCOIS KISSEL Classic French Chef

© Bob Peterson

They were still restoring the Pioneer Square pergola in the early 70s, but François Kissel was already here, having set up the city's first French restaurant in a seedy soup-kitchen previously known as the Pittsburgh Lunch. It was a cheery, half-basement space with tiled walls and floors that would have been hosed down nightly after the smelly indigents had been fed. "Tables for Ladies," it said on one window: shoppers could eat alone without being considered prostitutes. François transformed it by leaving the tiles alone, the cafeteria line intact, covering the tables with butcher-paper, and renaming the place Brasserie Pittsbourg, even though, truth be told, it was far more like a busy neighborhood bistro than a big, bustling brasserie.

You'd descend a few stairs, taking note of an impressive certificate proclaiming Kissel a professional member of the *Chaîne des Rôtisseurs*, and be greeted by glorious aromas unlike anything known to Seattle at the time: a billow of steam from the push-and-shove cafeteria line bearing a cloud of garlic, onions, rosemary and thyme, warm bread and simmering chicken stock.

The waiters were mostly French expatriates; they took your order with an accent. The salad dressing was a seductive vinaigrette that Francois himself concocted behind locked doors. (Its secret ingredient, never revealed publicly, was probably sugar.) The meats were unusual cuts for the time, like braised short ribs. For anyone who had traveled to Europe and eaten well, this was the real thing, the equivalent of a full-throated Beethoven symphony, albeit with white tile floors, a pressed tin ceiling, bentwood chairs, and antique copper pieces everywhere. Ris de veau, veal sweetbreads, were on the menu for $8.50, provençal leg of lamb for $9.

After François retired to the west coast of France, the Brasserie became an antique mall. Its longtime neighbor, Trattoria Mitchelli, stayed in business a block away for another decade until it, too, breathed its last. But a longtime employee, Axel Macé, took over the last surviving Kissel property, Maximilien in the Market. With his business partner Willi Boutillier he launched an unsuccessful expansion to Capitol Hill with a "very French" café called Le Zinc, now called Naka.

VICTOR ROSELLINI A Real Restaurateur

© Bob Peterson

The date to remember, if you're taking notes, is November 2nd, 1948, when Washington voters authorized the sale of liquor by the drink. Within a few short years, a number of restaurants sprang up. All at once, you had Peter Canlis opening a spot on Aurora Avenue, high above Lake Union; you had John Franco on the lake itself, at Franco's Hidden Harbor; you had Jim Ward opening the 13 Coins, a swanky 24-hour diner; and you had Victor Rosellini and his brother-in-law, John Pogetti, opening Rosellini's 610 at the corner of 6th & Pine.

Victor's parents had come to Tacoma from Florence, Italy. They opened a restaurant there, but later moved to San Francisco, where young Victor worked in several of the Little Italy restaurants and clubs of North Beach. When he returned to Seattle, he had the elegance and bearing of a patrician. The 610 was a hit with the downtown business crowd; even more so was the Four-10 in the White-Henry-Stuart Building a few years later. It was continental elegance at its best: waiters in tuxedos, starched tablecloths, heavy silver serving pieces, steaks flamed table-side. But it was Rosellini's welcoming personality that made the difference; he had an uncanny memory for faces and an astute understanding of local politics (which councilman or judge to seat where). Victor's cousin, Albert, was the professional politician in the family; he was first elected to public office as the legislature's youngest state senator, eventually serving as Governor from 1957 to 1965.

Victor adopted his wife Marcia's son from an earlier marriage, and Robert Rosellini followed in Victor's footsteps as a host and restaurateur. He also mentored newcomers like Mick McHugh and Tim Firnstahl, who went on to operate their own chain of restaurants. And late in life, Victor would pilot his white Cadillac around town, Marcia in the passenger seat, stopping off at local hotspots (like Dick's on Capitol Hill). A stereotypical "Italian" scene: Don Victor, retired king of Seattle restaurants, making the rounds, pressing the flesh.

LUCIANO BARDINELLI Another Classy Italian

© Bob Peterson

It was mid-morning on a Tuesday, and Luciano Bardinelli had just lit his first cigar of the day. On Sunday, Mother's Day, he'd served a full house; on Monday, he'd packed up his files and belongings. After a lifetime as an owner, headwaiter, manager, occasional line cook, waiter, busboy, Luciano was not going to work in one of his own restaurants. "My first day as a free man."

Luciano (no one calls him Signor Bardinelli for long) had come to Seattle exactly 30 years earlier, in 1982. There was no Tom Douglas, no Ethan Stowell. There were no websites to chronicle the comings and goings of platoons of energetic young chefs, no Eater.com, no NoshPit, no ChowHound.

Born on the shores of Lago Maggiore, in the northern Italian Alps, Luciano had already managed exclusive restaurants and private clubs in Las Vegas and the Hollywood Hills. One fine autumn day in 1981 he happened to pay a call on a friend in Seattle, and found that the landscape of red and yellow leaves reminded him of home. Within months, he had left the desert and driven to Seattle, the radio of his U-Haul tuned to the Kentucky Derby. ("The winner was a long shot named Gato del Sol," he recalls.)

Luciano became the Godfather to Seattle's Italian restaurant renaissance. He was not a chef by training or temperament; his strong suit was Armani (topped these days by a full head of white hair), served with an urbane elegance. French was the cuisine of prestige back then, but Settebello, his first Seattle restaurant, on Capitol Hill was decidedly Italian. Not low-brow, Spaghetti House meatballs-in-red-sauce but classy, suave northern Italian: osso buco, agnolotti stuffed with veal, tiramisu. In the course of its ten-year run, it changed the way Seattle thought about food–not just Italian food, but restaurant food in general.

13 COINS 24 Hours

It's hard to persevere in the restaurant game in a town that's still a-building. Canlis was a lucky exception; it's perched like a medieval fortress at the south end of the Aurora bridge, able to fend off attacks from developers.

Jim and Elaine Ward's original 13 Coins is just barely hanging on, however, though its offshoot at SeaTac is doing well. (Another one on the way, it's said, for Pioneer Square.) The Coins has been under new management for the last several years, but it's still a dark and welcoming spot you can visit after the bars close, sit up at the counter in those wing-back leatherette chairs, and watch the line cooks set your food on fire as they fry, scramble, flip and toss your order. You can't get cherries jubilee at 3 AM anymore, and the tureen of soul-satisfying bean soup isn't on the 24-hour menu, but the Joe's Special (a steak-and-spinach frittata) will keep a hungry drinker from starving.

The Wards also launched the original El Gaucho steakhouse (another sacrifice on the altar of building a Greater Seattle). Fortunately, one of their managers, Paul Mackay, kept their vision of elegant service alive as he migrated through other Seattle dining rooms. In 1995, he braved the troubled sidewalks of Belltown, partnering with Chris Keff to open Flying Fish. Then, two years later, a spot opened up at the corner of First Avenue and Wall Street.: a union hall for sailors on the main floor, a roach-filled tavern on the lower level, a mission for the homeless across the street complete with an on the for the drug dealers and winos. "That was Belltown, fifteen, twenty years ago," Mackay recalls. The rebirth of El Gaucho coincided with the dot-com boom, high-tech millionaires and celebrity chefs. A heady time. But the vision was fulfilled: elegant service for the rich, the famous, and the celebrators of special occasions.

A family tradition to tie all this together. The gent who ran the kitchen at the original 13 Coins, at El Gaucho and at Metropolitan Grill (and later as executive chef for the entire Consolidated Restaurants group) was a firm but beloved old-school taskmaster named Earl Owens. Almost single-handedly, he trained a whole generation of Seattle restaurateurs. Today, both his grandsons, the Anderson brothers, are in the biz, and both working for Consolidated; Joshua is the general manager at Metropolitan Grill, while Jeremy is VP of Operations for the whole company.

CARMINE SMERALDO Elegance in Pioneer Square

© Bob Peterson

It's hard not to use the word "icon" when talking about Il Terrazzo Carmine. Sheer longevity, if nothing else: it's 30 years old, for starters, an eternity in the fast-moving hospitality industry. The restaurant is tucked inside a handsome brick & stone building in the heart of Pioneer Square, at 1st & Jackson, overlooking a little patch of garden (the terrace, the *terrazzo*). The Carmine part, that's for Carmine Smeraldo, born in Naples, who worked his way up from cleaning hotel toilets to a spot at the right hand of the longtime restaurateur who brought northern Italian cuisine to Vancouver, BC, Umberto Menghe.

In the 1970s and 1980s, Menghe was opening restaurants at a furious pace, and he sent Carmine down to Seattle to test the waters. First came Umberto's Ristorante on King Street, then, in 1984, a block away, Il Terrazzo. Menghe himself withdrew from Seattle a few years later, and Umberto's closed, but Il Terrazzo remained and was given the additional name "Carmine's." For decades it has been the touchstone of a warm, elegant Italian style of dining. You wouldn't call it "rustic" because that implies bare tabletops and mismatched china, but it's hardly stuffy or starchy-formal.

At the heart of Il Terrazzo is the spread of *antipasti misti*, the display of vegetables and cold cuts so common in Italy (and finally at a couple of places in Seattle: The Whale Wins, Bar Sajor). A daily menu of fish, grilled meat, homemade pasta. A wine list that doesn't neglect famous bottles yet remains accessible. Service that's attentive without being overbearing.

Until he passed away suddenly at the beginning of 2012, Carmine himself ran the dining room with unflagging energy. Today his widow is at the podium, greeting a steady line of guests out for a celebratory lunch. This is not a parade of mourners but of regulars who return for the pleasure and familiarity of the elegant room and the superb food. And a 1,400-square-foot expansion, called Intermezzo, has opened on the First Avenue side of the building. It's a stylish wine-and-cocktail bar featuring *aperitivi* and *amari*, serving *cicchetti*, the Italian version of tapas. Its retractable street-side glass wall takes advantage of warmer weather, along with sidewalk tables.

"We see Intermezzo as a portal that will open our brand to the next generation of diners," said young CJ Smeraldo, son of Carmine. "People love Il Terrazzo for its old-school charm. The point of Intermezzo is to usher our business into the new culture." Soon to come: a new Carmine's on the east side.

CANLIS Swimming to Destiny

It's probably Seattle's best-known restaurant, and almost certainly the only one with three generations of history: the founder, Peter, who opened the aerie overlooking Lake Union in 1950; his son Chris and daughter-in-law Alice, who took over after Peter's death in 1977; and their sons Mark and Brian, who have run the operation since 2005.

But the Canlis story actually begins a full generation earlier, when a young man named Nikolas Peter Kanlis braved the elements and (legend has it) *swam* from Greece to Turkey. Presumably this was across the Strait of Samos in the eastern Aegian, about a mile. Still, a fateful dip.

Kanlis began making his way through the linguistic and cultural mazes of the Ottoman Empire, and by 1909 was working at Mena House, the most famous hotel in Cairo, when Teddy Roosevelt, the former US President, arrived in search of a cook for a year-long African safari. Not just a cook, but a steward and translator. Safari mission accomplished, Roosevelt's assistant joined him on the return journey from Egypt to America. On Ellis Island, Kanlis became Canlis. He moved west, to Stockton, California, married, and opened a restaurant.

In the 1930s, young Peter, who'd been a reluctant apprentice in his parents' restaurant, moved to Hawaii and got into dry goods. But he knew food and he knew purchasing, so he wound up managing the quasi-military USO (United Services Organization). After the war, he opened a ten-table sidewalk restaurant on a little-known beach, Waikiki, and finally, in 1950, Peter Canlis moved to Seattle.

He commissioned an up-and-coming architect named Roland Terry to design a restaurant that was virtually revolutionary. For starters, it was three miles north of downtown, on Aurora Avenue overlooking Lake Union. Through angled windows diners had a view of Lake Union, Lake Washington, and the Cascades. There was a stone fireplace in the middle of the restaurant! The kitchen wasn't hidden away; you could see the cooks! And the waiters didn't wear tuxedos; in fact, they weren't waiters at all but graceful Japanese women in kimonos.

Then there was the food. An iconic "Canlis" salad prepared tableside, with a coddled egg dressing, for $2 per person. (The *New York Times* finally printed the recipe in 2013.) Exotic Hawaiian fish, like mahi-mahi, flown in fresh by Pan Am pilots who were personal friends of Peter Canlis, $3. Top quality steaks cooked over charcoal. Canlis became a place for Seattle's new Boeing money to dine alongside Hollywood stars like John Wayne; it was elegant without being stuffy (like Seattle's venerable downtown institutions, the Rainier Club, the University Club and the Sunset Club), yet democratic.

Peter Canlis watched over the restaurant from his personal table near the front door (the one with a telephone) for the next quarter century. He even had living quarters installed in a "penthouse" off the main dining room so that he could stay close to his beloved restaurant.

Canlis developed friendships with Conrad Hilton (the hotel magnate), Victor Bergeron ("Trader Vic") and Don the Beachcomber (who popularized "tiki drinks"), and was persuaded to open a second Canlis in Honolulu, then another in Portland, then in San Francisco. Legend has it that Canlis wanted no more "expansion," so he showed up drunk at a Hilton board meeting, and the horrified board pulled the plug on plans to put a Canlis in every new Hilton in the country.

Peter's son, Chris, was working as a Wells Fargo banker in California when he was summoned back to Seattle in 1977 to take over the company. Where Peter was a showman, Chris and Alice were "behind the scenes" leaders. They would spend the next 30 years at the helm of the ship before their sons, Mark and Brian, assumed ownership. The notion that remains, though, is one of elegant, unfailing hospitality. Culinary star Greg Atkinson served as exec chef here; Brady Williams, a Wunderkind not yet 30, was recruited from Roberta's in Brooklyn to run the kitchen when Jason Franey, the previous incumbent, moved to California. He promptly devised a new, six-course tasting menu served on new tableware; Canlis didn't miss a beat.

Chapter 16 · TODAY'S BIG TOQUES

Every time we go out to dinner, we're getting into the restaurant business. We weigh the question of independent versus corporate, modern versus traditional, glamorous versus cozy, exciting versus predictable. More and more, we visit chain restaurants. The world's second-largest restaurant group, after McDonald's, with 22,000 stores worldwide, is headquartered in Seattle. That would be Starbucks, but the word chain doesn't appear anywhere on its website.

In industry-speak, chain restaurants are MUFSOs, multiple-unit, full-service operators. Starbucks is a specialty store; Mickey D is a quick-serve restaurant. But there are dozens of MUFSOs in Seattle nonetheless, a vital part of Seattle's economy, creating thousands of jobs while upping Seattle's attractiveness.

THE BIGGEST TOQUES OF ALL ?

The restaurant industry in Washington state is ubiquitous – a pizza parlor on every street-corner, you might think – but also fragmented: 14,000 locations, most of them relatively small (think strip-mall noodle shops, roadside burger stands, franchised taco joints). Overall, Washington restaurants employ almost a quarter-million people (an average of 15 workers per restaurant), ring up more than $10 billion in sales, pay $4 billion in wages and contribute $1 billion to the state's tax coffers.

What's driving the restaurant explosion? Well, every crane on the Seattle skyline represents a construction project, and every developer wants the project to have a signature restaurant. So landlords are chasing hot chefs as well as proven concepts. About half of Seattle's leading restaurant groups are headed by, for want of a better term, "celebrity chefs." These are culinary professionals who made the entrepreneurial transition from cooking in someone else's kitchen to running their own show. And did it again and again. The others are restaurants that grew out of smaller operations but have since evolved into "corporate families." Here are some of the best-known.

ETHAN & ANGELA STOWELL Seattle's Crown Prince & Princess

For a quarter century, Kent Stowell and Francia Russell, artistic directors of the Pacific Northwest Ballet, stood at the summit of Seattle's cultural elite. Russell had founded the company's ballet school; Stowell *père,* among his many achievements, choreographed Seattle's holiday favorite, *Nutcracker.* They had three sons, one with Oregon Ballet Theater, one with Teach for America, and the youngest, Ethan, who went to work at 16 making shakes at Daley's on Eastlake. At The Ruins supper club he started by taking out the trash and cleaning the garage. His first restaurant, Union, which opened when Ethan was only 28, failed when its downtown customer base (specifically, Washington Mutual) fell victim to the 2008 recession. Early success, early failure, but followed by a relatively swift and steady recovery.

In Union's wake, Ethan created new spaces, a dozen of them, all deep within Seattle's rich tapestry of residential neighborhoods: Capitol Hill, Belltown, Queen Anne, Greenlake, Ballard, Madrona. He had no over-arching marketing strategy, like "tourism." Not that he turns away tourists, but they're not his focus. There's no shame in courting hotel concierges, of course, or in courting the media, or in siting all your restaurants within walking distance of one another, as Tom Douglas has done with bustling big-city *brasseries.* Stowell's restaurants are designed to be cozy neighborhood *bistros.* They offer a menu that's neither fussy nor expensive; service that's courteous; ambiance that's warm and welcoming. Stowell recognizes he'll always be compared with Douglas, but he's really in a different world.

Stowell admits he used to focus on the top two percent of Seattle diners. That's a very small slice of the folks who eat in restaurants, and it's also a hugely competitive sector of the market. Almost everything you read about restaurants in Seattle (blogs, magazines, papers) is aimed that that top two percent. And Stowell wasn't doing badly, far from it. But when he was offered the chance to consult for Centerplate (the concessionaire who manages food service at 250 venues nationwide, including the Safe), he didn't pooh-pooh it as a chore beneath his abilities; he welcomed it.

Stowell has the wherewithal, technically, to recreate the experience of dining in Rome (Rione XIII), of making his own pasta (Lagana), of engaging his fans with special events and "Sunday Suppers." At Safeco Field, he broke out of the self-imposed box that limits the appeal of celebrity chefs to the followers of celebrity chefs. He's not on the Guy Fieri low road (thank goodness), but he's making a connection, at the ballpark, with a heck of a lot more diners than could ever squeeze into Bar Cotto or How to Cook a Wolf.

And there are moments of greatness from Stowell kitchens, such as a breathtaking ricotta gnocchi with beef tongue *sugo* at the Belltown Tavolata. The gnocchi are cloud-like, the tongue flavorful and meltingly tender. The dish has an evocative power, taking you back into a childhood of steaming kitchens, grandmothers, great-aunts and noisy family dinners (not that we grew up with any of that, but you get the picture). Mortadella and prosciutto di parma at Bar Cotto, washed down with a glass of slightly fizzy lambrusco. Puntarelle (winter chicory) at Rione XIII. Noo-Yawk-style pizza pies, 20 inches across, baked on the hearth of a Baker's Pride double-stack "SuperDeck" oven at Ballard Pizza Company.

It's getting harder to find parking along Ballard Avenue's Restaurant Row where Stowell already has Staple & Fancy Mercantile and Chippy's in the Kolstrand Building (sharing the space with Renée Erickson's Walrus & Carpenter oyster bar). And when Chippy's didn't quite work out, Stowell moved swiftly, replacing the fish & chips concept with a more mainstream Marine Hardware, and adding a gastropub called Bramling Cross down the street. He also teamed with Kolstrand's owner, Chad Dale, to form a new venture, Grubb Brothers Productions, that intends to bring better quality to classic American comfort food: sandwiches, fried chicken, burgers. Though Stowell's favorite cut of meat is the bone-in rib-eye, it's not an item for a restaurant menu. ("You don't want to show your Henry VIII side to other diners.") Skillet-roasted rabbit, on the other hand, makes sense for the four-course, fixed price menu at Staple & Fancy.

How does it all get paid for, these careful build-outs? Different ways, Stowell allows. Investors, partners, loans, self-funding. There's no single angel writing blank checks. Most often than not, it's the landlord who wants a hip, trendy restaurant in the building and makes Stowell an offer he can't refuse.

The payroll for Stowell's corporate umbrella ESR these days (13 restaurants, the event space, a wine storage facility, the pasta business) is over 200, the annual gross is nudging up against $20 million. Not nearly the size of "rival" restaurateur Tom Douglas's outfit, and besides, they're not rivals. Stowell has far fewer total seats, and his market is locals, not tourists. You could(almost) put all of Stowell's seats inside Douglas's Dahlia Lounge.

"It's a business and needs a business plan," both Stowells acknowledge. "An art, a craft, *and* a small business." And his wife, Angela Dunleavy Stowell, is the company's chief financial officer. Says one well-regarded industry observer: "Here's how the business of a neighborhood restaurant works: you go to work every day, you take your turn at bat, you keep your eye on the ball. Stowell and his wife strike me as savvy operators who understand how to build a brand." That brand, of course, is "Ethan Stowell." Confirmation at the national level: *Restaurant Hospitality* magazine named Ethan and Angela Stowell as the 2016 recipients of its Innovator of the Year Award for creating outstanding restaurants across multiple concepts. "We stay on top of things daily," says Angela Stowell. "The executive team gets an email every day with every social media post. You have to know what your guests are thinking, right or wrong."

The Stowells seem to have found that sweet spot between adventure and predictability. Take a look at the menu: it's sophisticated but unthreatening. Take a look into the kitchen: it could be a fraternity in the 1960s, with pale faces in lumberjack beards well-trimmed. Only in multi-cultural, multi-racial Seattle does this look bizarre.

TOM DOUGLAS "Best Restaurateur in America"

The best decision Tom Douglas ever made, industry observers say, was to hire Pamela Hinckley as CEO. She had worked for the company as a manager before leaving to run Theo Chocolate. Douglas already had a culinary wizard (Eric "ET" Tanaka) running operations; hiring Hinckley freed Douglas up to do what he does best: just be Tom Douglas (and be named Best Restaurateur in America by the James Beard Foundation in 2012).

Most Tom Douglas restaurants are within a short walk of major downtown hotels. It also doesn't hurt that two of his most popular spots, Cuoco and Brave Horse Tavern, are in the very heart of South Lake Union's Amazon country. The restaurants share a high-energy ambiance with great attention to details of service. They may have a reputation among local food snobs as being too "corporate" but that criticism misses the point. Visitors want a strong element of predictability when they leave their hotel rooms.

Does T-Doug have an outsize influence on Seattle's fine-dining scene? Probably. Is his cuisine as refined as a tweezer-wielding perfectionist in a two-person kitchen? Probably not. But, collectively, his restaurants make an enormous contribution to Seattle's reputation as a gastronomic destination, and on a purely practical level he employs so many prep cooks, line cooks, and chefs that his company, TDR, not only fields a deep bench of kitchen talent but a teeming pool for dozens of ambitious new restaurants.

ERIC TANAKA

Eric Tanaka, known since high school as ET, is T-Doug's executive chef and business partner, the guy who converts the big picture (T-Doug's strong suit) into the nitty gritty of getting it done. He grew up in Los Angeles, a Japanese-American kid who ate his way effortlessly through the melting pot (almond duck in Chinatown; avocado burgers in the Valley) of Tinseltown.

Though many of the dishes at Tanaka San have Asian names, the menu isn't meant to be "authentic" anything in particular. There's a braised oxtail, to be sure, and a wok fried crab, but also "family fried rice" and a trio of ramen dishes. The miso-dashi is made with matzo balls. House cocktails include a Ghost Dog concocted from gin, vermouth, and sake. And there's a slushee machine, too, with several boozy flavors. But it's ET's quiet mastery of logistical detail that makes him one of Seattle's unsung movers and shakers.

JOSH HENDERSON Huxley Wallace Collective

You can't pin a label on Josh Henderson, who is the "next big thing" on the Seattle restaurant scene. He began with a single food truck, Skillet, which morphed into two diners (Capitol Hill, Ballard), a catering company and a hamburger garnish called Bacon Jam. Skillet Street Food is now a freestanding company with its own CEO and culinary staff. Henderson embraces creativity that doesn't see food as high art but as everyday craft – "a new story about what Northwest cuisine is all about."

Two more independent ventures, Cone & Steiner General markets (Capitol Hill, Pioneer Square) and The Hollywood Tavern (Woodinville), preceded the formation of Henderson's current company, named for his sons. Huxley Wallace's hot spots are Westward (North Lake Union) and Quality Athletics (Pioneer Square). But Henderson is far from finished. He brought back from Chicago a former associate named Eric Rivera, to help break out with a blizzard of new projects but Rivera just moved on again. Poulet Galore (South Lake Union) is envisioned as a rotisserie chicken "window" that will serve whole or half chickens with a choice of sauces. Noroeste is envisioned as having a small, curated menu of tacos, ceviches, braised meats and salsas for a focus on a sexy late-night bar scene, also in South Lake Union. Great State is the name for Henderson's classic burger joint in Ravenna. Saint Helens is a neighborhood brasserie serving pastries and espresso upstairs. And Nest is the rooftop restaurant at the new Thompson Hotel across from the Market. And before the year is out, look for Vestal, at the northern end of Westlake.

ERIC RIVERA

A chef for eaters who think, that's Eric Rivera. He trained at the Art Institute and was working at Blueacre before moving to Chicago for a stint at Alinea as director of culinary research (not bad, eh?). Then he was "recalled" to Seattle by Josh Henderson to take charge of opening a series of new concepts for Huxley Wallace, among them burgers (Great State). No sooner done than he decamped to Tallulah's, on Capitol Hill.

NICK NOVELLO

At the Ballard outpost of Skillet Diner, exec chef Nick Novello tweaks the menu for the sunny season, for "the endless days of summer," with the scent of mesquite in the air (from all the backyard barbecues), hot days and cool nights. You can imagine all 102 seats filled up on those long summer evenings, with the windows open and the sidewalk tables filled with happy families. The tomato salad features heirloom tomatoes topped with slices of house-made mozzarella, the duck leg is infused with juniper, the soft-shell crab (from Boston this time of year) is edible down to the last morsel, the lamb chops come from Oregon animals raised in Australia (tasty, tasty, mate) served with a green harissa, the cod comes right out of Neah Bay. Special chef's dinners are offered on Fridays in May and June as well. Breakfast, lunch, dinner, there's no shortage of opportunity to snag a table.

MATT DILLON The Corson Building, Sitka & Spruce

The driving force of this family of restaurants is Matt Dillon, a passionate forager and two-time winner of the James Beard award, in 2007 as Best New Chef and 2012 as Best Chef Northwest. His current ventures put him at the center of the movement to revive Pioneer Square with innovative restaurants. As his spokesman put it, "We place high value on our community of farmers, purveyors, winemakers, fishermen, artists. We work hard to celebrate this community through food and the nourishment it provides." Dillon's properties include Sitka & Spruce and two Bar Ferd'nands (both on Capitol Hill), The Corson Building (Georgetown), Bar Sajor and The London Plane/The Little London Plane (Pioneer Square). The Old Chaser Farm on Vashon Island provides some of the group's provisions and serves as an event venue as well. An odd hybrid of haute cuisine and "picnic food," Bar Sajor failed to catch on in Pioneer Square (Seattle's Sandwich District) and was closed in mid-2016, but Dillon (and a partner, Marcus Lolario of Li'l Woody's) forged ahead and opened Ciudad in Georgetown.

JOHN HOWIE Seastar & Steaks

John Howie got his start at Restaurants Unlimited in the Rich Komen heyday and absorbed its ethic of unexpected hospitality, inspired cuisine and memorable dining experiences. Howie also maintains a strong association with the National Football League through the Seattle Seahawks. The biggest draw here are steaks, but Howie is also a big fan of sustainably grown and harvested salmon. A steakhouse at The Bravern, a seafood spot not far away, an informal sports bar in Seattle, and, most recently, a brewpub in Bothell.

FRIEDMAN & GILLIS Homegrown Sandwiches

Ben Friedman (photo) and Brad Gillis were longtime friends from Mercer Island, attending college in Boston. Friedman (photo) was getting a degree in advertising and marketing at BU, Gillis in environmental studies at Bowdoin, and in their conversations about what they wanted to do next, one of the things that kept coming up was Seattle's particularly keen awareness of environmental issues. But that sensitivity didn't seem to extend to restaurants.

"We saw that people were committed to buying local and organic at the grocery store," says Friedman, "but it was harder to keep that commitment when you went out to eat." Says Gillis, "You shouldn't have to give up your food ideals when you leave your home. Even for something as simple as a sandwich."

Sandwich! That was *it!* They would open sandwich shops, but sandwich shops with an environmental conscience, made with sustainably grown, locally sourced ingredients. Not yet 23 years old, they rounded up some funding over spring break, and, in 2009, opened the first store in Seattle's Fremont neighborhood. They called it Homegrown.

Before long they had more stores than they could supply from trips to local farmers markets, so they launched their own sustainable farm along the Sammamish River, about half an hour northeast of town. They called it Sprouting Farm, and it now supplies the seasonal produce for all the stores.

The leading factor for a Homegrown customer is their level of education, Friedman says. That's the biggest reason for their success. Not just environmental awareness but environmental commitment, as demonstrated by a willingness to spend more than ten bucks for a sandwich. "Whole Foods has come to the same conclusion."

The company has grown quickly and now has ten locations in the Seattle area. Not bad for two guys celebrating their 30th birthday this year. Their next expansion, thanks to a $2.5 million round of fund-raising, is planned for late 2016. It skips over Portland, instead targeting San Francisco with three stores: one in the Financial District and two in the East Bay.

GUILD SEATTLE The one you've never heard of

Sounds very mysterious, like an Ivy League senior society. In the beginning, almost everyone was involved with the Capitol Hill Block Party. A core group of three longtime friends and business associates transitioned from event management to the restaurant business: Jason Lajeunesse, Dave Meinert, and Joey Burgess. Lajeunesse is a music promoter, Meinert owns the 5-Point in Belltown, and Burgess worked his way up from server to operations director before joining as an owner. As Guild Seattle they developed Lost Lake Cafe, Comet Tavern, and Grim's in the heart of Capitol Hill, then turned the old Kingfish Cafe into Ernest Loves Agnes. The deity, as it were, is Mike McConnell, founder of both Caffe Vita and Via Tribunale, two virtually ubiquitous Seattle chains. Another relative newcomer is the oldest guy, Big Mario Vellotti, born in Italy, whose family runs pizzerias on the east coast. The "slice" pizzeria they all opened on the hill one short block downhill from the original Via Tribunali prospered, so they opened another on Lower Queen Anne. Mario also runs a specialty outfit called Vellotti Fine Foods, and he's in and out of a dozen restaurants a day, a great way to hear the latest gossip.

OPPER MELANG RESTAURANTS Matadors & More

Nathan Opper was a home builder in Michigan before moving to Seattle. Zak Melang, a bass player, came here from North Carolina to play music but wound up in the restaurant business (Floyd's Place, Ten Mercer). The duo hit it off and transformed a little bar in Ballard into the first iteration of The Matador.

By now they've got more Matadors than there are bull rings in Spain, and have added two more spots for 20-somethings in Ballard (Kickin' Boot, Ballard Oyster Annex).

JAMES WEIMANN & DEMING MACLISE Global Sparklers

On Capitol Hill, the sparks are German and Mexican; in Ballard, they're French and Scots. James Weimann and his business partner Deming Maclise have put together a mini-empire of sorts: they're the operators of Cafe Bastille, Stoneburner, and Macleod's Scottish Pub (Ballard), Rheinhaus and Poquitos (Capitol Hill).

Bastille is vast and handsome, shiny white-tiled walls with dark wood accents in the front rooms, exposed brick and a grand chandelier in the back bar. There's also a large patio, where smokers were huddling furtively in the moonlight. As Obermaier Machine Works, the building spent half a century at the heart of Old Ballard's industrial district; it's been beautifully reworked as French *grande brasserie*. The long bar is molded zinc, just like in France; found objects from Parisian flea markets abound. The menu also takes its Frenchiness seriously, listing moules, frites, baguette sandwiches, *soupe de poissons* and *salade niçoise*.

There's also a wacky, self-congratulatory note of locavore political correctness at Bastille, with a rooftop garden growing herbs and salad greens for the $8 *salade du toît*. We'd guess, with the price of real estate and the cost of "urban farm" labor, that a more realistic price for that salad would be $800, but that's another story.

There was also nothing in Seattle even remotely like Rheinhaus, a vast, 10,000-square-foot barn of a place on Capitol Hill, a former candy factory and furniture warehouse that's now been converted, at a cost of $1.5 million, into a 420-seat Bavarian Biergarten. Their genius is to assemble a giant garage sale worth of genuine vintage items and salvaged pieces, whether from Paris flea markets or Mexican market towns. Their inspiration was the Hofbräuhaus in central Munich, nondescript outside, lavishly decorated inside, with long wooden tables and painted ceilings. The designers added Viennese chandeliers, railings salvaged from the McCaw mansion in Medina, stuffed elk heads, leather club chairs, Belgian doors, and a colossal Austrian fireplace. Three bars, two mezzanines, and five indoor bocce ball courts, each 8 by 50 feet (complete with a bocce-ball concierge).

RESTAURANTS UNLIMITED

RESTAURANTS UNLIMITED

The company, founded in Seattle by Rich Komen five decades ago, today now encompasses 20 "brands" in 44 locations across ten states. Locally, the signs on the door say Cutters, Palisade, Maggie's Bluff, Palomino. Some casual, like Henry's Tavern and Maggie's Bluff, some upscale, like Palisade and Palomino. But it has not been an entirely happy half-century. Yes, the company grew, but not enough to remain independent. It was purchased in 1990 by Eli Jacobs, a stock market investor and owner of the Baltimore Orioles, but before long Jacobs was forced into bankruptcy by his creditors. For a time, Komen was back in charge, but in 2007 RUI was taken over by Sun Capital Partners, a private equity outfit that specializes in "distressed companies." John Howie, who joined RUI as a chef in 1988 (before the sale to Jacobs) lamented that outside owners just wanted to make money rather than take care of guests. Howie told the *Seattle Times*, "In the long run, that's going to hurt you. Rich [Komen] never intended the company to go in that direction." When the takeover by Sun Capital was announced, Komen resigned from the board and moved to San Juan Island, where he runs the Roche Harbor Resort.

McHUGH & FIRNSTAHL Rosellini x Harvard

At his iconic 1950s supper club, the 410, across from the Olympic Hotel, Victor Rosellini hired a couple of youngsters named Mick McHugh and Tim Firnstahl, taught them what he knew, and sent them into the world to spawn their own restaurants: F.X. McRory's, Jake O'Shaughnessy's, and half a dozen more. Where Rosellini was discreet and formal, with servers in tuxedos, McHugh and Firnstahl were flamboyant and publicity-driven. (Remember the Concorde flying into Seattle in November, 1984? That was their doing; they chartered a goddamn Concorde to fly the first cases of Beaujolais Nouveau to Seattle.) But they were also savvy Harvard Business School operators who ran their stores by the book, a manual that ran to some 2,000 pages. When they split up, they tossed a coin from the top of the Space Needle to claim "first dibs" on their restaurants. McHugh got FX, Firnstahl got Jake's. And though they've gone separate ways they remain good friends.

Among their innovations: a fanatical devotion to the specific, detailed origin of ingredients (now considered *de rigueur* but a real innovation 30 years ago), and to what might be called a restaurant's "razzle-dazzle" factor. At Firnstahl's new spot, **Von's 1000 Spirits**, at the top of Harbor Steps, it's not just a pizza, it's a French country sourdough "fric," baked in an 800-degree, almond wood-fired oven. At the far end of the room is the grand, mirrored back-bar from Jake O'Shaughnessy, in storage for the past 20 years. The menu has 9 "hamburgs," 8 frics, 19 footnotes, and, of course, 1,000 spirits. Firnstahl's daughter, "proprietress" Merissa Firnstahl-Claridge, and his son-in-law, executive chef Jason Amador, are in charge. Missy, as she's known, has been in the restaurant biz since the age of 15, got a degree in business administration, followed her dad's path to Harvard, and spent several years as VP Operations of the family company. Jason, married to Missy's sister, Terra, comes from the family behind Sugee's in Bellevue, purveyors of box lunches as well as bakers of the giant strawberry shortcake at Bumbershoot and Folklife. Jason's history includes sleeping on the flour bags at Sugee's as a teenager. In addition to culinary skills, he brings his family's 50-year-old sourdough starter.

Meantime, down in Pioneer Square, it's Friday night and the bar at F.X pulses with conversation and laughter. Thirty tap handles line the bar top, half of them dispensing beers from breweries in the Pacific Northwest. Alongside a giant Leroy Neiman mural of the back bar (painted in 1979), the mirrored shelves hold one of America's largest collections of premium spirits: American bourbon; Irish, Canadian, and Scotch whiskies; not to mention international vodka, gin, rum, tequila, brandy, cognac, and cordials, well over 1600 brands in all. And a dozen labels bear words that were simply unthinkable even ten years ago: a Seattle address, thanks to the Craft Distillery Act passed by the State Legislature in 2008.

PETER LEVY & JEREMY HARDY Ciao

In the annals of celebrity divorces, it may have been less made-for-TV than the McHugh-Firnstahl breakup but Chow Foods was, until 2010 or so, one of the most influential locally-owned chains in Seattle, defining for a generation the concept of the neighborhood restaurant. Driven by menu concepts that changed every three months rather than by a celebrity chef; small enough, individually, to feel intimate, yet big enough, collectively, to centralize back-office and administrative functions, the eight (at the time) Chow Foods stores ran parallel to the Tom Douglas and Ethan Stowell "empires." But they never made a big deal about being under the same ownership; their names weren't always know city-wide: Edolyne Joe's (West Seattle), Atlas Foods (U Village), Jitterbug (Wallingford), the Hi-Life (Ballard), Coastal Kitchen (Capitol Hill), 5-Spot (Queen Anne), Mioposto (Mt. Baker).

It had all started in Portland, where Peter Levy (he's on the left in the photo) learned the restaurant biz as a kitchen slave for the McCormick & Schmick organization, working his way up to GM. Returning to Seattle in the late 1980s, Levy found an underutilized spot on North 45th Avenue, an unsuccessful, ahead-of-its-time espresso bar and gelateria. He added a restaurant kitchen with a regulation hood and rechristened it the Beeliner, a diner with east-coast attitude (a sign said "Eat It & Beat It").

Levy added the 5-Spot atop Queen Anne a couple of years later, and took on a partner, Jeremy Hardy, who'd also been a GM for McCormick. In 1993 they opened Coastal Kitchen on Capitol Hill's 15th Avenue, then they tilted at the windmill of downtown sandwich shops with a concept that sounded much better on paper than in practice: Luncheonette No. 1. The Beeliner had also run out of gas, and was sold, only to see the buyer after buyer default. Levy and Hardy reopened it as Jitterbug, but that didn't help much. It's now back in Levy's hands, renamed TNT Taqueria.

As for Jeremy Hardy, he's still at it, as well.

"There are lots of reasons you fall in love with the restaurant business," says Hardy, "but you don't stay in it for the same reasons." Early on, there's a rush: the cash, the prestige, the groupies. Gets you through the slog of the dish pit at Lobster House in Boston, but eventually, you find yourself married and entangled. What saved Hardy from becoming cynical was his interest in music, in performance. "We create magic."

The customer only sees the tip of the iceberg, Hardy says. As the owner you need to control everything, to assert your voice, to frame the experience. He started Mioposto because he wanted a better spot to take his wife, Tiah, for date night. They developed the concept together; today's she's the company's CFO (Chief Food Officer). For one thing, all domestic ingredients: olive oil, cheese, tomatoes. Nothing wrong with the Vera Pizza Napolitana certification of places like Tutta Bella and Via Tribunali; Miposto's is "Seattle Certified Pizza." Hardy would like to have a dozen more stores, but he's realistic. "I wish I was 20 years younger."

So he'd have time to work on expanding the Mioposto concept, Hardy sold Coastal to the Tweten family of Tacoma, owners of a company called South Sound Restaurant Group. Over the years, the Twetens have owned the Lighthouse in Port Orchard and the Poodle Dog in Fife. They recently purchased the 1920s-vintage building on 15th, then made Hardy an offer he couldn't refuse. So he will leave Cap Hill after nearly three decades. Alas, early reports from Coastal suggest the tide has gone out. Way out.

WHO OR WHAT'S BEHIND THE NAME?

HEAVY RESTAURANT GROUP is the parent of Purple Cafe and Wine Bar (Seattle, Bellevue, Kirkland, Woodinville), Barrio (Capitol Hill), Meet the Moon (Leschi) Lot No. 3 (Bellevue), and The Commons (Woodinville). Larry Kurovsky and Karen Gibson, owners of a wine shop in Kirkland, added restaurant seating in 2001 and never looked back. The menus won't challenge you, but the wine lists offers plenty of opportunity to educate your palate (a flight of three Italian whites, $17; three northern Italian reds, $19). The company's wine director, Chris Horn, was named Sommelier of the Year at the 2015 Washington Wine Awards.

DERSCHANG GROUP is the umbrella for Linda Derschang's restaurant ventures around Capitol Hill (Linda's Tavern, Smith, Oddfellows, Bait Shop, Tallulah's). There's a music venue in Ballard, too (King's Hardware).

Then there's Seattle's love-hate relationship with south-of-the-border menus. **AZTECA** (21 locations in Washington) gets short shrift, rather like a fancier version of Chipotle.and Qdoba, both firmly on the Taco Bell slope of the curve. **CACTUS** (5 locations) fares better and has a more upscale vibe. But Seattle (otherwise generally tolerant, generally adventurous when it comes to eating out) generally won't support restaurants with a menu written in Spanish. One wonders.

Chapter 17 · TOP INDY CHEFS

Used to be, cooking in a restaurant was considered a decent first job after getting out of the Army or getting out of prison. Then the Food Channel made cooking look glamorous, and bogus academies started waving around "free" money to cover the cost of culinary school. Overnight, kitchens (traditionally populated by older brown-skinned people) were swarmed with bright-eyed young men (and a few women), tattooed, some fresh-faced, some bearded, proclaiming their "passion" for food. Overall, this evolution was beneficial, though it does tend to obscure the talents of the outliers.

EDOUARDO JORDAN An Impressive Sense of Flavor

Restaurant kitchens have evolved over the years, but they still don't reflect America's racial makeup. Plenty of women these days are exec chefs, run kitchens, and own restaurants. Asians, too. But you can count on one hand the prominent African-American restaurateurs in Seattle: Daisley Gordon, Wayne Johnson, Donna Moodie, Makini Howell. Nationally, the figure is a dismal 15 percent of back-of-house employees. African-Americans are twice as likely to be dishwashers as managers. So it's a tribute to his talent, enthusiasm, and people skills that Edouardo Jordan has succeeded in opening Salare, Seattle's hottest high-profile restaurant.

"The road I traveled was not easy," Jordan says, shaking his head at the unrealistic ambitions of all the young cooks he interviews. "They want $17 an hour and a three-day week. But if you're still trying to learn, you've gotta work!"

Jordan is a Florida-born African-American chef whose career has taken him from St. Petersburg to Michelin-starred kitchens in New York City (Per Se) and California (French Laundry); to Italy, for hands-on experience with cured meats; and to Seattle for stints alongside celebrity chefs like Jerry Traunfeld (The Herbfarm) and Matt Dillon (Bar Sajor).

Before dinner service begins, I found the boyish Jordan (he's actually 35) sitting in the dining room of the restaurant he converted, in a five-month flurry of low-tech shop tools, out of the the shell of a truly frightening greasy spoon called Patty's Eggnest & Turkey

House. Some seventy seats, including 14 at a walnut-topped communal table and another 6 overlooking the kitchen, all adorned with ceramic votives made by artist Jill Rosenast. The walls were festooned with wooden molds for *corzetti* (sand-dollar pasta) and a blackboard that recites daily specials.

So what will be on offer this evening, and does it answer the question, what sort of cuisine is this? Italian (handmade pasta, house-cured charcuterie)? Southern ("dirty rice," collard greens, boudin, gumbo, sweet potato fritters)? Northwest (oysters on the half shell, king salmon, fuyu persimmon)? African (egusi, dukkah, tsire)? Well, it's all those things. But a lot of it is Italian, the country cooking that Italians themselves refer to as *cucina povera:* the cooking of poverty. Well, not so much poverty as make-do-with-what-you've-got. Descriptors and ingredients like Tuscan kale, Calabrian chili, cappelletti, trompetti, burrata, and peperonata make appearances on the menu, which all point toward the Mediterranean.

And indeed Jordan's experience in the northern Italian village of 8,000 people called Colorno, outside of Parma, explains where his discipline comes from. He apprenticed in a highly regarded country restaurant called Al Vedel, down the road from Colorno's grand ducal palace, which houses the world-famous Alma cooking school. Al Vedel is the sort of self-reliant place we don't see in the US; for one thing we don't have a nine-generation tradition of *anything*, let alone handmade pasta and the in-house, artisanal production of cured meats like *culatello* and *prosciutto*. "It's all in the seasoning," Jordan explains, repeating the words of his Italian mentors: *Salare, salare!*

This, of course, is how culinary cultures evolve. Edouardo Jordan, brought up in a tradition of "southern" food, with its Louisiana *boudin blanc*, who trained at the Cordon Bleu in Orlando, finding his feet and learning his craft at Mise en Place in Tampa, then winning a coveted spot at the French Laundry. And that month in Italy, which seems to have come at precisely the right time. He arrived in Seattle at the invitation of Mark Bodinet, alum of the French Laundry, who was by then running the kitchen at Cedarbrook Lodge. On to a stint with Jerry Traunfeld at The Herbfarm, then to Capitol Hill's Sitka & Spruce before settling in as chef de cuisine at Bar Sajor.

He runs the kitchen with two line cooks. The menu is relatively short but requires precision, since each of the baker's dozen hot-side dishes has its own specific accompaniments and garnishes. The biggest seller is usually the duck, which gets (among other things) hedgehog mushrooms. Pasta, made in house, can be cappelletti (served with squash, endives, and cotechino sausage), or trompetti (served with gulf shrimp, kale and chili sauce). When an order for oysters comes in, Jordan moves off the line and starts shucking. If it's a pasta dish, or one of the vegetables, or the appetizer of sweet potato fritters, the job goes to a sous-chef, with Jordan checking the plate before it's sent out. An early reviewer claimed to hear a lot of shouting in the kitchen, but the need for "barking" orders--so common in show-off kitchens--has all but vanished. The three chefs now just get on with it like seasoned professionals, plating and sending out one dish after another without drama.

If you're not familiar with ingredients like the Fuyu persimmon (Greek), egusi sauce (Nigerian), dukkah (Egyptian), tsire yoghurt (West African), or ancient-grain einkorn, you can order them from Salare's "Garden" menu, which takes a bold step in the direction of global and vegan-friendly food culture. (Not even Capitol Hill's vegan Plum Bistro gets this exotic.) On the other hand, no one will reproach you for ordering the silky-smooth Dungeness crab with sea urchin beurre blanc and spaghetti; or the grilled salmon with broccoli, eggplant, lemon confit, and pine nuts. Still, it's the charcuterie that shines most proudly, with a "chef's selection" of house-cured meats (garnished with pickled vegetables and cornichons): rillettes and pâtés of duck and pork; lardo, salami, coppa, boiled ham.

THIERRY RAUTUREAU French Under His Hat

Born near Toulouse, his passport stamped with half a dozen top-ranked kitchens, Thierry Rautureau arrived in Seattle in the early 1990s. Soon thereafter, he bought a restaurant in a Madison Valley courtyard that had been started as a weekend hobby by the former headmaster at the Bush School a quarter mile down the road. He kept the name, Rover's, because, why not? And turned the little house into a temple of gastronomy. Buckets of Champagne, plenty of caviar, butter-poached lobster and seared *foie gras*. Thierry kept it going for two decades, ably assisted by his wife, Kathleen Encell. By the time he closed Rover's, he had opened a less formal spot, Luc, in Madison Park, and a splashy spot in the Sheraton Hotel downtown, Loulay.

Luc is on a lively block: there's takeout pizza, takeout teriyaki, a dry cleaner's, a French bistro (Voilà), an Italian trattoria (Cantinetta), a fancy vegan Thai spot (Araya's Place, replacing Rover's), an Asian cafe (Jae, replacing Chinoise). There's another vegetarian (Cafe Flora) a block in one direction, Spanish tapas (Harvest Vine) a block in the other. Good bread, too (Essential Bakery). There used to be a frame shop at the corner of East Madison and MLK; and you'd drive past it thinking it would be the perfect spot for a bar.

A neighborhood bar, then, in the French style with a zinc-topped counter, open late, not expensive, with local wines (literally, from Wilridge, just up the hill in Madrona) and familiar dishes like *boeuf bourguignon* available to go (on real china). Regulars from the Rover's mailing list were offered the opportunity to buy $1,000 shares (technically, gift certificates). The name? Luc, Thierry's father, who passed away four years earlier. The painting? A photo of young Thierrry, already thinking of his hat, surrounded by books, with chapter headings from the cookbook he would eventually write (with Cyntha Nims). The artist was Isa D'Arléans, a Madison Park neighbor, whose brother Cyril Fréchier was the sommelier at Rover's for two decades.

So on to the new adventure, Loulay Kitchen & Bar, in the 6th & Union corner of the Sheraton Hotel. It's named for the village where Rautureau grew up, St. Hilaire de Loulay. When the Sheraton opened its doors in 1982, it was home to Seattle's most prestigious eatery, Fuller's (long gone, but it's where Kathy Casey and Monique Barbeau got their starts). There's still a chain steakhouse, Daily Grille, at the 7th & Pike corner of the block, but the local owners of the Sheraton franchise have long wanted something fancier to attract and retain the more sophisticated convention crowd; Thierry is more than happy to oblige.

ENZA SORRENTINO Italian by Instinct

 She wears a silk scarf, not a white chef's coat, and looks like she just stepped off a movie set. She speaks in rapid-fire Italian to her Spanish-speaking kitchen staff. Enza Sorrentino, who works seven days a week at Mondello, a tiny Italian restaurant in Magnolia (named for the fishing port of Sicily's capital, Palermo). Mamma Enza, proudly Sicilian, arrived in Seattle 15 years ago ostensibly to be present at the birth of her first grandson, then to help out as the chef at her son's original restaurant in Belltown, La Vita è Bella. One thing led to another, and within a five-year period there were four more restaurants and four more grandchildren in the family. Mamma even had her own place, Sorrentino Trattoria & Pizzeria, atop Queen Anne. When the pizza oven died a natural death, she renamed the place Enza Cucina Siciliana, and when the lease was canceled she moved to Magnolia and started cooking again at Mondello. Nothing in Seattle can touch her lasagna with home-made pasta, bechamel, parmigiano, and bolognese sauce. Or her ethereal gnocchi, for that matter. She's not a "sophisticated" chef (no tweezers!) but an instinctive one, who starts her day baking two dozen loaves of bread before preparing the dough for lasagna, gnocchi, and fettuccine. Not surprisingly, she disdains most of what's passed off as "Italian" food in Seattle. Her broad network of fans includes such diverse admirers as Jeff Bezos (who arrived in a chauffeured sedan), Howard Schultz (who showed up after sampling her lasagna at Via Tribunali), Martin Selig (who has her cater his neighborhood parties), and Gordon Bowker (who also lives in Magnolia and obviously knows good food). "A client is a sacred trust," says Enza.

JIM DROHMAN Prince of Chicken Livers

Le Pichet, the French café on First Avenue, owes a lot of its charm to the neighborhood bistros of Paris, but perhaps even more to the informal *bouchons* of Lyon, where workmen gather noon and night to eat hearty plates of pork sausage, pike *quenelles*, and beef tripe in side-street storefronts that once housed stables and made themselves known by hanging a bundle of brush–known locally as a *bouche*–over the door. Hence *bouchon*, which means cork in Bordeaux and Burgundy; no corks at a bouchon, however; the wine comes straight from the cask. Chicken livers are also on the menu, not as a mousse or pâté but puréed and baked and served with tomato sauce.

Jump-cut to Seattle and a restive Jim Drohman, UW grad, aeronautical engineer at Boeing, who chucks it all, moves to Paris, and spends 18 months learning to cook professionally at the École Supérieure de Cuisine. Back in Seattle he begins to work as a line cook, eventually becoming exec chef at Campagne. His wife's uncle is Joe McDonald, who owns the private supper club The Ruins, where he meets his business partner, Joanne Heron. Together they open Le Pichet, and Drohman decides to adapt the classic Paul Bocuse recipe for chicken liver mousse for his new menu.

The chicken livers (free range chickens, naturally) come from Corfini Gourmet, a classy restaurant supply house. Poached, then emulsified and blended with cream, eggs and a Madeira reduction. Seasoned with orange peel, thyme, clove and allspice, the whole thing strained through a fine sieve to remove the fibrous bits. Then it's baked, like a terrine, in a bain-marie, unmolded, and served chilled: a thick, four and a half-ounce slice, topped with a line of *gros sel* that provides crunch as much as saltiness. At Le Pichet, the garnish is cornichons and two kinds of mustard; at Café Presse on Capitol Hill, it's served with a cherry compote.

"We take modest products and turn them into tasty food," Drohman says. Food that pleases Drohman himself. You can't get a Caesar salad at Le Pichet, certainly no caviar. It's not an "I want" restaurant for fussy diners, it's a "show me" place for 32 eaters at a time, lucky enough to eat whatever Drohman and his kitchen turn out. Fortunately, the *gâteau aux foies de volaille* is on the "anytime" Casse-Croûte menu.

Unctuous seems the right word for the *gâteau*, a mouthfeel much smoother in texture than traditional chopped liver, with richer flavors than a foam-like mousse and lighter than a traditional pâté. Spread it thickly on the crusty slices of Grand Central baguette that they serve alongside it, add a *petite salade* drizzled with hazelnut oil and wash it down with a glass or two of Beaujolais, and you will be happy.

MIKE EASTON No Guido-Wannabe

In a city where it's fashionable to be--or pretend to be--an "Italian" cook, Seattle is full of Guido-wannabes. Mike Easton comes as close as a non-Italian can to being the real thing.

In his tiny space across from the King County Courthouse, Il Corvo, Easton and a couple of helpers prepare just three pastas, nothing but Easton's own whims, whatever he finds at the Market and whatever he can crank out by hand with his trusty, antique brass pasta-making apparatus. He posts a picture on his blog, Il CorvoPasta.com, and a tasting note: "The aroma of garlic, anchovies, and chili flake, slowly simmering in olive oil, envelops you like a warm blanket on a chilly October morning."

There's room for maybe three dozen to sit at a time, and they often come based on what he tweets or writes. Three pasta choices, optional salumi plate, optional bread, optional wine, maybe some gelato for dessert, and, originally, cash only.

But look at the choices! From time to time, a superb *taglialini alla Siciliana*, which Easton describes as "a culinary hug." Not some huge, Olive Garden or Bucca di Beppo-sized monstrosity, but a perfect lunch size plate, under $10, of pasta flavored with tomato paste, chili flakes and anchovies, topped with the peasants' substitute for grated cheese (because the aristocrats kept the cheese for themselves): toasted breadcrumbs. And might I add a modest hurrah for the depth of flavor contributed by anchovies? Beats bacon any day.

On the other hand, like a True Believer faced with heresy, I wonder about the lack of eggplant in his caponata. Not *al dente* vegetables in a sweet-sour dressing; that's a *giardiniera*. But Easton should be forgiven, not scolded, for this one rare lapse.

Il Corvo (the Crow), was named Restaurant of the Year in 2013 by the readers of Eater.com. It's an exceptional spot, tiny, lunch-only, no reservations, and in the few, hectic hours that it's open it serves maybe 250 patrons. Subscribe to his newsletter to be alerted, mid-morning, to his menu for the day. He and his wife, Victoria, run the shop with five employees.

"We never created Il Corvo to be for everybody," he told Eater, "and so there's a bunch of people who come in and they're just like, 'Oh, I have to go order my food and grab my own silverware? Forget it. This place sucks!' I'm fine with that. Good riddance. If you can't appreciate what it is and what it does, I'm totally fine with you not coming in."

His new venture is pizza. There isn't any good pizza in Pioneer Square, he says. His pizza is going to be "Roman," the kind of pizza you'd find on the Campo de' Fiori. None of this thin-crust Neapolitan stuff, but very bready. The restaurant is in the historic Pacific Commercial Building at Second and Main Streets. The name: Il Gabbiano (the Seagull).

Two birds! Well, sorry to say it didn't work out. Unsentimental, Easton closed the pizzeria and rejiggered it as a pasta workshop.

Everybody's got a stereotype, and Italians are no different: wildly passionate one moment, indifferent the next. Political corruption? Cynical indifference. Matters of the heart? Passionate but fickle. Matters of the table? Ah, passionate to the core. Easton's an honorary Italian and a Seattle treasure.

MARIA HINES Would-Be Sicilian

There are more Italian restaurants than any other category in Seattle, so Maria Hines knows she has to beat the canned-tomatoes-and-garlic competition. That's Neapolitan, anyway, not Sicilian. Hines actually wrote the menu for Agrodolce (literally "sour-sweet") before she had ever visited the island. When she finally got there in the fall of 2012, courtesy of the US State Department (she's a US Culinary Ambassador), she went straight to the Vucceria market in Palermo and bought *pani con miusa*: a spleen sandwich. "This is Italy's soul food," she says. By this time she'd worked at Earth & Ocean in the W hotel, opened Tilth and Golden Beetle, won a Food & Wine "Best New Chef" award, and beaten Masahura Morimoto on Iron Chef.

So the surprise at Agrodolce, in Fremont, is timidity. The arancini and the meatballs can be almost flavorless, while the rabbit cacciatore is overwhelmed by the briny olives. Caponata was made with Brussels sprouts. (No way! Caponata *requires* eggplant.) Even if we share an admiration for the spleen sandwich in Palermo, uneven execution will deflate the balloon of ambition.

PERFECTE ROCHER & ALIA ZAINE Trusting the Chef

Two of the nicest people in Frelard are Perfecte Rocher and his partner, Alia Zaine, behind the counter at Tarsan i Jane. Rocher's grandfather was a shepherd and opponent of Franco who had to hide out in the hills between Barcelona and Valencia on the eastern coast of Spain; with a long beard and wild ways, they called him Tarzan. Even today, the people of Catalonia

maintain a fierce independence and even a separate language. When he visited his grandfather's mountain hideout, Rocher was in charge of the ducks, the chickens, the rabbits. On a day off at the beach he encountered Alia, a traveling American; they moved together to Los Angeles, where they both found work in restaurants.

Familiar story: they wanted their own place, they wanted a smaller city, so they came to Washington (Valencia is the same size as Seattle), and found a ready-made space where Heong Soon Park had been running his third restaurant, Tray. One too many; he had his hands full with a young family and two other spots, Bacco and Chan. Now the space will be home to the wood-fired cuisine of the Spanish countryside and the Mediterranean coast. And their logo is a rabbit.

"The dining experience at Tarsan i Jane is based on trust," it says on the menu. It's a challenge that goes in both directions. "We trust our diners to be open minded, adventurous, and inquisitive eaters. In return, guests can be confident our kitchen will provide a one-of-a-kind culinary sampling that draws on local producers, seasonal crops, and a deep passion for mixing modern techniques with traditional cuisine."

DUSTIN & DEREK RONSPIES Brother Act

Clearwater, Florida, 40 years ago, would not have been a culinary hotbed. (Not that Seattle was, either.) The best-known kitchen, Bern's Steakhouse, was a good half hour across the Tampa Bay causeway. And yet, from this land of stone crab and fried grouper, from ethnic neighborhoods like Ybor City featuring Cuban sandwiches and Greek salads, came the Ronspies brothers.

Dustin, lanky, goofy, older by two years, found work as a dishwasher, then as a line cook (six years at Outback Steakhouse), while earning credits toward a degree in architecture, which he traded for culinary school, and in whose alumni newsletter he found an ad for a chef with a luxury travel enterprise in France. As it happened, it was the famous Buddy Bombard hot-air balloon company, headquartered just across the peninsula in Boca Raton. The balloon gig was followed by a stint as private chef to a globe-trotting billionaire, then a tour as chef on a yacht. One port of call was Seattle, and Dustin disembarked. Eight years ago he found a rundown spot in Wallingford that became The Art of the Table. Twice now he has been named a finalist in the James Beard ranking of regional chefs. "It's about life, nourishing oneself, nourishing others."

Dustin's cooking is quite sophisticated. A typical plate: butter poached octopus, duck gizzard, shiitake, cilantro fried rice, carrot butter, chili oil, orange-vanilla vinaigrette. Twenty-eight seats, including the chef's table overlooking the kitchen. There's a manifesto of sorts: "Put away your phone, eat your fish skin, slurp your broth, gnaw your bone, eat your micro-greens, lick your plate, eat your cheese rind, have a cocktail, try everything, use your fingers when applicable, hold onto your silverware, enjoy your time here."

An early sous-chef was his little brother, Derek, more intense, who'd been working as a server in Colorado while taking computer animation classes. "I hated waiting tables," Derek told me, "but I loved working the kitchen." His particular interest was charcuterie. After a stint on Nantucket and a foray to Argentina, he turned up in Seattle. After hours, the brothers, along with Dustin's wife, pastry chef Shannon Van Horn, would go for beers and ramen at Showa, the upstairs annex above Chiso's in Fremont.

In 2013, Derek took over that very space, just half a mile west of AOTT, and launched his own restaurant; he called it Le Petit Cochon, the little pig. All of 39 seats. The menu makes a brief nod in the direction of the ocean (Neah Bay black cod), but is otherwise concentrated on the four-legged denizens of farms and ranches. A true snout-to-tail restaurant, in other words. Pork chops, of course. But also brisket, short ribs, offal, bone marrow. It's what Derek calls "Swine Dining." No dish is more iconic than his Phat-Ass Pork Chop, a hunk of meat five inches thick, served on a cutting board. The website is gettinpiggy.com. Order the Smokey Pig Face Fritter, with mussels and beans.

The brothers don't cook in the same kitchen very often these days, but they do get together. One gets the feeling they were not always such pals growing up, but now, as grown-ups, as chefs, as friendly rivals, good buddies they are. Switch kitchens? Not likely. Share a pop-up, why not?

COASTON SISTERS Southern Belles

Seattle is open, tolerant, and diverse, but has a poor record of support for "black" chefs or restaurants that appeal to people of color. Despite this puzzling problem, sisters Leslie and Laurie Coaston had a solid, 20-year run at a charming spot on the eastern slope of Capitol Hill with their New Orleans-themed Kingfish Cafe. Red beans & rice, jerk wings, fried green tomatoes, sure, but also gumbo, fried catfish, shrimp & grits. The desserts alone had a strong following, although they were too sweet and heavy for some tastes. When the Coaston sisters closed, the story was that they intended to develop a concept for several neighborhood cafes. So far, two years later, though, no word.

BLACK BOTTLE & BAR VALICANDO Hard-Working, Unpretentious

The latest "Black Bottle," on Capitol Hill's 15th Avenue spine, is actually called Bar Vacilando, joining siblings from the enterprising restaurateurs behind Belltown's Black Bottle and The Innkeeper. The name and logo suggest a wanderer ("going somewhere but not greatly caring about arrival"), and yet, 11 years after setting out, here they are.

'Twas a warm summer day on First Avenue in 2005 when the door opened to a space that had been under rehab for months. The ghastly Two Dagos tavern had been transformed, one square inch at a time, into Black Bottle. They called it a gastro-tavern, an izakaya. Nobody had ever heard of such a thing back then. Pubs served beer and stale sandwiches, we thought. And here were dinner-size plates of "unfussy, rustic" food for under ten bucks. A wall of hearty, "hard-working" wines for six or seven dollars a glass? Wow! The creators were hands-on owner Chris Linker, chef Brian Durbin, and designer Judy Boardman. After their initial success, they kept at it, first by expanding Black Bottle into the adjacent space, then by taking over Marco's Supper Club, down the street, and renaming it The Innkeeper. Eventually leaping across the Lake to open a clone, Black Bottle Postern, in Bellevue.

None of this Wallace-Huxley frenzy for this trio; they take their time, as much as they need. Two years ago, the cafe called 22 Doors shut all of its doors (City Light having some time earlier turned out the lights) and Capworks LLC (the Black Bottle crew) took over the space. It was, once again, a meticulous rehab. Then the lights came back on. Fortunately, Durbin was ready with an inventive menu: half a dozen each meat, seafood, veggies, plus three flatbreads and three desserts.

In Belltown, there's no finer dish than the braised oxtail. The raw material, 7- to 10-lb chunks of tail (minus the very tip) comes from MacDonald Meat in South Seattle, the same folks who deliver burger patties to Dick's. The pieces are seasoned, seared over high heat, then braised. (Durbin recalibrated the ovens to make sure the temperature was right.) When an order comes into the kitchen, a line cooks drops two or three pieces of meat into a pan, adds a scoop of the jellied glaze, and sets the sauté pan over high heat for several minutes so oxtail can absorb heat and moisture through the sauce. When all is right, the dish is plated, what's left of the reduced sauce is strained through a sieve and topped with a garnish of tarragon and rosemary before it gets sent out into the dining room.

Speak to the dish harshly and the meat will fall off the bone. It is exquisitely tender and intensely flavorful, redolent of beefiness. You can't stop yourself; you pick up the bones, nibble the cartilage and suck down every last skerrick of meat. What's left on your plate resembles the "Vertebrae" sculpture by Henry Moore at Safeco Plaza on Fourth Avenue.

JASON STRATTON Chameleon

He is by turns boyish, creative, confident, shy, a social media darling (@bambichronicles), a *Food & Wine Top New* Chef, a serious contender on Top Chef, a media darling who can do no wrong, a media outcast who does nothing right. Jason Stratton does not head a culinary empire; he has always worked for others (and there are plenty who want to hire him). He was first noted in the kitchen at Cascina Spinasse, which the mercurial chef Justin Niedermeyer had abandoned, and where Stratton was on hand, as *maître d'hôtel* on opening night, while he waited to start a sous-chef gig at Poppy. Accolades aplenty, and new frontiers beckoned.

Before long, Spinasse begat Artusi, and then made the leap off Capitol Hill to the Market, taking over the Thoa space at the bottom of Union and imposing on it a country-Spanish theme. (Uh-oh; Seattle does not love Spanish food.) As Aragona, it was a colossal flop. Reimagined after a few months as Vespolina, with a country-Italian theme it slightly fared better but remained on life support until its cord, too, was cut.

His next project was eastern Mediterranean, working with **Wassef and Racha Haroun** to bring the cuisine of Syria and Lebanon to Capitol Hill at Mamnoon. And then to the heart of Amazonia, with Mamnoon Street. And shortly with mBar, atop the 400 Fairview Building in South Lake Union (and overlooking downtown Seattle as well).

It matters little whether the new ventures catch on; with his tajarin in butter and sage, Stratton has already signed his name to one of Seattle's great dishes, as iconic as the ageless Canlis salad or Shiro Kashiba's oft-imitated kazu sake cod.

JOHN SUNDSTROM Lark Ascending

He may not be as flashy as some, but he's tenacious. After graduating from culinary school in Vermont, John Sundstrom apprenticed in a series of prestigious kitchens around the world, worked alongside Tom Douglas at Dahlia Lounge, opened Earth & Ocean in the W Hotel, and, in 2001, was named a James Beard best chef. He opened his own restaurant, Lark, on Capitol Hill, where he produced a dazzling menu of small plates. He then took over a decrepit building nearby and turned it into a more elegant, full-service Lark, complete with raw bar and private event space on the mezzanine. At the same time, he was converting the original Lark into an elegant pizzeria, Southpaw. (I know, yet more pizza for the Hill.) He also published a new cookbook titled, not surprisingly, "Lark: Cooking Against the Grain."

THE VARCHETTA BOYS

Before "Mamma Enza" Sorrentino started cooking authentic Sicilian food in Belltown, Queen Anne, and Magnolia, there was "Mamma Melina" Varchetta, matriarch of a restaurant family, although it was actually her three sons, Leo, Salvio, and Roberto, who started the restaurants. Buongusto atop Queen Anne, Mamma Melina in the University District, Leo Melina downtown. Mamma came over from Naples to visit, and ended up staying for years. Today there's still a Mamma Melina's, where you can get a decent pizza and a reasonable approximation of southern Italian

fare (even though cream sauces with seafood are decidedly not authentic).

Mamma having once again returned to Naples, the brothers continue to work together They opened the upscale Barolo in 2006, where osso buco, branzino, and cinghiale are on the menu every night, along with a wine list of fine bottles from the Barolo region itself. And in 2016 they took advantage of an offer to expand their downtown footprint with Cinque Terre, a northern Italian seafood restaurant in the heart of Amazonia. (Salvio and Leo pictured.) More fine wines from the top vineyards in Italy, obviously, but there's also an oyster bar (with three kinds of caviar), excellent house-made pasta, and whole branzino, among the specialties turned out by former Cicchetti and Serafina chef John Neumark.

WILLIAM BELICKIS Mistral's Soft Wind

William Belickis was the first of the new wave of chefs who (two decades ago) challenged the old notions of what fine dining was supposed to look like and taste like. Not the Grand Hotel, classic *brigade* school of *haute cuisine*, with *chefs de partie* and *garde-manger* and on and on, but the other classic of kitchen lore: one man, one whisk. Of course it's not really possible to run a kitchen entirely by your lonesome, although, lord knows, enough people try. Belickis did better than most, at the original Mistral on Blanchard Street in Belltown, with Charles Walpole at his side. Dieter Schafer, recently retired from the Rainier Club, ran the dining room, offering diners a choice between the 5-course "Market Menu," the 7-course "Tasting Menu," and the full-on "Mistral Tasting Experience." The guests never saw a printed menu; every dish was a surprise, set down and described by Schafer or Belickis himself. A succession of tiny, fussed-over plates, embellished with foams or paper-thin decorations. That scallop in the middle of a dish was actually the garnish for a parsnip soup; the orange foam was whipped up from tobiko.

Eventually Belickis left Belltown for Westlake Avenue, where expense account wallets and free-spending conventioneers were more likely to wander in off the street. But Belickis himself has never wavered. David Boulay in New York. Fuller's in Seattle. The Salish Lodge. High end gastronomy without without self-importance, but without compromise, either.

CIRCADIA

Eagerly awaited upscale eatery just up the street from Mistral and across from the Federal courthouse, yet another high-end spot. Sommelier Jake Kosseff and partner Jeanie Inglis plan to open a posh new place called Circadia; the chef will be Garrett Melkonian, late of Mamnoon.

Chapter 18 · "BIG PHO"
How Seattle Became an Asian Outpost

If you live here, you no doubt recognize pho, a dish of rice noodles in a clear stock with thinly sliced beef brisket (or tendon, or tripe, or even oxtail). Sauces (sriracha, nam pla) on the left, basil and bean sprouts tucked under the bowl to the right. Elsewhere in the country, this would be considered exotic; here, it's as local as hot dogs and apple pie. Elsewhere, they might call it "foe;" Seattle knows it's "fuh."

But it's not just Vietnamese noodles, of course. Korean, Chinese, Cambodian, Laotian, Thai, Taiwanese, Filipino: the list goes on and on. The world of Asian noodles is complex almost beyond comprehension. Back in the old days, Chinese restaurants served "Chow Mein," and that was that. Eventually, diners learned that "mein" were noodles made from wheat, "fun" were made from rice.

In Seattle's ethnically diverse Asian communities, each has its own relationship with food, its own culinary traditions, its own sets of noodles. Udon and ramen, pansit and soba, banh canh and banh pho. And that doesn't even touch the influence of Japan's culinary culture, notably the Japanese reverence for sushi.

PHO BAC Where it Started

In 1974, after the fall of Saigon, Gov. Dan Evans sent an aide to California's Camp Pendleton with an offer of welcome to the Vietnamese refugees who were being housed there: come north and rebuild your lives in Washington State. And they did. Today Washington is home to the third-largest Vietnamese community in the nation, Vietnamese is the most-spoken foreign language in Seattle. What's no less impressive is that there are more pho parlors in the city than Starbucks cafés. (More pizza joints, too.)

By 1982, Yenvy Pham's family had opened a sandwich shop at Rainier and Jackson, serving a fragrant rice noodle soup called Pho on weekends. Didn't take long until the soup displaced the sandwiches. There are now four Pho Bac stores, all owned by family members.

Pho itself originated in the northern part of Vietnam, where cows were used as bests of burden, but the French colonizers of the country had a penchant for eating beef. The word "pho" sounds like "feu" or fire, and that's the basis of the soup: beef bones, caramelized onions, star anise, roasted ginger. (The French *pot-au-feu* is a boiled beef dinner.) It's a relatively new phenomenon and there's no standard recipe; in the south, for example, people would only eat pho for breakfast.

JAY FRIEDMAN Seattle's Mein Man is a Fun Guy

Jay Friedman goes where even the most jaded Caucasians rarely venture, down narrow alleys and dingy strip malls, ducking into unmarked noodle parlors and darkened butcher shops. He's particularly keen on offal, and when the owner raises his eyebrows as if to say, "You no like," Friedman answers confidently, "Oh yes, I do like."

At Dong Thap, a shop in the ID that makes the noodles for many of Seattle's Asian cafés, he dives into the bun bo hue, served with a cube of pork blood. At Bar Bar, it's simply "the best pho in town." At Hoang Lan, it's "a carnivore's delight of pork sausage loaf, pork blood cakes, beef tendon, and a huge ham hock." At Hokkaido, it's the pickled plum. At Huong Binh, the braised duck. He orders tripe and kidney at King Noodle, and devours freshly shaved noodles La Bu La. At Phnom Penh Noodle House, he revels in slow-cooked pork tripe and intestine; at Revel, he loves seaweed noodles with Dungeness crab. He travels to Edmonds for biang-biang noodles at Qin, and to Lynnwood for cold Korean noodles at Sam Oh Jung.

Dazed and confused? Fortunately, there's an expert on hand, an Eastcoaster who voted for Bernie Sanders when he was running for mayor of Burlington, a world traveler with a Japanese wife, a writer about the finer points of food (not just noodles), who also happens to have a full-time job as a sex educator.

Friedman, author of "The J-Spot," grew up on Long Island and took courses at the Cornell hotel school. He got a cooking job in Vermont, and ended up working for Planned Parenthood for seven years. He didn't like the "apologetic" approach to sex ed, so he went freelance on the college lecture circuit, but always, always, took the time to eat well.

He would frequently fly from the west coast to Asia. And one day in 2002, instead of passing straight through Narita he spent a couple of days in Tokyo, where he'd been set up by a PR firm with a personal tour guide, a young painter named Akiko Kino. By 2004 they were married and living in Seattle, where Friedman had settled in 1999. He wrote a book about his life on the road, the title taken from his lectures ("The J-Spot–A Sex Educator Tells All") and continues to travel the country speaking to college audiences and delivering "sex-positive" messages.

As it happens, one of Friedman's longtime colleagues in the sex-ed/sex advice business (one hesitates to call them competitors) is Dan Savage, who was for many years the editor of Seattle's alt weekly *The Stranger,* whose earliest Q&A advice columns were titled, simply, "Hey Faggot." Eventually, as society grew more tolerant of gay lifestyles, Savage became a sought-after media figure; in 2010 he launched the nationally recognized "It Gets Better" project to give hope to LGBT youth, and in 2011 he was named Seattle's "most influential person" by *Seattle Magazine*. This occurred while Friedman also had a sex advice column, "Sexy Feast," in the competing *Seattle Weekly*. Both men were also on the college lecture circuit, Friedman full-time, Savage sporadically (and commanding much higher fees). "I think we are both advocate of sexual health and sexual freedom, and we are both passionate about sexual politics," Friedman says. Savage's primary forum is publication, while Friedman is better known as a performer and public speaker.

But Friedman also has a separate career as a food expert. In addition to his Sexy Feast column ("What Our Favorite Foods Teach Us About Sex ," including the debate over spitting v swallowing), he has a popular blog, Gastrolust. He co-authored the "Fearless Critic" guide to Seattle restaurants and is a regular contributor to the Serious Eats website; he also curated the Seattle edition of a lively newsletter, "Eat Drink Lucky," during its all-too-brief Seattle run. Friedman documents virtually everything he eats with terrific photographs, too. What got him the most attention is a post he wrote two years ago on Gastrolust titled "What's Wrong with Ramen in Seattle?"

"I really hate to be a wet noodle about our ramen boom," he begins, "but as someone who's spent considerable time in Japan, I've been feeling a little sad about the state of ramen in Seattle."

During one of his dozen trips, Friedman tuned into a TV show dedicated to ramen. In it, three experts traveled from restaurant to restaurant, judging ramen quality. A bad bowl? The expert would simply say *Gomen na* ("I'm sorry,"), and walk out.

Friedman scolds the Seattle chefs who westernize the ramen. "You won't find ramen made with sous vide short ribs and candied carrots in the Land of the Rising Sun. But, all too often, that's the direction the dish is taking in the United States."

So he calls for a change in nomenclature. "If you're not trying to be authentic, then let's call your creation something new: Wramen. Pronounced double-u ramen, it indicates a version that you wouldn't expect to see in Japan." He cites examples of wramen joints, some perfectly fine, like Brimmer & Heeltap (delicious, but spongy noodles), Tanakasan (strange soba-like buckwheat noodles). But not Mighty Ramen (weak soup), Bloom (more weak soup), and Boom Noodle ("mushroom soup"). The real thing? Tsukushinbo (but only for lunch on Friday), 4649 Yoroshiku (again, lunch), Kuzuki (especially the yuzu-shio), Junya (tonkotsu), and Santouka (again, tonkotsu).

Friedman's ramen gold standard would be "Three Tens:" ten seats, ten minutes, ten bucks max. On the other hand, he most definitely doesn't recommend the same quick in & out when it comes to, ahem, more intimate relations.

ERIC BANH & SOPHIE BANH · Vietnamese with a French Accent

Eric and Sophie Banh, brother and sister, fled their native Vietnam in 1978, while young teenagers; the family settled in Edmonton, Alberta. (This explains the poutine on the menu at Ba Bar.) In Seattle, the siblings started Monsoon restaurants on Capitol Hill and in Bellevue, two Baguette Box sandwich shops, and then Ba Bar.

Eric trained as an accountant and sold real estate for seven years, but had worked as a busboy in a classical French restaurant in Edmonton called Bentley's, where he cleaned the ashtrays and loaded the table-side salad carts. When he moved to Seattle in 1996 to start a restaurant, his parents were furious. "We didn't risk our lives to leave Vietnam so you could become a *cook*," they said, though they relented a bit when Sophie joined him.

Ba Bar is in the mold of French-Vietnamese bistros in Saigon that open early for pastries and stay open past 10 o'clock at night. The building once housed Watertown Coffee, across from the Seattle University campus. It's on the east end of Little Addis Ababa, a bit isolated from the rest of the Capitol Hill buzz. Eric especially loved the cloudy-hazy glass windows on the north side and the floor-to-ceiling windows in front. "There's nobody upstairs, so nobody's going to complain about kitchen odors or noise, the way they did when we opened Monsoon East in Bellevue." Except for the windows, he gutted the space. There's new insulation, and a whole new kitchen. "It was unbelievably expensive; we had to sell Baguette Box to raise the money."

Vietnamese food appeals to maybe five percent of the public, not the broad base of people who enjoy Italian or French; it's not even in the top ten of ethnic cuisines. He and Sophie do a lot of charity events, but they don't advertise. "We tried one coupon program at Monsoon East (Living Social), to let people know we were there, but we won't do it again. Good honest food at an affordable price, that's the best advertising."

Eric Banh thinks the hardest part of running a restaurant is finding good people, which requires a skill set of its own, and one he acknowledges is not his strongest suit. What he looks for are team players, not prima donnas. "A restaurant has a lot of moving parts, and you can't run it on so-called passion alone." Meantime, Banh's new steak house called Seven Beef, has opened just around the corner, and plans have been announced for another Ba Bar in South Lake Union.

BA BAR CREPES Only on Weekends

Walk into Ba Bar on a Saturday or Sunday and you'll see this man standing in a cloud of steam. His name is Mr. Chau, and on weekends he prepares a dish called Banh Cuon. It's a Vietnamese rice crèpe, filled with ground pork (Carlton Farms) and wood mushrooms, topped with slices of *cha lua* (Vietnamese ham) garnished with cucumbers and bean sprouts, and a generous sprinkling of the sweet dipping sauce called *nuoc cham.*

The trick is getting the crèpe to the proper, gossamer-thin consistency, which Mr. Chau does by grinding rice and adding just enough water to make a slurry. ("Rice only; cornstarch is cheating!" he says.) He steams a ladle of the (slightly fermented) batter on a cloth stretched across a of pot of steaming water. Taken off too soon, they fall apart; left on too long, they become chewy.

An order of three Banh Cuon is $10. Perfect for breakfast, but only on the weekend.

RICK & ANN YODER Wild Ginger & Hawker Delights

More than 25 years have passed since Rick and Ann Yoder opened the original Wild Ginger, an unusual little café with a pan-Asian menu on the Western slopes below the Market. In 2000 they moved uphill and took over the spacious Mann building at 3rd & Union, remodeling the upstairs in to a multi-sectioned 450-seat drinking & dining emporium and converting the lower level (a one-time porn theater) into one of the city's leading music venues, the Triple Door. In 2013 they expanded again, to the Bravern in Bellevue, a ready-made village of ultra shops, power offices and millionaire condos. And now they're getting ready for another expansion, partnering with Whole Foods to open Wild Ginger Kitchens in four of their supermarkets.

On the east side, just like downtown, they crack their own coconuts, grind their own spices, blend their own sambal. And they have a wine list, one of the best in town: Grüner Veltliner and off-dry riesling by the glass. An Enomatic wine-machine with

Yquem by the ounce. Riedel stemware. Industrial chic decor, which will define this decades as much as brick-&-fern did the 70s. Yoder himself is on hand, shyly offering guidance to cooks and servers. No impatient, uniformed ladies pushing steam carts of mysterious substances. (On the other hand, no garlic pea vines, either.) Four pieces of dim sum ("touch your heart") for 6 bucks max. If the deep-fried prawn & sesame cracker seems a bit like diet food for your taste, there's an alternative: delicious hum bao, beef dumplings, shu mai, wrapped scallop & chives, and an array of dipping sauces.

Then the "hawker specialties" sold in Asia's open-air markets. Soups like pho (rice noodles), laksa (seafood), jook (rice again). Seven Element soup, a staple of the downtown Ginger, makes an appearance in Bellevue: egg noodles, turmeric, red curry, coconut milk and another dozen or so ingredients. You get a bib (so the turmeric won't stain your Armani). In Thailand, this dish is known as *khao soi*, also called Chiang Mai Curry Noodles, although we suspect it's considerably more pungent on its home turf. The biggest seller remains Seven-Flavor Beef, flank steak with lemongrass, chilies, hoisin,basil, garlic, peanuts, and, yes, ginger. ("We certainly like our cow in this country, don't we?" says Yoder. "It's pretty darn good.")

At Wild Ginger downtown the main dining space is ringed by a balcony for overflow crowds. There's a lively bar with sturdy wicker furniture overlooking Union Street, popular with office workers waiting for traffic to subside.

At lunch, long lines outside the Triple Door box office, now dubbed Tiffin (and shortly to become Wild Ginger Kitchen): the tiffin concept originated in India, as a packed lunch for office workers. In big cities, housewives would send lunches packed in metal boxes to their husbands by a network of "tiffin wallahs." The menu is short and sweet: rice bowls, noodles, stir-fries, spring rolls, and desserts. It changes every couple of weeks but remains "Asian" in outlook, ingredients, and spicing. The incumbent exec chef is David Yeo, with Ashley Santo Domingo in charge in downtown Seattle, but they are not prima donna celebrities; their job is to transmit a pan-Asian culture and spirit. Perhaps our palates have become more familiar with some of these flavors in the past two decades, but that's a compliment, not a criticism.

The cuisine spans the entire eastern Pacific Rim (think China, Indonesia, Malaysia, Vietnam). You could start with laksa, a Malaysian version of Bouillabaisse, or with the popular Siam lettuce cup filled with chunks of seabass seasoned with Thai basil, lime juice, chili, and tamarind. Then proceed to the Vietnamese Hawker Beef or young mountain lamb, served on a skewer with a peanut dipping sauce. The house special is a fragrant dish of roast duck spiced with cinnamon and star anise, served with steamed buns and a sweet plum sauce. (I only wish the duck had been more succulent.) There are also some interesting seafood items: Thai spicy clams, black pepper scallops, Cambodian-style Mediterranean mussels, prawns, tuna, and seabass. Regardless of your choice, you should also get a side order of Sichuan green beans.

Wild Ginger has an extensive wine list; the restaurant has won the Wine Spectator's Grand Award and Award of Ultimate Distinction too often to count. For many years, the emphasis has been on wines that showcase the subtle flavors of many Asian cuisines, especially rieslings from Germany and eastern Washington. The incumbent wine director, Martin Bealy, started as a chef and moved to the front of the house, and was eager to share an unexpected and modestly priced treasure: an Oregon Muller-Thurgau from Anne Amie for $30 a bottle.

The Triple Door is where Wild Ginger provides a traditional happy hour, with $7 cocktails, $5 wells, and $5 bites. It's not the same kitchen as upstairs, but many similar dishes are featured, including a three-bun version of the duck. If all you want is a tallboy and some taro chips, this is your spot.

This is Seattle's version of Asian street food, not so much dumbed down as cleaned up. "Authentic"? If you mean aggressively spicy, no. The Ladies Who Lunch, who let the valet park their Lincolns, probably won't come in for the full-on Thai treatment, which you can find elsewhere (on the fringes of the ID, or along on Bellevue's back streets, if that's your preference). But let's give Yoder and his crew (300 employees!) big points for going where mainstreet Bellevue hasn't gone before, even if it's where the Eastside is already heading: there's a huge Asian community out past Crossroads, and the young fashionistas cruising the Bravern's shops look more like China Beach than Jersey Shore.

Wild Ginger is a culinary interpreter of that cultural shift, feet firmly in both camps, nowhere more obviously than inside the 365 Market that Whole Foods is opening this year in Bellevue on the site of the old JC Penney's. And Wild Ginger itself is moving out of the Bravern into Kemper Freeman's new Lincoln Center expansion early in 2017. "I always wanted greater exposure," Yoder says. "The food of Southeast Asia and China is so forward-looking, healthy and flavorful."

MARK & PICHA PINKAOW Thai Curry, Shaved Ice

For several years now, Mark and Picha Pinkaow have operated a popular lunch spot in the International District called Thai Curry Simple. (Weekday lunch only, menu posted on Facebook, minimal décor, less than $10 for specials like sautéed minced pork with spicy chili and basil). Now they have opened a second location, in the U District, featuring shaved ice desserts called Wann Yen. Says Picha: "Our concept is to introduce Thai gourmet shaved ice with housemade flavors."

Wann Yen is a Thai term that doesn't have an exact translation. One interpretation of the phrase is "slow life." Another is "sweet & cool." Says Mark, "Think of shaved ice like the Good Humor truck, But even in Thailand, it's getting harder to find this traditional treat." The distinguishing characteristic of a Wann Yen dessert is actually lightly sweetened fresh fruit rather than gooey syrup. In any event, this is Thai shaved ice, fruit on the bottom, ice on top.

Picha Pinkaow, who created the menu, has six flavor combinations to start, from a sweet coconut milk with ruby water chestnuts and jack fruit, to a mixture of tropical fruits with red date, toddy palm seed, sweet yam, and cendol topped with sweet coconut milk.

WILEY FRANK & PK Right-Sized Uncle

Her full name is Poncharee Kounpungchart, but her husband Wiley Frank (and almost everyone else) calls her PK. As a team they've run food trucks, catering operations, hole-in-the-wall take-out kitchens, good-sized sit-down spots, not to mention a line of Thai spices and condiments (Peek's Pantry).

Their sweet spot has counter service and maybe two dozen seats, and a kitchen that fits three or four cooks (who double as dishwashers, and as bussers for patrons who forget or can't be bothered to clean up after themselves). In other words, the current Capitol Hill incarnation of Little Uncle at 15th and E. Madison.

There wasn't enough space at the original Uncle; there was too much in Pioneer Square, and they've got two kids at home, so they can't keep the late-late night hours of, say, Ba Bar. So they stick with what they can do. "We're growing, but within our means," is how Frank puts it. Lunch dishes are meant for one, dinner plates are to share. The signature Phad Thai is spicy and vegetarian (don't bother asking for chicken), but there's also a beef noodle dish, a "jungle curry" of wild boar, a Dungeness crab stir fry. Closed on Mondays.

SHIRO KASHIBA Master of Sushi

When Shiro-San first arrived in Seattle, sushi was almost unknown outside the Japanese community. Shiro would hike the Puget Sound beaches and dig his own geoduck; he would take unwanted octopus and salmon roe from fishermen along the Seattle waterfront. He would go clamming on the shores of Puget Sound and dig his own geoduck because there was no commercial catch. Eventually, it would start selling for 89 cents a pound in local markets; now, 30 years later (with increased demand and the rise of a sushi-mad Chinese middle class), geoduck is $20 a pound.

By training and temperament, Shiro is a traditionalist, and his namesake Belltown restaurant, Shiro's, was the archetype of a traditional sushi parlor. Guests who expect (and demand!) unusual preparations like "fusion rolls" are politely shown the door with the suggestion that Wasabi Bistro, a block south, might be more accommodating. Myself, I remember telling Shiro, after half a dozen visits, that I was ready for something "more adventurous." I might as well have asked Bach to improvise "An American in Paris." At any rate, Shiro set me straight: the adventure is created within a formal framework, in the pleasure of each piece of fish, in the satisfaction of the experience.

His memoir, "Shiro," is an unaffected gem. The first two-thirds recount his journey from Kyoto to Seattle, passing via years of slog in Tokyo's Ginza district. Ambitious, he persuaded a Seattle restaurateur named Ted Tanaka to hire him, and, in 1966 he arrived in Seattle. Within four years, he had opened the city's first full-service sushi bar, The Maneki. Four years later, he married Ritsuko, a fellow foreign student at Seattle Community College. In 1972 he opened Nikko (which he would sell to Westin Hotels); in 1986, Hana; in 1994, Shiro's.

The book itself is a physical delight. It *smells* good, a refreshing cedar aroma. (The book's designer, Joshua Powell, explains that the paper used for the memoir section is known as "Yu Long Cream woodfree" and the for the recipe section "Chinese Woodfree," both uncoated.) The content is full of memorabilia: snapshots, old menus, airletters from his patron, maps, calligraphy, sketches, watercolor illustrations. The memoir, told with good-humored modesty; it's a tribute to Shiro's character that there's not a trace of braggadocio; perhaps because it's about an unfamiliar culture that none of

this gets boring. (Credit, too, to Shiro's Seattle-based translators, Bruce Rutledge and Yuko Enomoto.) Shiro himself comes across as an ideal, rather formal host, whether he's preparing your dinner at the sushi counter or at Bill Gates's annual CEO dinner in Medina.

And then, just when you're pleasantly sated, along come another 100 pages of recipes and tips: how to cook short-grain rice, how to prepare it for sushi, how to make nigiri sushi (with lovely photographs by Ann Norton), how to clean smelt, how to cut fish for sashimi, how to season and eat sushi (no dunking in soy sauce!). Plus a handy list of terms to use at the sushi counter. (*Oaiso*: Check, please!)

There are storm clouds on the sushi horizon, however. More of the Chinese middle class have discovered the allure of sushi, driving up the price of fish; more middle-class Americans find it sushi too expensive; fewer of Japan's trained sushi chefs want to work in the US; there's less good fish to go around. And Shiro himself has moved on, selling his interest in the Belltown location and setting up inside the Inn at the Market, in a space called Sushi Kashiba. (The former location is still called "Shiro's," though, and is run by disciples.) His memoir should be read and taken to heart by every food lover for its celebration of simplicity and its reverence for nature's bounty.

"I hope that long after I'm gone, traditional sushi will find a way to adapt to different regions of the world," Shiro concludes. "With smart stewardship and respect for the oceans, the Pacific Northwest can remain a paradise for sushi lovers."

HAJIME SAITO Sustainable Sushi in West Seattle

If Sherlock Holmes could solve a crime because of the dog that didn't bark, Hajime Sato is running a sushi bar in West Seattle, Mashiko, without the industry's most famous animal. Call it the fish that didn't swim. At the heart of the international sushi experience, supposedly, swims *maguro*, the foie gras goose of sushi, the giant bluefin tuna with a fatty belly. But it was not always so; the ancient samurai considered bluefin unclean. And bluefin today is overfished, endangered, the subject of vitriolic debate. The Japanese taste for soft, buttery bluefin tuna began only after World War II, when Japanese fishing vessels could venture further afield and track down the elusive bluefin, which now sells for astronomical prices at the fish market in Toyko.

No one questions the fact that o-toro is delicious, but "We are loving it to death," writes the environmental activist Casson Trenor in his 2008 book, "Sustainable Sushi." The oracle of the ocean (a Washington native who now lives in San Francisco), Trenor found an eager disciple in Hajime Sato, a lad from the Tokyo suburbs who opened his own place in West Seattle 17 years ago and who followed Trenor's suggestion to transform Mashiko from one of 200 sushi parlors in Seattle alone to one of only three "sustainable sushi" restaurants in the entire country.

A couple of years ago a diner here could swoon over a gorgeous dish of pink monkfish liver medallions atop thinly sliced octopus. No more. Neither is sustainable; they're both off the menu. But there's no self-conscious political correctness at Mashiko. You don't miss the fish because, after all, you're eating fish. It's not like going to a vegetarian restaurant and ordering "pork chops" made from tofu.

So let's look, instead, at a couple of the fish that Chef Sato does serve. Catfish, first. Farm-raised, And it substitutes for, of all things, eel. Now, you might not think that eel, wriggly things that ought to to survive anywhere in the universe, would be endangered, but they are. So Hajime (as he prefers to be called) looked for a sustainable alternative and found catfish, long considered a junk fish raised in muddy ponds of backward, backwater southern states. But no. Mashiko's catfish come from the ecologically correct Carolina Classics catfish farm in North Carolina, where a closed system is used to purify the water, and the fast-growing fish are raised without antibiotics (they're the rabbits, if you will, of the sea). The catfish makes an appearance atop a Southern Roll: tempura sweet potato, avocado, and "namagi," a made-up word that combines namazu (catfish) and unagi (eel). Salmon at Mashiko is a farmed coho from SweetSpring Salmon, a Washington State company that's also using a closed system to avoid polluting coastal waters by operating miles inland.

Mashiko is actually far more than sushi bar. There's a whole izakaya side of the menu with Japanese gastropub fare. I counted half a dozen folks in the kitchen, and, at Hajime's side, a female sushi chef, Mariah Kmitta. Well, why not, unless you're an unreconstructed segregationist, in which case you probably wouldn't have set foot inside Mashiko in the first place. After all, Rule #1, posted on his website, is "Mashiko is a non-discriminatory establishment" and Rule #2 is "Because Hajime said so." There's also a sign at the door that says "Please wait to be seated, unless you are an idiot and can't read." Point being, this is not a traditional spot like the old Shiro's or the defunct Saito's, nor a hybrid like I Love Sushi or Wasabi Bistro. It's irreverent. The website is called SushiWhore.com. Hajime's email moniker is sushipimp. There's a live webcam of the diners at the sushi bar, for heaven's sake. Mashiko's motto, after all, is "Shut up and eat."

A final note: yes, there's one of those hi-tech Japanese toilets in the ladies room, the kind that, I've been told, gently spritzes and blow-dries a guest's lady-parts. Standard fixture in Japan, apparently. The men's room urinal, on the other hand, is a traditional American Standard.

THOA NGUYEN Rolling Sushi in Bothell

Chinoise made a name for itself with vermicelli bowls and unfussy sushi rolls in Madison Park and Queen Anne, restaurants that don't exist anymore. So what's the deal with the latest Sushi Chinoise at Beardslee Crossing? "I know this area is ready for sushi," is how Thoa Nguyen describes her decision to open a sushi parlor in Bothell. The population of this sleepy suburb has grown to include Asian–and non-Asian–residents who want options nearby without having to travel to Seattle or even to Bellevue. She also anticipates a robust demand for "to go" and catering orders.

And Bothell is sleepy no more. The population is pushing 50,000; there's a real downtown, complete with stop lights. Sure, a lot of fast-food and chain restaurants, but serious places, too. Russell's, Preservation Kitchen, Purple, Amaro Bistro, the remodeled Anderson School, five thousand students at the UW satellite campus, shared with Cascadia Community College.

Nguyen is no innocent-eyed newcomer. She has launched six previous restaurants in the Seattle area over the past two decades, each with its own character. "This space spoke to me when I first saw it," she says of the new location, adjacent to John Howie's newly opened Beardslee Public House. You underestimate those innocent eyes at your peril. Mid-2015, she competed on the Food Network's "Beat Bobby Flay." She made short shrift of the semi-finalist, then went on to knock out Mr. Flay himself with her version of the Korean rice bowl Bibimbap.

So, yes, there's a "Beardslee Sushi Roll" on the menu (salmon, shrimp, snow crab), alongside the much-loved vermicelli bowls with their distinctive rice noodles and lemongrass sauce. Thoa Nguyen's market is not the sushi purist's bulls-eye but the broader target of folks who appreciate "Asian fusion" cuisine, where you can mix and match gyoza and Vietnamese egg rolls, honey-walnut prawns and Shanghai noodles. There's a Volcano Roll, a Sunset Roll, and a Rainbow Roll. But other locations–in the Issaquah Highlands, and in Columbia City–serve delicacies like seaweed salad and grilled salmon collars.

Chapter 19 · PIZZA, PIZZA

Seattle is now the U.S. city with the highest density of certified Neapolitan pizzerias. (Take that, Noo Yawk!) Almost like pho parlors and takeout teriyaki, it can seem like there's a pizzeria on every corner. Which is surprising when you realize that the NY Times still felt it necessary, even in the late 1940s, to tell its readers that pizza pie wasn't a "pie."

MIKE McCONNELL Coffee & Pizza

Mike McConnell, soft-hearted and long-haired, a fan of good coffee and rock music, opened Caffè Vita 20 years ago with the then-novel notion of forging closer bonds between coffee growers in third-world countries and coffee buyers. (Starbucks was doing the same thing.) McConnell expanded his network business to include music venues and pizza parlors; his Via Tribunali pizza chain is one of Seattle's best-known, with stores in Capitol Hill, Belltown, Fremont, Georgetown, and Queen Anne. The gimmick, now shared with Tutta Bella, is that the pizzerias are "certified" by a Neapolitan organization called the Associazione Vera Pizza Napoletana.

AVPN's purpose is to ensure that pizzas are made the traditional way. It allows the use of its collective certification trademark (i.e., brand name and logo) only after a rigorous set of regulations are met, including specific standards for ingredients, cooking and production methods, and the characteristics of the finished pizza. Take Article 3, entitled "Required equipment", subsection 3.3, entitled "Wood" describes the wood permitted to heat the bell-shaped ovens (which, yes, according to subsection 3.3.1 and entitled "The pizza oven" must be bell-shaped, as it has been for centuries): "Wood that does not hold any moisture, smoke or produce odours that alter the aroma of the pizza in any way is required to cook Verace Pizza Napoletana. (The Association recommends oak, ash, beech and maple.)

JOE FUGERE Prince of Pizza

Call him Viceroy of AVPN. Joe Fugere is a home-grown entrepreneur who launched the Tutta Bella pizza chain ten years ago in Georgetown. But not just any pizza. He flew to Miami and spent a week in the company of a pizza master, Pepe Miele, who had signed on with VPN as its director for North America. Before then, to be sure, there was plenty of pizza in Seattle, but none that followed the strict VPN standards for flour, for tomatoes, for mozzarella. Nor were there any authentic southern Italian ovens. Fugere had a pair custom-made and shipped  from Naples, and when he opened he was rewarded with the first VPN certification in the Northwest, "Attesta Numero 198."

By late 2013, Tutta Bella had opened its 5th store, this time in the Crossroads Shopping Mall in Bellevue. Time for another ceremony. The three top officers from the VPN are in attendance, along with the CEO of the family-owned company that supplies Tutta Bella's flour, and a rep from the company that provides its tomatoes. (They'd all spent the previous week hanging out with Fugere at Pizza World, the industry's annual trade show in Las Vegas.) Every store has two 7,000-pound ovens, and follows minutely detailed standards for the elasticity of the dough, for the number and dimensions of burnt bubbles of crust, and so on. In charge of the ovens, exec chef Brian Gojdics.

Over the course of its 30-year existence, VPN has certified fewer than 500 authentic Neapolitan pizzerias worldwide.

One key question: is there an "official" way to eat an authentic margherita? Do you pick it up with your hands, or use a knife and fork? The "official" answer: if the pizza is served uncut, use utensils; if sliced, you're allowed (but not required) to pick it up. On the other hand, pizza *is* the street food of Naples, where it's often picked up whole and folded over, not once but twice, in a style called *al' libretto*, like a book.

Nothing against his legion of competitors, though Fugere is clearly on the side of thin-crust. "In Naples, they say there are only two kinds of pizza: VPN and imitation VPN." And when President Obama had a hankering for pizza during the 2012 campaign, Fugere and his crew set up a mobile oven at Paine Field in Everett and delivered two dozen "Il Presidente" pizzas to Air Force One.

MARIO VELLOTTI Big Mario & Friends

Lower Queen Anne, late morning, these four pals are just hanging out. Big Mario Vellotti on the left, originally from Naples by way of Noo Yawk, where his extended family runs a string of pizza joints. Dave Meinert, one of Seattle's least pretentious and most savvy saloon keepers. Joey Burgess, GM of the Comet and its Cap Hill neighbor Lost Lake. Jason Lajeunesse, Cap Hill Block Party. Mario's got a day job, too, running Vellotti Fine Foods, an importer and distributor of specialty products for the restaurant trade. He's in and out of every Italian restaurant in town several times a week. Good guy to know, even if he didn't have a couple of pizza places named for him. The other gents are known collectively as the Seattle Guild.

On to the pizza. Noo Yawk style, as mentioned. Nothing too fancy. Big pies, but most people order slices, then move into the bar.

The New Haven pronunciation is something like "a-BEETS." The first Big Mario's opened four years ago on Capitol Hill, a short block from the Caffè Vita on the Pike-Pine corridor. Mario was running his Italian food-importing company in Georgetown and counted the Via Tribunali chain among his best customers. But Tribunali is authentic Neapolitan, with all the mystique of a wood-fired oven certified by an industry board of examiners, with more of a sit-down-for-dinner clientele. Big Mario's, like Vellotti himself, is large, loud and brash; get your slices at the front counter (as they come out of the Baker's Pride ovens) and take a stool at the bar in back. The new spot was put together by the same crew, Guild Seattle, that also launched the exquisitely detailed Ernest Loves Agnes on the eastern slope of Capitol Hill.

WORLD PIZZA

Two brothers, Adam Cone and Aaron Cosleycone, run World Pizza in the International District. They originally opened in Belltown, at 2nd and Lenora, in 1992, and kept it going for four years. "But restaurants are like dog years," says Adam, "so it felt like 28." They were on a month-to-month lease with a demolition clause, so when the landlord tore down the building in 1996, they were out of business. Says Aaron, "We like to say we were abducted by aliens, and they just dropped us off 15 years later." Seriously, what did they do in the interim? Adam ran two bakeries on Vashon Island;

Aaron got into antiques and the professional appraisal business. And now they're in Chinatown! How weird is that? Says Aaron, "The entire International District is landmarked. We love it here, it's an eclectic neighborhood."

They had kept the two slate-floor Vulcan pizza ovens from their Belltown days. "We took them out of storage, and it was great to fire them up again!" says Adam. He found their original dough recipe in the back of an old book; it calls for high-gluten flour from Pendleton Mills. They make dough twice a day, and bake at 450 degrees (the antithesis of the super-hot VPN method). They often pre-bake the crust, maybe 3 or 4 minutes, before they put on the sauces, and they use a whole milk American mozzarella that bakes up nice and dark. One size, 16 inches. Everything is vegetarian; the most popular is a potato pizza. And the surprise, for the neighbors, is the "Italian" aroma that wafts out into the Asian sidewalk.

BRANDON PETTIT Delancey & Dino's

He's Brandon Pettit, Dino to his friends, a musician and composer from New York, who moved to Seattle for love (Molly Wizenberg, author of *A Homemade Life*" and the blog Orangette) and opened a pizza parlor called Delancey in Ballard, and now another, Dino's, on Capitol Hill. The pies are huge, although you can get slices after 8 PM. To see Pettit hovering over his pies like a mother hen, constantly checking their crusts and shuffling them in the custom-built oven, is, frankly, exhausting. You may not be a fan of the result, but you can't blame Pettit for not paying complete and total attention.

MAD PIZZA

For some, a successful restaurant company is the objective. Not for the Hanauer family. An immigrant from Stuttgart, Jerry Hanauer arrived in Seattle with enough resources to buy a small bedding company, Pacific Coast Feather, and transformed it into a $300 million heavyweight. His sons, Nick and Adrian, took full advantage of their inheritance. They started Museum Quality Discount Framing to capitalize on the franchise craze and the popularity of "do-it-yourself" projects. On his own, Nick invested in Amazon, then in an online advertising company that Microsoft bought for $6.4 billion. He's also a very public spokesman in a variety of progressive causes, including a higher minimum wage and opposition to income inequality. No slouch, his brother Adrian eventually bought the Seattle Sounders and launched Mad Pizza Company. The latest plans from Mad Pizza: expanding nationwide through franchises.

BAR DEL CORSO

One of the best independent pizza parlors in town, but it hardly ends there. Roman street food like *suppli* (rice balls), grilled octopus, house-made Calabrian sausage.

Owner and chef Jerry del Corso is a local lad, with his wife, Gina, contributing the Italian creativity. Corso himself traveled the world before returning to Beacon Hill and opening his restaurant, where roughly half the business is pizza.

FLYING SQUIRREL

Brian Vescovi is one of the partners in this eight-year-old company, which now has three locations (Seward Park, Maple Leaf, Georgetown). The name is pure invention ("We just knew we didn't want an Italian name"), but the product is squarely traditional. Fifteen-inch pies, with ten predetermined combo choices, and a huge business in custom toppings. Nothing outrageous (no small mammals), just a family-friendly neighborhood joint.

Chapter 20 · FISH ARE JUMPING

Fish houses are where you take Aunt Minnie from Minneapolis, right? Maybe she's never tasted a raw oyster, but when she comes to Seattle, you've got to take her out for seafood.

RENEE ERICKSON Eating Sea Creatures

All different names, but a clear theme: Boat Street, the Whale Wins, Narwhal, Sea Wolf, Walrus & Carpenter, Barnacle, Bateau, Bar Melusine, General Porpoise. The corporate umbrella, no surprise, is Eat Sea Creatures, the name of her company (with Jeremy Price and Chad Dale). Then again, their 30-acre property on Whidbey Island is called La Ferme aux Ânes. So we have the slight cognitive dissonance that Bateau (French for boat) will serve beef from the donkey farm. The Melusine of folklore is actually a water sprite; think of the Starbucks mermaid and you'll get the picture.

Should mention that Erickson was honored this year by the James Beard Foundation as "Best Chef, Northwest," no mean feat. And Bateau, her Capitol Hill steakhouse, received the first-ever four-star review from *Seattle Times* writer Provi Cicero.

By the way, no tipping needed, since there's an automatic service charge. Part of Erickson's move toward greater equity between front- and back-of-house employees as the economy moves toward a $15 minimum wage. The menu explains that there's a 20 percent service charge, 55 percent of which goes to the employees directly serving the customer. Are we going to see more of Ms. Erickson? You bet, in the next chapter, on steakhouses.

IVAR'S ACRES OF CLAMS

© Bob Peterson

Founded by the puckish Ivar Haglund to feed visitors to Seattle's original aquarium, Ivar's has grown and grown. Typically, diners frequent half a dozen restaurants, but Ivar's customers stay close to home, visiting every 10 days and spending half their dining-out dollars at Ivar's. The company donates generously to local organizations and provides full benefits to its employees, who stay with the company an average of 20 years. The company's slogan, need we remind you, is "Keep Clam."

It may have started downtown but there are now Ivar's properties up and down the Puget Sound waterfront: Salmon House, two dozen Seafood Bars, seven stadium locations, seven Kidd Valley stores. The recent Pier 54 remodel for Acres of Clams alone represented a $20 million investment. Next up: an Ivar's in Burien, as well as a series of menu enhancements, like seasonal catches of deep-water halibut, Copper River salmon and Quinault River Coho.

ANTHONY'S RESTAURANTS

The big rival to Ivar's, and more upscale. Budd Gould, with a day job at Seafirst Bank, went looking for business opportunities. His first venture was a steak-and-lobster concept in Bellevue called The Fox Restaurant, followed by a prime rib house called Mad Anthony's. In 1976, Gould opened a third spot on the Kirkland waterfront, Anthony's HomePort, and it proved to be a home run. A dozen similar spots would open within the following decade, featuring waterfront locations and fresh seafood. The total number of properties is now approaching 30. Gould started his own seafood company at Pier 91 in Seattle's Interbay neighborhood to supply the restaurants. Various names as well: Harbor Lights (Tacoma); Chinook's at Fishermen's Terminal; Hearthfire Grill Woodfire Grill, Bell Street Diner.

KEVIN & TERRESA DAVIS Catching the Big Fish

A dedicated catch-and-release fisherman who ties his own flies, Kevin Davis promises you'll never find steelhead on the menu at his three restaurants, Steelhead Diner (in the Market), Blueacre (across from the new Federal Courthouse), and Orfeo (in Belltown). You'll find plenty of succulent seafood, though: a transcendent crabcake, a moist and flaky kazusake black cod, spice-rubbed Alaskan king salmon, beer-battered cod & chips, the sorts of dishes you'd expect from a guy who has cooked his way through more fish than almost anyone in town.

Then again, Davis also spent years behind the stoves of Oceanaire and Sazerac in Seattle, and five years before that as executive chef at Arnaud's in Nawlins, so he's into things like a complex gumbo, juicy po'-boy sandwiches (he calls his a "Rich Boy"), meltingly tender short ribs, pecan pie.

With quiet conviction, he has put together a menu that is, above all, local. (It does help that Steelhead Diner's pantry is the Pike Place Market.) Flash-fried cheese curds from Beecher's, down on the corner. Sausage from Uli, across the way, and Salumi, in Pioneer Square. "Frank's Veggie Meatloaf" named for Pike Place produce vendor Frank Genzale. Theo chocolate, Olsen Farms potatoes, Full Circle Farm lettuce.

And it goes on: bread from Jürgen Bettag's under-appreciated Golden Crown Bakery in Everett. Soft drinks from Seattle's sophisticated Dry Soda. A wine list composed entirely of 60-some Washington and Oregon wines which avoids easy choices, opting for adventurous bottles like Windfall Asian Pear, a bright, citrusy accompaniment to seafood.

Working alongside Davis is his wife, Terresa, a chartered accountant from Australia, who earned a law degree after arriving in Seattle and is also raising twins and two toddlers. Steelhead's poutine is based on her childhood snack of "chips & gravy."

Davis himself is not a fussy innovator. "There's a reason for culinary classics, dishes that stand the test of time," he says. "When it's done right, a crabcake can be as good as anything you'll ever eat. There's an emotional response."

And while her husband is the one with kitchen talent, Terresa is the one with financial skills. When Kevin got a call asking if he'd be interested in taking over the space vacated by the bankruptcy of the Oceanaire chain (and that would become Blueacre), Terresa didn't hesitate. "This is our family business, and it's our one shot," she said. She put together a successful application for a half-million dollar Small Business Administration loan to start the new restaurant. Then she put together the business plan to renovate and run the gorgeous space sitting empty in Belltown when Tamara Murphy moved to Capitol Hill. They named it Orfeo, for the Italian Orpheus, and decorated it with murals inspired by the

Giorgione painting. How heartbreaking to read early reviews (in glossy monthlies, in Seattle's wretched, ink-stained daily) that complained it was "designed for tourists." Tourists, eh? Lifeblood of an entire industry (lodging, transportation, restaurants), the very group targeted by Tom Douglas? When T-Doug does it, it's okay, but not Davis? Every concierge in town is looking for inviting restaurants, what's wrong with that, pray tell?

DUKE MOSCRIP Chowder Houses

We food writers sometimes forget that Seattle's restaurant scene consists of far more than a couple thousand self-described "foodies" who buzz around a handful of trendy bistros. In fact, it's a significant industry of almost 10,000 restaurants that collectively feed a populace of over half a million.

Take Duke's, for instance. Duke Moscrip's six restaurants seat over 900 indoors, with fair-weather outdoor seating for another 500, and employ a peak staff of 300. The company grosses $15 million a year, roughly the same dollar volume as the Space Needle, roughly the same as Salty's, but harder to do when the average check is $25 rather than $50 (Salty's) or $60+ (Needle).

Duke's maintains a strong mailing list (40,000 names) to get the word out to his regulars about specials like the weathervane scallops, a three-month fishery. He and his executive chef, Bill Ranniger, are also regular bloggers on topics that range from environmental sustainability to culinary (chowder recipes) to political (minimum wage versus tip credit).

"Nobody else goes to Alaska," says Duke. "The fishermen up there never see any of their buyers."

But Duke goes. He goes to Westport to check on the shrimp and crab operations on the Washington coast; he goes to Alaska for the salmon, the halibut, and the scallops, and he's found three scallop boats (with their own websites, even) that will handle the catch his way: small lots, hand-shucked and frozen on board immediately after they are pulled from the icy Gulf, packed in five-pound boxes clearly marked with name and date to ensure traceability. Each boat has an independent, at-sea observer on board to ensure that Alaska's rigorous practices of sustainability are followed. Unlike other scallops on the market, the weathervanes are free of phosphates, preservatives, and unwanted chemicals.

"The product is incredible." he says. "There's nothing like them. We sear them to a caramelized golden brown, and then we stop. They don't need a tricky sauce, and they certainly don't need overcooking."

A former Bothell High basketball star, a former stock broker, one of the original owners of Ray's Boathouse, at the helm of Duke's Chowderhouse for 35 years, Duke Moscrip has become an evangelist for sustainable seafood. "Nobody else drills down like this," Duke admits. It's almost an indulgence, this intense level of personal, on-site research.

He certainly wouldn't have time to do it if he didn't have his son, John, running the company's day-to-day operations as well as a fanatically loyal corporate chef Ranniger.

DUKE'S WINDJAMMER

Shilshole Bay is a Seattle treasure: a mile-long expanse of waterfront promenade between the mouth of the Ship Canal and the beaches of Golden Gardens. The Marina itself is managed by the Port of Seattle, no fly-by-night outfit. The cost of moorage is a buck-and-a-half a day, per foot, if you're just visiting, or you can lease a slip by the month for your own yacht; $500 and change for a 40-footer, with an electrical hookup (metered separately) at each berth. The spot offers astonishing views facing the Olympics from across the water, with sunsets that don't quit.

Alas, only one classy waterfront restaurant survives here after several decades of commercial activity: Ray's Boathouse. The most recent casualty was Anthony's Homeport, which expired quietly earlier this year. That was following the sad decline of Hiram's on the Locks (now an event venue) and Azteca (remodeled as condos).

So it's welcome news that the Windjammer, which was once one of Seattle's poshest eateries, is being given a new lease on life. In its heyday, the Windjammer was part of Walter Clark's family of restaurants. Clark himself reigned supreme over mid-market dining in Seattle with an assortment of Dublin Houses, Red Carpets, Village Chefs, and Crabapples. And the Windjammer, at 7001 Seaview Ave NW, featured dancing (!) as well as an elevator to the second level years before anyone thought to provide an alternative to stairs.

Well, the Windjammer is no more, but the Port of Seattle still owns the land. So they put out a request for bids from anyone who might like a crack at restaurant's old building. Now, ask yourself who, in Seattle, has a string of waterfront seafood restaurants and you'll figure out who jumped in with both feet: Duke Moscrip, founder of the Duke's Chowderhouse franchise. He's going to build a new Windjammer from the ground up.

Chapter 21 · THE STEAKS ARE HIGH

Clubby and dark, with stiff drinks and even stiffer prices, the traditional American steakhouse is a fail-safe choice for corporate first dates. You know the names: Ruth's Chris, Morton's of Chicago, Capital Grille, and, at a lower level, chains like Black Angus (founded in Seattle; there's a profile of founder Stuart Anderson on page 171), Outback Steakhouse, Claim Jumper. But in recent years the number of purely local steakhouses has grown apace. The demand for showy, expensive dinners is expanding, thanks to Seattle frenzied business climate.

BATEAU

What all is on the menu at Bateau, the new Renée Erickson steakhouse on Capitol Hill? Well, octopus, sweetbreads, tartare, and the like. A pork chop, a butter-poached fish. Then five kinds of beef. Filet, onglet, bavette, New York, and the *pièce de résistance* (as the French would say): Côte de Boeuf, the double-thick, bone-in rib-eye. The Italians call this cut Fiorentina; it's also known as a tomahawk steak (though that just means the butcher doesn't saw off the long rib bone). Set you back $125, it will. The doughnuts (General Porpoise next door) are far, far less, but probably not as satisfying. The blackboard tells you what cuts are available that night. The beef comes from Whidbey Island, a 30-acre property called La Ferme aux Anes, that's owned by Erickson and her partners, Jeremy Price and Chad Dale.

Now, you can't write about Bateau without mentioning that it received the first-ever four-star rating from *Seattle Times* reviewer Providence Cicero. "Elegance abounds," she wrote., noting that it's not your grandfather's steakhouse. More like a butcher shop in a fancy French food hall. If you're not fussy about which specific cut you want, go with the tasting menu, $75 for five courses; it's the best deal in town. And let us not forget to acknowledge that Bateau was named one of the top new restaurants in the country by Eater.com.

BUTCHER'S TABLE

Kurt Dammeier's day job is running a string of food businesses under the Sugar Mountain umbrella. Beecher's Handmade Cheese, in the heart of Pike Place Market, and its offshoot in a handsome brick building in Manhattan's Flatiron District. A couple of Pasta & Co. shops to provide synergy: Mac n Cheese! A food truck (Maximus/Minimus), two mid-market restaurants (Liam's, Bennett's). And, more recently, a passion for Wagyu beef.

Sugar Mountain's meat distributor, Mishima Reserve, rounds up American Wagyu cattle from a cooperative of Northwest and Colorado ranches. ("Wa" means Japanese, "gyu" means beef.) Seattle is already the nation's number four market for Wagyu (after Las Vegas, San Francisco and LA), and Dammeier is confident that it will get even stronger. The meat is currently for sale at Metropolitan Markets and on the menu at several of Ethan Stowell's restaurants (notably Red Cow and Goldfinch Tavern). Meantime, at street level, the construction crew from Mallett has been putting the finishing touches on Dammeier's most ambitious project: a luxurious steakhouse to be called The Butcher's Table.

A raw bar for local shellfish, a retail meat counter, an upstairs bar that encourages solo dining, a vast subterranean space with ornate tufted-leather nooks and crannies. A big place, in other words, to serve the ever-more-vibrant South Lake Union neighborhood. Dammeier is bringing in a hotshot chef from San Francisco, Morgan Mueller (and his wife, Ellie, a pastry chef). Another veteran, Anthony Casiello, from Mastro's Steakhouse in Beverly Hills, will run the wine program. It's a big bet, but, thanks to the sale of his family's printing company, Dammeier came to the table with a lot of chips.

DANIEL'S BROILER

Started in 1970 by Bill and John Schwartz with the opening of the Butcher Restaurant in Bellevue, and run today by John's son, Lindsay, Schwartz Brothers Restaurants operates on this simple philosophy: "Listen to your customers; they'll tell you what they want." Today, the company focuses on high-end dining – its Bellevue Daniel's Broiler has the second-highest check average in the state – in tony settings like the South Lake Union waterfront, the Leschi waterfront, and high atop Bellevue. Plus Chandler's Crabhouse, Spazzo Italian Grill & Wine Bar (Redmond), Gretchen's Shoebox Express (catering) and Schwartz Brothers Bakery (Renton, Seattle). The best view is from the view lounge in Bellevue called Prime 21. Veuve Clicquot by the glass, a prime filet sandwich or a traditional steak tartare, and a view that toward the east and the west that will take your breath away.

EL GAUCHO

One of the managers at the original 13 Coins, Paul Mackay, kept that restaurant's vision of elegant service alive as he migrated through other Seattle dining rooms. In 1995, he stuck his toe into the roiling waters of Belltown, partnering with Chris Keff to open Flying Fish. Two years later, a spot opened up at First & Wall. There was a mission for the homeless across the street with an outhouse on the sidewalk for the drug dealers and winos. Not that he had anything against the Peniel Mission, you understand, but the aromas of stale beer and urine didn't exactly attract high rollers. The rebirth of El Gaucho coincided with the dot-com boom, high-tech millionaires and celebrity chefs. A heady time. But the vision was fulfilled: elegant service for the rich, the famous, and the celebrators of special occasions. "A night to remember" is the objective. It certainly doesn't hurt El Gaucho's image that it was known as a late-night haunt for Seattle's pro basketball stars. Paul Mackay's son, Chad, runs the company today. Tip: if you've got a couple of spare Benjamins in your wallet, order the Chateaubriand, carved tableside. And drink one of the sensational Washington reds on the wine list.

NINA MICHAELENKO Artist of the Pampas

Nina Mikhailenko is the Russian artist whose oils adorn the walls of El Gaucho. Her style has its roots in a late-19th century Russian art movement called Peredvishniki, a loose group of itinerants who rebelled against the formal restrictions of the tsarist academy. Instead they painted populist themes: peasants, religious celebrations, landscapes. Her most successful works are commissions: murals of life on Pampas, bullfights, chefs, cigar smokers, jazz musicians, well-fed urbanites, and the folks in the kitchen.

BRAZILIAN STEAKHOUSE MEAT-UPS

The style is called *churrascaria*, which refers to the slow grilling of a dozen or more kinds of meat. The local example with the greatest longevity was first called the Buenos Aires Grill in Belltown. The concept moved downtown as Ipanema, then returned to Belltown as the Grill from Ipanema. All owned by Marco Casas Breaux.

In the interim, there was a joint called Fumaça, which didn't last long. Meantime, in South Lake Union, there's Novilho's, which offers beef, pork, chicken and sausages, carried through the dining room by a platoon of skewer-wielding gauchos, who carve thin slivers of meat at your table. They keep coming until you turn over your coaster, from green to red. Hungry again? Flip the coaster and start all over. Before you get started, there's a salad bar, too.

If you're familiar with Brazilian steak houses in Seattle, you won't be shocked by the price, about $60.

JOHN HOWIE STEAK

That's actually Mark Hipkiss in the photo, the exec chef at John Howie Steak in Bellevue. He's the carnivore behind such items as the breakfast burger (bacon & eggs), not to mention Wagyu steaks (from Japan's Miyazaki Prefecture, from Australia's Darling Downs, or from Snake River Farms outside Boise, Idaho; you can sample filets from all three for $250), along with pork belly confit sandwich, or a New England lobster roll. (Don't worry, the guy with his name on the door has his own write-up on the fish side of the ledger.) Should you find yourself half-starved at lunchtime, be aware that the Triple Bypass starts with 12 ounces of prime chuck ground in-house, cheddar cheese, topped with three pieces of tempura bacon. There are also tempura onion rings in there somewhere, and what's described as "drive-in sauce." (Lovers of Dick's will understand.) No bun; it's served between two grilled cheese sandwiches. And do come back for dinner and try the Wagyu.

METROPOLITAN GRILL

Eric Hellner is a lifer, not a bad thing if you're in charge of the kitchen at Metropolitan Grill, Seattle's top steakhouse; he's been part of the team for a quarter century now. The Met is part of Consolidated Restaurants, a storied local chain founded in 1951 by David Cohn as Barb's, at Fourth Avenue and Seneca in downtown Seattle. There were a dozen Barb's restaurants before Cohn opened the Polynesia on Pier 51 in 1962. At that point, Barb Enterprises was the largest owner-operated restaurant company in the Northwest. In the 1970s, Barb's gave way to two landmark restaurants under the Consolidated banner, the Metropolitan Grill and Elliott's, and David Cohn's son, Ron, took the reins. Short of a private venue like the Rainier Club, there's nothing that says "tradition" in Seattle like The Met. (And nothing says "seafood" like Elliott's, for that matter.)

Hellner sears a 6-ounce ohmigyu tenderloin, seasoned with only salt and pepper, on a cast-iron griddle, brings its internal temperature up slowly to keep the fat unctuous.

Served with a drizzle of veal demi-glace and a few Yukon gold potatoes poached in garlic butter, it's $100. (You can also get raw Ohmi as a carpaccio appetizer for $20.) Don't listen to people who say it's not worth it, the best steakhouse meat is never cheap.

Thanks to its elevated glutamate levels, not to mention inosinic and oleic acids, Ohmi provides an umami experience like no other. It's like cutting into a perfectly seared lobe of foie gras, redolent of meaty char, rich blood and exquisite liver. If you pay attention to taste, you will remember this for the rest of your life.

SEVEN BEEF

The latest Eric Banh venture to open is Seven Beef, just around the corner from the original Ba Bar. the name comes from *Bo 7 Mon*, a ceremonial seven-course presentation usually reserved for weddings. The tasting menu, priced at $35, includes lesser-known cuts of beef (but regularly found in classier southeast Asian restaurants around town), served grilled, ground, steamed, wrapped, and so on. Seven Beef occupies a 4,000-square-foot building that once housed an architect's office; it seats about 100 guests, with a private dining room and outdoor patio still to come.

The centerpiece is the dramatic open kitchen equipped with an Infierno wood-burning oven (smaller than the one at Miller's Guild, but still impressive) alongside a combi-convection oven. What you don't see is the cooler in the back that houses the restaurant's sub-primal cuts of prime, grass-fed beef, delivered weekly by Heritage Meats from their ranch in Rochester, Wash. (They'll cut you off a three pound, bone-in Côte de Boeuf for $120.) Watching over the kitchen is Scott Emerick (right), a longtime friend of Eric Banh's recently returned from Washington, DC, whose former spot in Madrona, Crémant, became Ethan Stowell's Red Cow. Ba Bar's pastry chef, Roger Martinho, is in charge of bread and desserts.

The restaurant's polished concrete floors are softened by white table cloths. The central portion of the main dining room is lit with bistro lights that remind you of a country festival in France or Italy; the overflow space at the back–usually referred to as Siberia in other restaurants–becomes a jewel with an ornate chandelier. The bar, deliberately darker, is brightened with white marble.

Steakhouses everywhere are expensive–beef is expensive, folks, and grass-fed cattle the costliest of all–so you shouldn't come here if you're both hungry and broke. The signature Bo 7 Mon is quite reasonable, but everything else is à la carte. On the other hand, where else are you going to find aligot ($9), the French mountain amalgam of Cantal cheese and potatoes? Or braised leeks in brown butter ($10)? Look, if the Côte de Boeuf is a bit rich for your budget, you can step down to the Porterhouse or the T-Bone or the teres major or the *onglet*. But c'mon, it's a steakhouse. It's on Capitol Hill. Shut up and go. There's even a valet to park your Tesla.

MILLER'S GUILD

The centerpiece of Miller's Guild in the Hotel Max is a nine-foot, custom-built grill called "Infierno." It comes from a company in Michigan called Grillworks, founded 30 years ago by Charles Eisendrath, a former foreign correspondent for *Time Magazine,* who was Inspired by the open-fire cooking techniques of Argentina. Chef Jason Wilson, winner of the James Beard award as best chef in the Northwest, is now involved with Portland's leading restaurateur, Kurt Huffman, at Miller's Guild. Wilson's own place on the eastern slope of Capitol Hill, Crush, is now a development kitchen for a project called Coffee Flour, leaving Wilson time to concentrate on the Infierno. It has a central fire station, as it's called, that puts out 1,100 degrees. It feeds the two side grills that you can adjust for height, and the hearth baking platform. The hood is constantly cooled by water. "It costs about as much as a BMW," Wilson admitted. "Instead of a new BMW, I'm driving a 15-year-old car, but this is way more fun."

SMITHCO And Where Does It Come From?

All this meat is from an outfit called Smithco, located in the sleepy, north Pierce County city of Sumner, population 10,000, where Sumner Chevrolet sales lots anchor the town's principal intersection, and the high school's Sunset Stadium bears the Chevy logo. A mile or so down the road stands a modest, one-story building without signage, home of Smithco Meats. "We don't sell retail, so we don't want to attract attention," says owner Jay Keener, who bought the company from the Smith family three years ago, after he "retired." He'd grown up as a "sawdust kid" in his own family's business, Keener's Meats in Bothell, that was bought out by increasingly anonymous national firms. Now he's happily back at work, running Smithco as a regional distributor specialized in delivery to restaurants.

The meat business is high volume, low margin. A company like Smithco buys what are called subprimal cuts, rather than, say, half a steer, and breaks them down, takes them apart, trims them, losing volume every step of the way. By the time they have, say, a tenderloin dry-aged and ready to deliver to a high-end steakhouse, it's worth $24 a pound.

Seventy percent of America's beef is sold in supermarkets and butcher shops, where a piece of meat is priced according to its weight. In food service, on the other hand, you've got to provide what the restaurant asks for: a 10-ounce New York cut, for example, or a 12-ounce cut. The price is "per each," so Smithco's cutters place each piece on a scale after they trim it, to be sure it's up to spec. At $24 a pound, an almost-imperceptible deviation of half an ounce would quickly turn into financial disaster.

Everyone's afraid of what a corn shortage might do to livestock prices and availability. The nation's cattle herd is down by 1.5 million animals, and the number of "placements" going into feed lots is declining. The flavor of a steak, Keener will tell you, comes from the animal's feed in the last three months of its life. "Grass-fed" beef may sound warm and fuzzy, but doesn't have the same rich taste. That means corn-fed beef, from the corn belt of the Midwest, although the potatoes, barley and soybeans of eastern Washington make a reasonable substitute.

ETHAN LOWRY · JOE HEITZEBERG Cow Tippers

You know that really smart friend, the one you only see every few years, but he's always doing something new and it's always awesome? That would be Ethan Lowry (right), last seen as the guy who started Urbanspoon, the first online restaurant site that later evolved into a reservation app. He sold it to IAC Interactive for millions and took off for a trip around the world. Now Ethan is back in Seattle with a new thing, co-founded with fellow techie Joe Heitzeberg, called Crowd Cow. Kinda like Farmstr or Barn2Door, but just for cows. Local beasts from the Skagit Valley.

The idea is a sort of Kickstarter that pools money from online contributors to jointly purchase a steer "on the hoof." Once the price is reached, the cow is "tipped" and it's taken away to be butchered, cut into useful pieces (steaks, roasts, organs, ground beef), vacuum-packed and aged, and, when the time is right, shipped to its buyers. Price looks to be about double what the supermarket charges, but this is the real thing: grass-fed, no-hormones. "We're offering a convenient way for customers to get great tasting beef from sustainable local farms, just the cuts and quantity they want, delivered straight to their door," says Lowry. He and Heitzeberg focused on meat because they think that a lot of people are frustrated with the lack of transparency and the practices of the industrial meat-production system. One recent example: you'd think "grass fed" meant the cow ate only grass and foraged plants from weaning to slaughter. Hah! The US Department of Agriculture actually rescinded that requirement in 2015 under pressure from politically powerful feed lots (which finish the cattle on grain). And it's the grass-fed ranchers who are lobbying to have the stricter rules reinstated.

Grass fed simply tastes better, its advocates say. And it's better for your health, too. And the environment (no bloated cows farting methane.) Oh, Cow Tippers do sell tongues and tails, cheeks and bones, hearts and livers, kidneys and leaf fat. "All the parts the USDA will let us. In fact, those are often the first items to go," says Lowry. They'd sell the tripe, too, if the processing facilities were properly licensed. "We certainly don't want any of the animal going to waste!"

Chapter 22 · BIG PICTURE WINDOWS

Why, you ask, doesn't Seattle have any great waterfront or view restaurants? Answer: Because it doesn't really have to.

Good, sure; great, nah. None of the restaurants with great locations offer particularly bold flavors or innovative dishes; you really can't do that at Seattle's top view and celebration restaurants. The clientele is just too diverse, too untrained in more sophisticated dining, too unwilling to make a stretch. Still, here's a look at some of the most popular spots for visitors as well as local folks looking for something special.

SPACE NEEDLE

Sky City is the formal name of the restaurant atop the Space Needle, owned and operated by the family of the contractor who built it in the early 1960s as the symbol of the World's Fair. The construction company was sold a decade ago; what remains is now called Seattle Hospitality Group under the direction of Howard S. Wright III, a civic-minded executive who helped broker the city's move to a $15 minimum wage. The Space Needle is but one element; there's also the attraction of art glass at ground level (Chihuly Gardens & Glass), a motor coach company, the Seattle Trolley, and so on.

What the management expects of its kitchens, and generally gets, is a predictably high level of execution: ingredients of good quality properly prepared. At the Space Needle, this task falls on the shoulders of Jeff Maxfield, and the result, not unexpectedly, is an operation that ranks at the pinnacle of Seattle's list of top-grossing restaurants. With close to 300 seats and an average tab of over $60 at dinner, Sky City feeds over 50,000 visitors a year and grosses $15.5 million.

Maxfield specializes in "celebration" menus: crab cakes, lobster & tenderloin combos. The fanciest dessert is called the lunar orbiter (dry ice, sparklers, roman candles). A three-course brunch is $50.

But in the prime locations, to justify the high prices, there must also be drama, and the drama must come from the presentation. So you get polished service, you get food towers, you get careful plating, you get sizzle (That dry ice! Those sparklers!) What you probably don't get is a taste, even a mild one, of what Seattle's vaunted food scene is all about.

SALTY'S ON ALKI

In 1985, Gerry Kingen bought a tumbledown waterfront building called the Beach Broiler on the West Seattle waterfront and added it to his portfolio of seafood restaurants in Portland and the South Sound. It's called Salty's on Alki and sits on Harbor Avenue two miles across Elliott Bay from downtown. "It's a million-dollar view," says Kingen. It's also a $10 million-plus a year restaurant, in the top 100 nationwide.

Salty's also has a well-developed event and catering business with as many seats (on its lower level) as the ballrooms of Seattle's downtown hotels. It also offers a popular weekend brunch, with plenty of crab and shrimp. Best of all, Salty's sits on prime real estate, leading to speculation that the underused space (like the parking lots) would be an ideal site for a small, luxury hotel.

Of the Big Three, Salty's is probably in the best position to weather the storms of fickle public opinion. Earlier in his career Kingen had launched the Red Robin concept of gourmet burgers. The guy who started the Blue Moon Tavern, Boondock's, and Lion O'Reilly's also has another project up his sleeve: barbecue. He and his wife, Kathy, partners in the family business, have bought out Pecos Pit, the 'cue joint in Sodo, and plan to spread the concept throughout Seattle. Their daughter, Kate, left a job with DeutscheBank in New York, to pilot the project. The first Pecos Pit barbecue opened in West Seattle in the summer of 2016. Expect more.

PALISADE

Situated at the base of a bluff at the southern tip of Magnolia, Palisade overlooks the Elliott Bay Marina and Smith Cove. The twinkling lights of downtown Seattle–sometimes blocked by cruise ships –are three miles to the southwest.

Parties looking for a "celebration restaurant" are the target customers. As the sun sets, Mt. Rainier comes into greater relief. Says former GM Doug Zellers, "People had kind of forgotten about Palisade." (At one point, the vaunted Sunday brunch lost its signature seafood buffet, but it was quickly reinstated.) The revitalized kitchen was given a mandate: "Elegance on every plate." So there's been a refreshing coat of paint and a new layer of upholstery; the signature Ocean Tower (oysters, lobster, crab legs, prawns, etc.) now arrives tableside on a customized metallic stand shrouded in a cloud of dry ice, as dramatic an entrance as one can imagine.

Palisade, for all of its uniqueness and prestige, is the flagship of a $150 million chain called Restaurants Unlimited. RUI is also the parent company, locally, of Palomino and Cutters, and has nurtured a goodly share of local talent (John Howie, for example). And RUI in turn is one of dozens of companies (hospitality, retail, industrial) in the portfolio of private equity firm Sun Capital.

RAY'S BOATHOUSE

On Shilshole Bay in Ballard, it began life as Ray Lichtenberger's boathouse 60 years ago with a glowing neon beacon (RAY'S) to signal sailors approaching the waterway leading to the Ship Canal locks and Lake Union. The immutable attraction here is the stunning sunset view across the water to the Olympics, but it's more than location that beings people here today. Upstairs, in the informal café, there's reliable fish & chips plus a bar with craft beer. Next door, a full-on catering venue. Downstairs, in the Boathouse proper, two iconic dishes: Alaska King Salmon and Sake Kasu Sablefish (adapted from the original Shiro Kashiba recipe) by Ray's first chef, Wayne Ludvigsen, who now sells organic produce at Charlie's.

Ordinary seafood is not enough, though. "Today's diner is more worldly," says co-owner Russ Wohlers. So techniques from the Nathan Myhrvold school of modernist cuisine are being applied to traditional recipes. Ray's "wasn't broken," the owners point out, but needed a face lift, as much to cater with post-2008 economics as anything, so smaller plates, lower price-points, more exotic flavors. And cocktails that appeal to the target audience (decision-makers when it's time to select a destination): women in their late 30s.

"We'll still have around 50-percent tourists," Wohlers acknowledges, but more locals willing to spend $50 per person without feeling overcharged. So how do you modernize without scaring away your regulars? At Ray's, it looks like they're going to try rocking the boat a little bit. Not too much, just a little bit., but enough "to be on the leading edge again."

SIX SEVEN

The Edgewater Hotel's restaurant, Six Seven, has as impressive a location as any restaurant on the Seattle side of the water. An unobstructed sunset view of the Olympics and the arrival, in summer, of the Clipper from Victoria; an unobstructed southbound view as well into the forest of Port of Seattle cranes and the reassuring silhouette of Mt. Rainier. Its neon "E" is almost as recognizable a Seattle landmark as the Space Needle. You can fish from your room at the Edgewater, which was constructed on a pier. Ir was briefly (and fittingly) called the Camelot, and what with environmental regulations, there will never be another structure built over the water. As it happens, the State of Washington owns part of the Edgewater's lease, which runs through 2018.

The Beatles stayed at the Edgewater when they visited Seattle (and ordered room service). Led Zeppelin, too (the notorious "mudshark" incident took place here in 1969).

The food is pretty much what you'd expect: egg dishes at breakfast, fish & chips at lunch, grilled salmon at dinner, a wine list from corporate headquarters in Kirkland. The décor is a bit bizarre: what appears to be a forest of antlers attached to the walls with what looks like high-tech boat hardware. But the view! Ah, the view.

And still more waterfront

AQUA BY EL GAUCHO on Pier 70. Easy to overlook, which is a shame. First of all, there's parking, a big plus in this crowded part of the world. And then there's the fact that this spot, at the tip of Pier 70, sees itself as offering the most ambitious and prestigious menu (read: priciest) of the string of downtown waterfront restaurants.

ELLIOTT'S OYSTER HOUSE on Pier 56 is part of Consolidated Restaurants and a longtime supporter of locally sourced seafood and shellfish. Home to the annual Oyster Olympics. Less dramatic views of the Sound, but great oysters and perfectly prepared salmon.

ANTHONY'S PIER 66 is part of the ubiquitous Anthony's HomePort chain. There's another outlet in Kirkland, on the east side of Lake Washington, that also provides a democratized (read: less expensive) dining experience. Excellent wine list, excellent seafood. If you're not hung up on the prestige factor, this may be your best choice.

Chapter 23 · EXCURSIONS

Fire up the Packard, Gramps, we're going to hit the road. North, south, east, we've got a table waiting. We'd go west, too, but that would require a boat ride. We'd go all the way to Lummi Island's Willows Inn if it didn't take a three-hour drive.

THE HERBFARM Culinary Drama in Woodinville

At most restaurants you'd be asked to choose: pasta or fish, chicken or beef. Not at The Herbfarm. No choices, first of all. One seating, four nights a week, nine courses, six wines. On a recent evening, the first course was spot prawns, the second a rich pasta with savory onions. The Columbia River king salmon was seasoned with lemon thyme from the garden; the chicken was no ordinary broiler but one of the Poulet Bleu birds from Lummi Island you've been hearing about. The T-Bone of lamb was beautifully grilled. Still to come: an intermezzo of noble fir ice, a cheese course, and a dessert of strawberries and wild elderblossom, followed by coffee, tea, and tiny dessert treats from the pastry kitchen. No wonder dinner takes almost five hours.

The cellar holds over 25,000 bottles, the most extensive collection of Oregon and Washington wines anywhere, period. Yes, there's a formal wine list, but each dish is accompanied by a nigh-perfect glass that you might never discover on your own (a 2013 Walter Scott chardonnay from the Amity Hills of the Willamette Valley to accompany the salmon); over a year's worth of dinners, Zimmerman opens some 8,000 bottles. Was there a pinot noir among the dozen wines served? No. Did I miss it? Nope.

There's nothing even remotely like The Herbfarm in Seattle: the very highest level of gastronomy and service, and an unmatched commitment to local sourcing. Over-decorated? In this age of minimalist concrete, perhaps. But don't let that stop you.

It began a generation ago, when Bill and Lola Zimmerman bought a farm in Fall City. Lola would sell her surplus chives and other herb plants to passers-by, and soon had a thriving business. When Bill retired from Boeing, he built a shed so people would have a place to picnic. Their son, Ron, was an outdoorsy type who co-founded Early Winters and wrote their catalogs. In 1986, he and his wife, Carrie Van Dyck, turned the shed and part of the farm house into a restaurant. It was Seattle's first farm-to-table restaurant, Ron in the kitchen and Carrie as hostess, and for years there was never an empty seat. Disaster struck in early 1997, when a fire destroyed the premises. The Herbfarm moved into temporary quarters until, four years later, it reopened in Woodinville.

The model for this concept was the Auberge of the Flowering Hearth, a self-sufficient country inn romanticized by the food writer Roy Andries de Groot. For much of the year, the Herbfarm's own kitchen gardens and a nearby, five-acre farm supply the restaurant with produce. As the culinary director, Ron writes 20 or so themed menus a year ("June's Silver Song," "Nine Songs of Summer") featuring wild mushrooms, handmade cheeses, artisinal caviars, heritage fruits.

The Herbfarm's first "outside" chef was Jerry Traunfeld, an alum of Jeremiah Tower's Stars in San Francisco who was working at the Alexis Hotel in Seattle when he was recruited in 1990. After he left in 2007, Keith Luce took over for a couple of years; the current incumbent, moving up from sous-chef, is Chris Weber, who, at 29, is now the youngest chef at a Four-Diamond property in the country.

There's a theatrical element to the Herbfarm dinners that some guests don't understand. The rationale is that you can feed your face in hundreds of places; you can eat good food and drink fine wines in more places than ever, and maybe even spend the $200 to $250 it's going to cost, wine included. But the Herbfarm is as much a temple as a table, where you are not just a pampered guest but also a participant in a what can sometimes seem like a sacred ritual to honor the earth itself. The social construct of "dinner" unfolds like a vaguely decadent religious ceremony, officiants bearing trays and goblets for your delight, yet, mixed with the dazzling pleasures and bright tastes, there's an (unspoken but solemn) reminder that we enjoy this bounty only because our planet is so generous.

ROY BREIMAN & MARK BODINET Gastronomy in the Wetlands

Mark Bodinet grew up on the south side of Chicago and attended culinary school in Arizona. But if Chicago was too bleak, Phoenix was too hot. He jumped at the chance to work on Martha's Vineyard, where his boss was a lanky dude named Roy Breiman. The French Laundry, Meadowood, and Per Se followed. Breiman, for his part, landed a spot at the Salish Lodge before moving to the French Laundry as well.

Meantime, Washington Mutual's conference center, in the woods just east of SeaTac, came on the market. Chase, the bank that had rescued WaMu, wanted no part of its woo-woo culture. No problem, though, for Coastal Hotels, a company owned by Howard S. Wright, the man who built the Space Needle. For Coastal, the 170-room, 18-acre site, renamed Cedarbrook, was an ideal alternative to airport motels and city-center skyscrapers, a perfect spot for discreet regional conferences. Natural wetlands and lush cedars surround the property, which boasts its own herb and vegetable gardens.

So here it was that Bodinet, more hands-on, became installed as executive chef at the restaurant, Copperleaf, while Breiman, more cerebral, became culinary director. In many establishments, one person plays both parts, a casting necessity, perhaps, but rarely successful. At any rate, Bodinet is excited to "show people what we can do, starting with the urban chef's garden."

Cedarbrook has a lot in common with resort hotels (a spa, plenty of catering, 24-hour room service), so there's a banquet chef and a platoon of line cooks. The "dining room" itself seats only 50 and virtually disappears into a patio-level extension of the lobby; there are another three dozen seats in the bar, and, when the weather is right, a few outdoor tables overlooking the meticulously tended grounds.

The Copperleaf tasting menu provides a good look at the restaurant's commitment to local farms. (Breiman's the bird-dog, flushing out farmers, produce, sources of fish and game.) He was one of the first to tout the virtues of Riley Starks's Poulet Bleu from Lummi Island, for example. The restaurant's Facebook page follows the path of edible roots as well as edible animals on their way to the kitchen. The tabletop salt & pepper shakers are a snail and a frog. The wine list includes treasures from Walla Walla with names like Leonetti and DeLille. But lest you think this is all for stuffy bankers, there's a "Young Adults" menu with homemade pasta and chocolate chip cookie ice cream sandwiches. If I had layover at SeaTac, I'd hike half a mile through the woods (to work up an appetite) and sit myself at the bar for an artisanal cheese plate with a glass of local ale. Or maybe I'll just get there early for my next flight.

BRIAN SCHEEHSER Growing His Own

When Brian Scheehser arrived in Seattle two decades ago, trained at the CIA via Chicago, to take a post on the line at the Hotel Sorrento's highly regarded restaurant, the Hunt Club, the city's culinary reins were firmly in the hands of a cohort of highly capable women (Monique Barbeau, Emily Moore, Kathy Casey, Tamara Murphy, Chris Keff, Kyle Fulwiler, Sally McArthur), not to mention Barbara Figueroa at the Hunt Club itself. Remember those days? Today? Renée Erickson and Maria Hines for sure, but mostly dudes.

Scheehser toiled dutifully at the Hunt Club for many years, never letting standards slip, but, a decade ago, he "moved east" and took command of the kitchen at a luxury boutique hotel across Lake Washington in Kirkland, the Heathman. The mother ship, the venerable Heathman Hotel in Portland, was where James Beard-winner Greg Higgins got his start before setting out on his own. Higgins pioneered the novel approach to the whole farm-to-table conundrum: to ensure a steady supply of high-quality produce, he had started his own mini-farm. In Portland, there are clear boundaries between suburbs for housing tracts and suburbs for agriculture; easier said than done in the Seattle area, with lax zoning regulations that seem to encourage construction, development, and urban sprawl. Still, Scheehser found 18 acres in nearby Woodinville (part of an urban agriculture project called South 47 Farm) which he has planted with a variety of fruit and produce for the hotel's restaurant, Trellis.

From winter squash soup and beet salad at lunch, arugula and zucchini carpaccio for the salad plates, to fried sage leaves for the house-made ravioli, there's a steady stream of vegetables, tree fruit and berries from the farm to the kitchen.

The latest project at Trellis is that classic British standby, the cream tea (sometimes called High Tea by confused Americans, but that's another story.) Popularized on the West Coast of North America by the grandest *grande dame* of all, the Empress Hotel in Victoria, BC, the cream tea features an assortment of finger sandwiches, along with pastries, fruit, and a generous bowl of clotted cream. (At Trellis, they call it *crème fraîche*.) So far, the tea service is only available on weekends; we hope it catches on. Why should Canadians have all the fun?

SALISH LODGE: Twin Peaks, Snoqualmie Falls

Twin Peaks, a cult TV show from the early 1990s, has risen again, filming a comeback season's worth of shows in and around North Bend last year. "A damn fine cup of coffee," says agent Dale Cooper, clutching his mug of joe at Twede's Cafe, called the "Double R Diner" for TV and renowned for its cherry pie. Nearby stands the "Great Northern Hotel" overlooking Snoqualmie Falls, in reality the Salish Lodge, whose claim to fame is its "honey from the sky" country breakfast. Once the new show starts its run, tourists (Japanese, German, French) will return by the busload.

Until then, the Country Breakfast ritual is well worth its own morning drive out I-90 to the town of Snoqualmie. There's a lot going on after dark as well: a full gourmet menu in the main dining room, smaller bites and pizzas around the fireplace in the cozy Attic. Also 84 guest rooms and a full spa. But for sheer drama, nothing beats the four-course breakfast overlooking the 270-foot waterfall where you can see rainbows rising from the mist: a mimosa to start; then coffee, pastries and house-made jam; a bowl of oatmeal; eggs, bacon, sausages, potatoes, and a freshly baked biscuit. Once you've cut open the roll and buttered it, the server arrives bearing a chalice of honey from the colony of Salish bees (yes, there's a colony 12 hives on the hill behind the parking lot); she raises her spoon to the ceiling with practiced precision, and the honey lands atop the waiting biscuit. Normally this extravaganza runs $75 for two; there was a $19.16 promotion in early 2016 to celebrate its centenary. On your way home you can stop at the gift shop for a supply of steel-cut oats, pancake mix, biscuit mix powder, as well as honey.

Reservations About Gambling

Further upriver is the town of Snoqualmie, as well as a spectacular casino overlooking the entire valley. It's not the biggest gambling hall in the state; that's Tulalip Resort, north of Seattle, but still: 175,000 square feet of gaming, 1,700 slot machines, 50 poker tables, and a fine-dining restaurant called Terra Vista. You might wonder what 15 casinos are doing along the I-5 and I-90 corridors until you recall some history revealed a decade ago. Jack Abramoff, then a lobbyist close to President George W. Bush, and two cronies, Ralph Reed (Faith & Family Alliance) and Grover Norquist (Americans for Tax Reform) eventually pleaded guilty to taking $85 million in bribes from Native American tribes in connection with their applications for casino licenses. Now, gambling is not normally not tolerated by the feds, but has been legal on the "sovereign territory" of Native American reservations since Abramoff pushed through the Indian Gaming Regulatory Act in 1988. Some 300 casinos in 38 states now generate over $30 billion a year in revenues, and create some 600,000 (mostly low-level) jobs for tribal members. No surprise that the scale of this windfall has attracted vultures: mega-building projects (Snoqualmie Casino is said to have cost $400 million), huge fees for night-club talent, lavish spending on advertising and ultra-high-end dining. In all the years I've lived in Seattle, I've never once heard anyone say, "We wanted to go somewhere special for dinner so we went to the casino." Nope, these places are for high rollers, big winners and chastened losers in need of cheering up. The whole point is high overhead, which generate big fees for the casinos' (predominantly white) consultants.

HOLLY SMITH Cafe Juanita

Roma, Roma on the vine, who's the one who will be mine? Campari? There's actually a tomato cultivar named Campari? Anyway, here's Holly Smith, owner and chef at Cafe Juanita some 25 miles to the north, straight out of a fairy tale, unquestioned princess of the Tomato Faire at Cedarbrook Lodge in the sheltered woods east of the SeaTac runways. Smith herself, James Beard winner, alum of T-Doug's empire (Dahlia Lounge), took over the venerable spot overlooking Kirkland's Juanita Bay some 20 years ago; until then, it had belonged to Cavatappi wine maker Peter Dow.

Under Smith's stewardship, Cafe Juanita has maintained the highest standards for northern Italian cuisine. When she redid her menu a while back, she divided up the tri-fold page into neat categories. Aperitivi (Krug Grande Cuvé with bone-marrow bruschetta) and antipasti (veal sweetbreads) on the left; salads (smoked eggplant panzanella) and pastas (goat cheese gnocchi) down the middle; fish, meat, and fowl (the famous rabbit braised in white wine) on the right. And then she realized she still had room for five or six items. Bingo, contorni! Side dishes! Cauliflower with cumin, organic green beans, roasted carrots, heirloom tomatoes. Well done.

After 15 years in the space, Smith closed the restaurant in 2015 for remodeling but continued to cook at the old Lark space on Capitol Hill (technically a pop-up, with a multi-course tasting menu four nights a week). Now the spiffed up and redesigned Kirkland spot is open and running again, a strong candidate for best restaurant in the Seattle area. There's a 10-course tasting menu for $135, but I'm happy with a plate of sage-&-butter tajarin, $15, and the one dish I cannot leave without tasting again, the rabbit poached in Arneis, $36. Rabbit, not *coniglio*. You're here for dinner, not a language lesson.

GREG ATKINSON Marché on Bainbridge

We said we weren't going west. Well, shucks, here we are at Colman dock, so let's stroll onto the ferry, stand at the prow for half an hour and walk off. Head up the hill, turn left at the traffic light and you're "downtown." This is Winslow Way, quintessential American small town, feed store, ice cream stand, arts & crafts shop. And a very fine restaurant, Marché, hiding at the back of one of the newer developments. Eat here. Read more about the chef, Greg Atkinson, and his cookbook, in the Feeding Back chapter.

Chapter 24 · FORKING IT OVER

They say that the secret of success is giving people what they want. Even if that's a $2 ear of corn dipped in liquified butter not 100 yards from a supermarket selling corn at 10 for a dollar. Because it's the appearance of value that matters, not the thing itself. If you were DeBeers, you'd try to control the supply (the mines) as well as the message ("Diamonds Are Forever"). Besides, it's just a little bite.

AL SILVERMAN: Bite of Seattle

It began innocently enough, three decades ago, with a street festival called Bite of Chicago. Back then, Al Silverman, who owned an Olde English joint behind the Factoria Mall called Barnaby's, smelled the bratwurst...and an opportunity; he launched a modest festival at Greenlake.

These days, Bite of Seattle, still owned by Silverman family under their corporate umbrella, Festivals, Inc, takes over Seattle Center for three days at the height of summer, feeding some half-million visitors. Most of them look well-fed to start with, which doesn't prevent them from lining up for elephant ears, funnel cakes and churros. A respected French chef like Thierry Rautureau (left) just adds window dressing.

To make ends meet, the Silverman clan some years back sold their banner sponsorship to the single most destructive force in the restaurant industry, Groupon. With Orwellian hypocrisy, Groupon's VP for North American Sales says: "As evidenced by the awesome restaurant and food deals featured daily on Groupon, we really love food. We're very excited about our three year commitment to celebrate the amazing food, restaurants and culinary talent of the Seattle area, and we're delighted the festival supports the great work being done by Food Lifeline to give more people in Western Washington better access to nutritious food." But will Groupon renew?

Yup, Groupon has paid to attach its name to Seattle's most bloated food event. Pass the antacids, please. And bite me.

Silverman's daugher Jody Hall runs the family business these days. "A lot has changed," she says of the evolving food festival scene. The Nibble of Northshore is a real thing. Every day, some sort of food tasting is announced on social media, and restaurants, increasingly, are taking the initiative to promote their own places. "We were the ones doing the work in the early days, and the restaurants were happy to break even." Which explains, perhaps, why so many of the exhibitors and concessionaires aren't really restaurants at all but pop-ups, sandwich shops, and food trucks. Unlike volunteer events like Folklife, Hall has to pay for staff, and there are only two income sources: vendor fees and sponsorship.s. A food truck might pay $600 in rent, a vendor selling ice cream cones from a 10 by 10 tent might have to cough up $1,800; a full-on restaurant with a 20 by 20 tent as much as $3,000. In return, Bite pays for all the permits, Seattle Center overhead, even ice. Still, I've always wondered what the City of Seattle gets out of this, aside from a crowd of cheapskates swarming over the lawn at Seattle Center, stuffing themselves with unhealthy food.

Most disturbing of all at the most recent Bite was a non-food booth selling toys: toy swords and guns. Glocks and AK-47s. Sure, the actual weapons are legal; sure, the toys had muzzles with bright-orange tips. But in a Seattle public park? Shame on you, Silvermans.

RETCH OF SEATTLE

Remember back to October of 2012, if you can, and a scam called the Seattle Underground Market. Its perpetrator, Michaela Graham, had previously tried something similar in Atlanta, but moved on after people got sick. It was described online as "a venue for passionate food entrepreneurs to share their food creations with others and get valuable feedback, as well as the opportunity to build up their fan base. It's an incubator and food testing ground." The Seattle event, at a warehouse in Redmond, was not, apparently, properly authorized. Simply calling an event a private function (even if patrons sign a waiver acknowledging that the food may not have been prepared in a licensed kitchen) doesn't eliminate the need to comply with the regulations. If admission is charged, and if food is for sale, it needs a permit. (In fact, all food sold at public events must be prepared in commercial kitchens that have passed safety inspections.) The King County Public Health Department has a long check-list of requirements for temporary food-service establishments: triple sinks for dirty dishes, clean water for hand-washing sinks, thermometers to watch the temperature of food. The Health Department's inspectors are zealous in their enforcement of the rules, as many a neighborhood festival (and even farmers market) can report. Most surprising was Graham's reaction to the complaints: she blamed food bloggers for drawing too much attention to the event.

DICK SPADY Burgers Deluxe

For an assignment (Burger Week, or some such), we wanted to know about Dick's, so we sent a message to John Spady, the son of founder Dick Spady, whom we had met once, on neutral territory. By this time Dick's Drive Ins had been around for five decades, starting with 19-cent burgers in Wallingford.

How many burgers do you sell in a week? How much meat do you order a week for the burgers? Who's your meat supplier? Liters a week of ketchup? Mustard? How much lettuce, tomato, onions, pickle? Lbs of potatoes? Cheese? What's your most popular burger? Milkshakes: most popular flavors? How many gallons? How many milkshake machines? Is there ever a line out the door?

We got a very nice reply from Mr. Spady's representative. "We will need to decline your request for by the numbers. Dick's is a private, family-owned business and all sales information is confidential." A private, family-owned business that's also a Seattle institution, of course. Personally, I often found the fries limp, cold, and greasy, but the Deluxe itself, oh Lord, nothing tastier. .

Some months later, Dick Spady celebrated his 90th birthday. He sent a message to the people of Seattle: "Thank you to our customers. We wouldn't have lasted a week, let alone 60 years without you! Ever since we opened our doors on January 28, 1954, you've embraced us with your support and loyalty. Thank you to my family, and especially my wife of over 58 years, Ina Lou, for your support and understanding. And finally, I would like to say thank you to all the people who share this beautiful place we call home. We are all blessed to be able to live here, for as much time as God allows."

Dick Spady passed away not long thereafter, having made a lasting contribution to Seattle dining. California's In & Out burgers may someday metastasize their way north along the I-5 corridor, but they will never replace the glory that was (and still is) Dick's.

STUART ANDERSON: Mister Black Angus

There's a second Seattle beef story that started out with lots of sizzle: a steak, a baked potato, and a green salad for under three bucks.

The man behind that concept was Stuart Anderson, who returned to his native Northwest after World War Two and took over a small hotel. He enjoyed running its bar and coffee shop more than renting rooms. A city boy who'd driven a tank during the war, he made himself into a Ponderosa-style cowboy (southern drawl, boots, leather jacket, horse, ranch), and in 1964 he opened a Western-themed steak house he called Black Angus. The three-dollar steak dinner was hardly gourmet, but the concept, pioneered by Tad's in New York and San Francisco was already familiar. Black Angus was an instant, line-around-the-block success; and expansion was rapid

By 1972 Stuart Anderson had sold his company to Saga, and in 1986 he retired to his sprawling ranch outside of Ellensburg.

There were over 100 stores at that point, but the chain spiraled into an unfortunate series of ownership changes and eventual bankruptcy. TV commercials featuring a dandified cowpoke named Travis were disastrous; by 2004 the parent company of Black Angus, American Restaurant Group, declared the chain bankrupt; five years later, ARG itself declared insolvency. Still, a private equity outfit specializing in "distressed" companies, Versa Capital Management, snapped it up and today runs what's left, some 45 stores (including one in Lynnwood, another in Federal Way) that manage to generate $400 million a year in revenues.

"The restaurant industry has lost a legend," Anthony Anton of the Washington Restaurant Association told the *Seattle Times* when Anderson passed away at the age of 93 in 2016. A legend who loved the restaurant business, to be sure, even though he could barely fry an egg if his wife wasn't home.

Chapter 25 · COMIC RELIEF

Not every dinner house in Seattle is a minimalist hipster emporium with tattooed bros working the line and earnest wannabes serving the food & drink. Sometimes, you just wanna have fun.

CAFE NORDO A Little Satire With Your Dinner

From Fremont to Pioneer Square, from the International District to Washington Hall on the fringe of the CD, the Cafe Nordo players found novel ways to tell their stories twice a year, with limited runs. Now they have their own space in Pioneer Square, a "culinarium" where the zany crew can spread their good cheer year round.

It started when Terry Podgorski and Erin Brindley, alums of a successful variety show known as Circus Contraption, created the persona of a fictional martinet, Chef Nordo Lefeszki. Their first production, in Fremont, brought together a cast of semi-professional entertainers for a show called "The Modern American Chicken." The tuxedoed and feathered cast performed the saga of a hapless, happy hen named Henrietta. "A hen is the egg's way of making another egg," said one character, energetically whipping egg whites. "And what makes a good egg? A good hen."

Technically, Chef Nordo was stabbed to death (offstage) in the Twin Peaks satire Somethin' Burning, but his presence is still felt. The shows have a homespun lack of pretense; their characters remain resolutely in character, even during breaks. The scripts regularly assail the soul-destroying purveyors of fast food even as the performers double as waitstaff. Brindley and Podgorski nuzzle right up to the line of self-parody but don't cross it.

You shouldn't come to Cafe Nordo expecting haute cuisine, but it does rise to the level of good, neighborhood bistro fare. Restaurants fall into broad categories, but once you get past the stuff-your-face-quickly places, they all have an element of the theatrical. What could be more dramatic, for example, than the simultaneous raising of the *cloches* in a Michelin-star fine-dining palace, revealing in one stunning moment the dishes of every guest at the table? Café Nordo, Seattle's homegrown enfant terrible of dinner theater, will have none of that artifice, thank you, but that doesn't mean they're averse to serving a meal whose entertainment value laces honest food and stiff drinks with a message of political satire. And, now, straight drama too. Now that they have a permanent space, Nordo is co-producing plays by outside companies as well.

TEATRO ZINZANNI Professional Wackiness in a Spiegeltent

Let's go back to 1972, when Seattle hired a quirky local non-profit called the One-Reel Vaudeville Show and its longhaired founder, Norm Langill, to produce a festival at Seattle Center called Bumbershoot that is still a highlight of the city's arts calendar. In the off-season, Langill went on to a career as an actor, playwright and theatrical impresario. Then, in Europe 20 years ago, he stumbled upon a Spiegeltent, an intimate, bejeweled circus tent with a wooden frame, canvas and mirrors, easily assembled by traveling roustabouts. In 1998, having imported a pair of Spiegeltents from Belgium and from Austria, he produced his first shows in Seattle and San Francisco.

Now, with a permanent location in Seattle's "Entertainment District," ZinZanni has become a shiny-shabby people's palace of raucous and bawdy entertainment across the street from the Opera House on Mercer. Some 285 guests, four nights a week, are served a five-course dinner (well-paired with matching wines) by a troupe of actors (the "Galaxy Girls") while the entertainment unspools: music, pop songs from the Sixties, PG-rated jokes, suggestive dances, and the spectacular aerial acts.

These are Cirque du Soleil-level performers; that is to say, at the very top of their trade, which is to make you gasp. We saw the amateur gymnasts on TV at the Olympics; these are professional-level athletes, up close and astonishingly personal.

The professional kitchen was originally under the direction of Tom Douglas and got high marks. For the past couple of years the exec chef has been Erik Carlson, who'd worked in the Gordon Biersch organization and at Bellevue's Twisted Cork. "Food is one of the characters in the show," he says. His colleague Jamie-Paul Rizzo curates the wine and cocktail list.

No table-side photography is allowed at Teatro ZinZanni, "for the safety of the artists." So we're showing you one of the backstage bulletin boards instead. This is a good place to take Aunt Minnie (you know, the one from Minneapolis) if she wants to spend an evening immersed in Seattle's diverse, slightly wacky cultural community.

Chapter 26 · PHONING IT IN

We've all heard the line on TV: "It's not delivery, it's DiGiorno." Leaving aside the tone-deaf notion that any old pizza "made today" is worth eating at all, there's no question that, for many households, "delivery" is more than just dinner, it's Deliverance.

There's not just one app for dinner, there's a dozen. Delivery services like Bite Squad, Postmates, and Eat24 will pick up from restaurants; menu services like Blue Apron will do your shopping; Chef'd drops off complete meals; Peach delivers lunch to your office; others, like Munchery, cook dinner for you. The target audience is not harried urban housewives so much as tech workers who stumble home sometime after 6 (or 7 or 8) no longer interested in doing anything but zone out. For them, deliverance is spiritual.

AAKHIL FARDEEN Lish

The founder of Lish is a former product manager for Amazon who knows what it is to come home from the office late, tired, and hungry. Weekends, Aakhil Fardeen would go out, weeknights, nah. But traditional takeout was all-too-often mediocre and unsatisfactory, even from good restaurants. His solution: ask good chefs to create meals *designed* for delivery, designed to be delivered chilled and heated at home.

Unlike Munchery, which has chefs on staff, Lish lets local independent chefs offer their own menus, and each dish gets rated by customers. So you have chef Max Borthwick (from Thailand) and ginger chicken; chef Prakash Niroula (from Nepal) and Moroccan grilled beef; chef Nasreen Sheikh (from Pakistan) and Khara Masala beef stew, all perfectly delicious. Chef Garrett Doherty (Massachusetts) is a veteran of Kraken Congee and a semi-celebrity. But Lish adds first-rank celebrity chefs: Ethan Stowell, Ericka Burke, and Jason Wilson. Stowell's signature dish, rigatoni with spicy Italian sausage, is regularly featured on Lish.

Fardeen says the freelance chefs have the potential to make $100,000 a year, since they are independent entrepreneurs and earn each time someone buys their meals. Right now his drivers (also indy contractors) are delivering to 15 zip codes that cover 80 percent of Seattle. More coming, but he needs more space than the commissary on Capitol Hill allows right now.

The celebrity chefs use their own kitchens, mostly "idle capacity." He's not cheapening their brand but enhancing it, allowing customers to continue their relationship with the chef in between visits to the restaurant itself.

Lish charges the chefs a hefty 25 to 30 percent commission for his "meals marketplace," but makes sure meals are delivered when and where the customer wants. Although they can be ordered as late as 7 PM, half Lish's orders come in ahead of time; Sunday nights are busiest, when customers often order for the entire week.

Meals are dropped off in special coolers. "It's not soggy," Fardeen says. Not surprisingly, he's looking at expansion beyond Seattle (Portland, the Bay Area).

UBER EATS

Comes now a new service from the ride-hailing app Uber. The company jumped in the restaurant delivery game in various cities last year, and has now docked in Seattle. The *Wall Street Journal* has reported on Uber's plans to "disrupt the food-delivery business as much as it has with taxis," and now we're about to see for ourselves.

UberEATS promises to deliver lunch in ten minutes ("Faster than a microwave") to subscribers who live in half a dozen downtown Seattle area neighborhoods.

The opening week menu included items like drunken chicken from Monsoon, pulled pork from Skillet Diner, and a trio of salads from Volunteer Park Cafe. Dishes will be priced between $8 and $12. Restaurant partners will do all the cooking, but UberEats will use a facility in SLU to pre-position popular meal options. Some 20 restaurants signed up as partners for the launch, with more coming.

Registered Uber users will see the UberEATS options available for their locations on their mobile devices, and meet the drivers curbside to pick up their meals. Delivery is included in the price; tipping is not necessary. Seattle is the tenth city with access to UberEats. says David Rutenberg, who's in charge of the program in Seattle. "We think this will be a game-changer," he said.

AMAZON PRIME

In cooperation with scores of local restaurants, Amazon Prime launched an Uber-style delivery service in 2015 for central Seattle. The field is crowded, with competition from Bite Squad, GrubHub, Munchery, Postmates, Instacart, Caviar, Lish, Peach, Groupon (Groupon-to-go), and Yelp (Eat 24), but that doesn't seem to stop the wave of meal delivery services.

TRENDSPOTTING Rise of the Grocerants

When you've finished your shopping at Costco but it's clear you're not going to make it home without immediate sustenance, you can get a slice of pizza or a hot dog while you're still inside the store, to tide you over until you can nuke something in your kitchen. But if you buy your groceries at Whole Foods or Met Market, you're in luck: before you even check out, you can pile your plate high with marinated vegetables or order up a noodle bowl and slurp it down on the spot. A full-service restaurant it's not, but that's the point. (And Wild Ginger is adding choices later this year.) Sales of prepared food inside supermarkets (known in the food-service industry as "grocerants") is growing apace (over 10 percent a year) while full-service operators and even quick-serve spots (like Chipotle) are reporting flat numbers.

Delivery services are obviously growing as well, though that part of the biz isn't yet sophisticated enough to provide nationwide figures. However, the market is changing (and isn't likely to go back). Half of Americans over the age of 18 are single. They're the ones buying prepared foods, rather than dining out or cooking large meals for themselves. Not every day, not every meal, no. But that's who's going through the line at the Whole Foods deli counter.

JULIEN PERRY Chefodexing

In mid-2015, a short-lived outfit called Dyne peddled an app for pop-ups (private, one-time-only, fixed price, fixed menu, limited-seating private events). Pop-ups, as we've learned over the past couple of years. are a great proving ground, whether for new concepts or for aspiring exec chefs. What's more, they can fill up a restaurant on a slow (or dark) night. Dyne didn't get it right, but that doesn't disprove the theory.

In the meantime, a local food enthusiast named Julien Perry has been running a real pop-up venture called the ONO (for One Night Only) Project. Along with a longtime pal, Melissa Peterman, Perry partners with top local chefs (Thierry Rautureau, Josh Henderson) to stage monthly dinners at established restaurants or catering spaces (Mallett, in Sodo, is a favorite), almost always on behalf of a high-profile charitable cause or non-profit. ONO was pretty-much a full-time job for both Perry and Peterson. Now, Pderry has doubled down, creating a concept called Chefodex. Sound like a gig you'd like? Here's the path Perry took:a UW degree in communications; internships in Tacoma, Seattle and New York; a stint at the Art Institutes; work at *Seattle Weekly* writing food gossip for Jonathan Kauffman; herding cats and wrangling freelancers at Eater.com; food editor at *Seattle Magazine*. Chefodex puts those industry contacts to good use.

Hey, I'll Drink to That!

Libations

Chapter 27 · BIG GRAPES
Washington's Wine Industry

Fifty years ago, there were only a handful of rusting wineries in Washington State, relics of Prohibition. Grapes were Concords, used for juice. Today the state is the second largest premium wine producer in the country. Its wine industry supports more than 27,000 jobs and contributes in excess of $15 billion to the state's economy. How did that happen? An unholy alliance with Big Tobacco played a big part; so did the foresight of a bow-tie-wearing Seattle attorney and a bolo-wearing WSU researcher.

WALTER CLORE: The Johnny Appleseed of Washington Wine

It's hard to overstate the importance of Washington State University in the development of a "food scene" in Seattle. Originally a land grant college named the Washington Agricultural College and School of Science, established shortly after Washington declared statehood at thOpdyckee end of 1889, the school was endowed with nearly 200,000 acres of public land and a federal mandate to educate farmers and conduct research to would benefit agricultural interests. Virtually every state had a similar institution, but no other state had Walter Clore.

He was nothing less than the Johnny Appleseed of Washington's wine industry. Born in Oklahoma to teetotaling parents (his mother was part of the Women's Christian Temperance Union), Clore arrived at the WSU campus in Pullman shortly after the repeal of Prohibition with a degree in horticulture, and was quickly hired on at what was then called the Irrigated Agriculture Research & Extension Center in Prosser. For the next 40 years Clore worked on "small fruit," including *vinifera* grapes, testing what would grow where, and under which conditions. Mind you, when he started, there were virtually no vineyards anywhere in the state, but Clore was persuasive when he found the right site. One skeptical owner of a cherry orchard in the Columbia Gorge ("Candy for gophers!") ripped out the cherries and planted gewurztraminer instead, on Clore's advice. Yet he never came across as a high-falutin' professor; to the end (except for his official portrait) he wore a simple, midwestern bolo tie. His authority came from the painstaking quality of his research, specifically the challenges of growing European, *vinifera* wine grapes. After he retired from WSU, Clore worked as a consultant to the wine industry, most notably for Ste. Michelle Vineyards.

After Dr. Clore passed away in 2003, his colleagues, recognizing his indispensable contributions to the industry, rallied to create a new institution in his memory. The Walter Clore Wine and Culinary Center in Prosser. And the Washington State Legislature in Olympia officially recognized Dr. Clore in 2003 as the "Father of the Washington State Wine Industry" for his research contribution to Washington viticulture.

ALEC BAYLESS Funds for Vineyards

No history of Washington wine would be complete without a nod, at the very least, toward Alec Bayless. A tireless civic leader and founder of a progressive law firm, the jaunty Bayless put together the original group of investors behind Sagemoor Vineyards. Without capital, no plantings; without vineyards, no grapes. Without grapes, no wine. Bayless made it happen. Whenever his travels took him away from his Pioneer Square office, Bayless returned to Seattle with news for local winemakers whose bottles he had found in shops around the country. "He was like a proud father, seeing those Sagemoor grapes turn up in Denver, Houston, Miami," recalls John Stoddard of Paul Thomas Winery.

He also carried local wines on his travels overseas. London-based wine writer Jancis Robinson speaks of Alec Bayless as a "charming ambassador" for Washington wine. "His warmth and breadth of vision [for Wasington wine] were all the more convincing because of his appreciation of the world at large," says Robinson.

"Every conversation with him, even if it was about the sun coming up, would be about fairness," says Stoddard. "Dealing with Alec Bayless was one more reason to keep doing this."

WALLY OPDYCKE Washington Viticulture's Deal of the Century

You could make a pretty good case that the defining moment in the history of Washington wine came in 1973, when Wally Opdycke met with the chief executive of a smokeless tobacco company based in Greenwich, Conn. Opdycke was a finance guy with an MBA from the University of Washington; in the course of running Safeco's investment portfolio, he had noticed that land in the Yakima Valley was plentiful and relatively cheap, and there was even a PhD scientist from the WSU research station in Prosser, Walter Clore, who claimed you could grow decent grapes for table wine there, not just Concords for juice. Intrigued, Opdycke had rounded up a couple of friends (Mike Garvey, Kirby Cramer) and bought the virtually defunct North American Wine Company, NAWICO. His daughter came up with a catchy new name for the company, "Ste. Michelle," but Opdycke needed more than a brand name; he needed capital to keep the company going.

Which brings us to Opdycke's other insight: that tobacco companies throw off huge amounts of cash. Copenhagen and Skoal, the most popular smokeless brands, had profit margins close to 40 percent. They were part of a low-profile company called United States Tobacco run by a gent named Louis Bantle. In one of the industry's great acts of salesmanship, Opdycke and his wine maker, Joel Klein, flew to Connecticut and made a pitch to Bantle: you guys take over NAWICO and you shelter your tobacco profits by plowing them into new vineyard acreage in Washington State. After a decade or two you'll be the dominant player in a new business (one that's regulated by the same federal agency, Alcohol, Tobacco and Firearms)! The cost: about one year's profit from the tobacco biz. Genius.

Of course, vineyards alone don't make a winery, so Opdycke's business plan had another side to it: marketing. You can grow good grapes and make fine wine, but you can't "push" the wine through the distribution pipeline, you have to suck it out case by case, bottle by bottle. To that end, Ste. Michelle built its own national sales team, present in virtually every state, at a cost of $50 million or so. By the time UST was done, they had spent between $125 and $150 million, and in return for their investment they became the dominant player in Washington's then-nascent wine industry.

Before long, a young man from Oklahoma, Charles Finkel, became so proficient at selling Chateau Ste. Michelle wines that he was hired as director of sales. Opdycke then hired an executive who was unhappy in his job at Boise Cascade (but who had been a successful brand manager for Gallo) to run the company; that was Allen Shoup, arguably the most successful wine executive in Washington history.

ALLEN SHOUP Planting the Flag for Premium Wine

When Allen Shoup was recruited to run a newly organized wine company outside Seattle called Chateau Ste. Michelle, the state's most widely planted grapes were Concord for the juice market and a noble German variety, riesling, for table wine, popular primarily because the wine was sweet. You can't blame the customers, they didn't know any better, but Shoup would help consumers make the transition to drier wines from varieties like chardonnay, merlot, and cabernet sauvignon,

Shoup had been a brand manager for Gallo (remember Sangria? That was his.) and worked in luxury marketing for Max Factor. He was running a company in Idaho when the headhunters called. He took one look at the faux-French "chateau" that had just been inaugurated on the bucolic Stimson Estate northeast of Seattle, with a few token vines planted across from the parking lot. "At first I hated it," he confided to me recently, "but now I see it was absolute genius." For the better part of a decade, the Chateau stood as a challenge to the nascent Washington wine industry: the biggest dog in the yard. Today, there are over 100 wine making facilities and tasting rooms within a five-mile radius of the front gate. What made it work for Shoup was the company's unexpected sugar daddy, an outfit in Stamford, Connecticut, called UST, manufacturer of Skoal and Copenhagen smokeless tobacco. "We built the Washington wine industry with UST cash," Shoup acknowledges. Not just the biggest dog, but the richest as well. He could have ridden roughshod over the competition but quickly realized that the region's strongest suit was going to be quality. From the start, Ste. Michelle's commitment to quality would mean that they had to *help* their competitors, not obliterate them. Any bad bottle, didn't matter whose, would reflect poorly on the entire region, and Ste. Michelle's name was on most of the bottles.

Today's challenges involve issues no one contemplated 40 years ago. Water rights, for example. The Columbia River watershed drains a quarter-million square miles (an area the size of France). The river itself is 1,250 miles long; its heavy flow is interrupted by a dozen dams used for both hydroelectric power and irrigation, but it's worth noting that 98 percent of its water flows into the Pacific Ocean. Still, everybody wants some. You can't blame them; look what irrigation has done for the Yakima Valley and for Red Mountain.

TED BASELER Ste. Michelle's First Citizen

In 2015, the Seattle-King County Board of Realtors named Ted Baseler, the CEO of Chateau Ste. Michelle, as its **"First Citizen"** for his community leadership. He joins a roster of worthies (Norm Rice, Lenny Wilkens, Dan Evans) from the worlds of politics, sports, the arts, and business.

Baseler refers to the current lineup of wineries in the Ste. Michelle Wine Estataes portfolio as a string of pearls. This is meant as a good thing. Ste. Michelle's corporate parent (Altria) has deep pockets; the prestigious California brand Patz & Hall is the most recent acquisition. ("But we don't overpay for trophy properties," Baseler insists.) Erath Winery in Oregon, a premier producer of pinot noir, was able to expand its production four-fold after it was bought by SMWE a decade ago.

Baseler grew up in Bellevue, attended WSU and got a graduate degree in marketing at Northwestern. He returned to Seattle and worked for an ad agency, Cole & Weber; one of his accounts was Chateau Ste. Michelle. "It was fun to go out to Woodinville, drink wine and philosophize."

In 1986 he joined the winery's marketing staff, and his first major project was a cookbook, *Taste of Liberty,* that raised money for the restoration of the Statue of Liberty. Recipes from early immigrant families were paired with Ste. Michelle wines. If it sounds like a corny idea today, it was anything but that 30 years ago: the book made the New York Times bestseller list. When Allen Shoup was promoted to run the company, Baseler took his slot, and when Shoup left to start his own venture, Baseler moved up.

Even if the tobacco connection has been played down, Ste. Michelle was always part of UST, and one day UST found itself swallowed up by Altria, the parent company of Philip Morris (Benson & Hedges, Chesterfield, Marlboro). Even though it's sneaking up on 10 million cases of wine a year, it's still a drop in the corporate bucket (as it were).

It's quite a success story, though. A dozen winemaking facilities, almost a thousand employees, $700 million in revenues, exports to more than 100 countries. The state now has 60,000 acres of vineyards, triple what it had only two decades ago. "Washington will always be in our DNA," he promises, but Baseler is keeping his eyes open to new opportunities. "We like what we don't have," is how he puts it. Nothing in Sonoma, for example. Not yet, anyway. Meantime, more alliances with international wine makers (Italy's Antinori, Germany's Dr. Loosen, a respected house in the Rhone), imports from France, Spain, Chile, New Zealand.

Ste. Michelle is a prime sponsor of the annual **AUCTION OF WASHINGTON WINES**. Socialites and wine producers from all over the state come together every year to attend a series of charity events (picnic, dinners, auctions) that raise several million dollars for Seattle Children's Hospital and WSU's Viticulture & Enology Program. It's modeled on the historic *Hospice de Beaune* events in Burgundy that benefit the local old-folks hospital.

ANDREW BROWNE Precept Brands

It's a name you may not recognize–Andrew Browne--unless you've made a careful study of the history books. Just a footnote is another name, Associated Vintners. In the 1950s, Professor Lloyd Woodbourne and three colleagues from the University of Washington made wine in Laurelhurst with grapes they'd bought from the first *vinifera* vineyards in eastern Washington. When they hired a professional winemaker (David Lake, who had earned Master of Wine honors in England) they renamed themselves Columbia Winery. Eventually they took on new investors and the company became part of Corus Brands. In 2001, Corus was sold to Constellation Brands in New York, and the Columbia label was eventually acquired by E.& J. Gallo. (Yes, Columbia property in Woodinville, across from Ste. Michelle, is owned by Gallo.) You really do need a scorecard.

The head of Corus was businessman Dan Baty, whose investments are mostly in in the healthcare industry. But he's still involved in the wine business with a company called Precept Brands that he and his star salesman, Spokane native Andrew Browne, founded in 2003. ("Stick with me," Baty said to Browne, "You'll learn a lot more than you would with a Harvard MBA."). Well, Precept today is the largest privately-held wine company in the state, selling a million and a half cases of wine. It owns well over 4,000 acres of vineyards, operates nine or ten wine-making facilities, and markets dozens of labels. "We went counter to what a lot of wineries did," Browne says. "They went super-premium, and we took the middle of the road."

Browne is a romantic. "We live in Renaissance times," he believes, with Bill Gates, Paul Allen, Jeff Bezos, and Dale Chihuly all contributing to the quality of life in Seattle. A lot of the wineries now under the Precept umbrella would no doubt have sunk had Precept not rescued them. But I'm not 100 percent convinced by the latest project, West Side Wine, which is wine in 8-ounce cans. Plenty of place you don't want glass, of course, but I wish the stuff inside were less fizzy, less sweet. Not super-premium, just better. Still, most of the labels are big hits. Steak House Red and Fish House White are more than drinkable. Waterbrook has turned into a production powerhouse, and Browne Family Vineyards produces excellent reds.

BOB BETZ Wine After Retirement

Some 40 years ago, Bob and Cathy Betz stood on a country lane in Burgundy's Côte de Nuits, looking at a low, unremarkable hillside topped with pine trees whose vineyards, over the centuries, had produced wines of astonishing quality. The monks whose abbey owned the land in the 7th century, and who kept written records, had given the vineyard a name, the first-ever *named* vineyard in history: Clos de Bèze.

Bèze, Betz, the similarity struck home. "At some point in my life," Bob recalls telling his wife, "one of my own wines will be called Clos de Betz."

It would take three decades, but he did it. One of the top wines from the Betz Family Winery is indeed named Clos de Betz. But this story is about what came in between.

Betz is a Seattle native (Blanchett), UW grad (zoology), outgoing yet reflective, a gifted communicator, who became the official spokesman for Chateau Ste. Michelle and the unofficial public face of Washington's wine industry. He was a sort of politburo ideologue at Ste. Michelle, with the grandiose title of Vice President for Enology and Research, the one who kept the winery's focus on wine, wine, wine. And when he left Ste. Michelle (where he had hired me), it was to start his own 1,200-case operation, Betz Family Winery.

It's been two decades since we worked together, and his beard has more salt than pepper now, but Betz has lost none of his enthusiasm for wine. In recent years, after grueling exams, he earned the prestigious Master of Wine certification. "Seamless syrahs and cabernets," cooed *Wine & Spirits* magazine, naming Betz one of the best small wineries in America.

Still, Betz and his wife, Cathy, are in their 60s now and thinking about retirement. Their daughters Carmen and Carla had both worked in the business but have careers of their own. The exit strategy was to sell, though only to the right buyer. And so, when the South African owners of the Phoenix private equity firm InSync, Steve and Bridget Griessel came along, promising to keep his baby a family-owned company, Betz said yes. An offer he couldn't refuse. He has just renewed his contract to be the winery's consultant, with his former deputy Louis Skinner, taking over "head wine maker" duties.

Crafting wine, a locution that implies some mechanical wizardry, is a misleading term much favored by non-winemakers who try to dumb down the process. It's really a series of incremental decisions, small steps taken every day in the vineyards, every day in the cellar, that affect how the wine will taste and mature. As for his uncanny ability to read a wine the way some people can critique a work of literature, he credits his breadth of experience with classic wines, much of it gained as a Master of Wine. Not just a German riesling, but one from the Pfalz. How a chardonnay from Meursault differs from a Chablis. "A wider lens," he calls this perspective. And he tastes constantly, so he knows where his syrah, whether sourced from Ciel du Cheval vineyards on Red Mountain or Boushey Vineyards near Grandview, fits into the continuum of syrah samples from the Rhone valley in France, from California, from Spain.

So back to the Clos de Betz. It's not a Burgundian pinot noir, like its Clos de Bèze "namesake," but a Bordeaux blend based on merlot. For all that, it's a splendid wine, with rich flavors of black cherries and overtones of dark chocolate. Would it ever be mistaken for French? The question isn't relevant; Betz wasn't out to make a French wine. Clos de Betz is the expression of its own terroir, of the unique combination of grape varieties, soil, climate, the entire season's growing conditions, and only then the human intervention that turns the grapes into wine.

CHARLES SMITH Washington Winemaking's Enfant Terrible

It's been three and a half decades since Chateau Ste. Michelle opened its showplace winery on the former Stimson estate in Woodinville. The idea, almost revolutionary at the time, was that it would become a tourist destination. "Wineries are just factories," the snobs intoned; "you wouldn't leave the house to visit a toaster production line in South Seattle, would you?" Ah, well, turns out the snobs were wrong. Over 100 wineries now fill the Sammamish River Valley, a few of them having made gestures toward their agricultural roots by planting a symbolic vineyard (that takes spaces away from the parking lot), but most firmly in the toaster-factory production facility mode. The difference for the producers is "access to the market," and, for visitors, "free samples." Wine-touring in the Seattle area has come to mean a trip to Woodinville.

Now the locus of this paradigm has shifted from the northeastern suburbs to a close-in neighborhood of South Seattle. The state's most innovative wine maker, Charles Smith, has opened a winery that houses a 32,000-square-foot production facility and tasting room. A video at CharlesSmithWines.com introduces visitors to Smith's irreverent attitude toward wine, not as an "aspirational" object to be approached with awe but to be consumed, to be drunk, to be enjoyed: "It's just wine," says the site, "Drink it."

For all the "aw shucks" and "pshaw" attitude, the Smith empire is extensive. The original K Vintners winery in Walla Walla has spawned a supermarket label, Charles Smith Wines, a brand called Sixto (chardonnay only), another called Wines of Substance, another called Vino (pinot grigio), an Italian-style sparkler called Seco, and a partnership with wine maker

Charles Bieler called Charles & Charles. It's no wonder that Smith was named Winemaker of the Year last year by *Wine Enthusiast*, the first time the honor has been given to anyone in the Pacific Northwest. "Amazing," was Smith's reaction.

Although he had worked as a sommelier in several prestigious California restaurants, he had no grand plan to get into the wine business. Instead, he followed a girlfriend to Denmark and spent the better part of a decade as the manager of rock musicians in Europe. Eventually he made his way back to Washington and took over a tiny wine shop on Bainbridge Island. And after a while, he made a few hundred cases of wine himself. That was 15 years ago. Today, Smith's various labels produce half a million cases.

In the beginning, he worked with Frenchman Christophe Baron; now he has hired Efeste's Brennon Leighton for the chardonnays and Andrew Latta in addition to partnering with Bieler. (Replacing Leighton at Efeste is a Canadian, Peter Devison, who's got a good grip on eastern Washington vineyards.) Smith quickly found critical acclaim, perhaps because Washington vineyards provide an antidote to the pro-California bias of the national press and international wine judges. They cannot deny the quality of Washington grapes ("So amazing," says Smith, "because we can make great wine from every grape: Bordeaux varieties, Burgundies, the Rhone, aromatic whites").

The defining moment, what he calls his "masterful hands" epiphany, came in 2007. By then, Charles Smith had been in the wine business for over a decade. He had won prizes and accolades, and really no longer needed to prove himself. It was the moment he realized that he had become a master of his chosen craft, that he really *did* know how to make wine.

And now he's moved into Seattle's oldest commercial neighborhood, Georgetown, "where Seattle has always made things." The designer for his new facility was the architect Tom Kundig, who had won awards for his remodel of the tasting room in Walla Walla.

As he adds production, Smith is moving beyond Walla Walla. In fact, many of the vineyards are as close to Seattle as to Walla Walla, so the move to Georgetown makes lots of sense. Much of the riesling, for example, comes from the Millbrandt brothers' Evergreen Vineyard in the Ancient Lakes region (a relatively new AVA adjoining the Columbia River near Quincy). The *Wine Spectator* named Smith's Kung Fu Girl Riesling to its annual list of the world's top 100 wines.

Now, firmly ensconced in his "Jet City" winery at the north end of the Boeing Field runway with Mt. Rainier in the background, Smith is moving into popular Italian varieties, even a Prosecco-style sparkler, and Spanish varieties like Tempranillo. "It's just Wine," he reminds us, and we remind you. "Just drink it."

TOM & ANNE MARIE HEDGES Red Mountain's First Family

 For Tom and Anne-Marie Hedges, who have a condo in Belltown, an office in South Lake Union and a place in Arizona, it's the chateau in the vineyards of Red Mountain that they call home. When they bought the land, 20 years ago, Red Mountain was no more than a geological anomaly, a modest bump in the desert landscape above Benton City at the east end of the Yakima Valley. It turned out, of course, to be an incredible location, and for the past two decades the entire Hedges family--their kids Christophe and Sarah, along with Tom's brother Pete--have dedicated themselves to creating and maintaining for Red Mountain a reputation as the best vineyard site in the state, with Hedges Family Estates casting themselves as guardians of its terroir and tradition.

You won't find Hedges Family Estate wines "rated" anywhere; Chris, in particular, calls numerical ratings "clumsy and useless." What you will find, on the Hedges Family Estate website, are half a dozen terrific short videos that show you the vineyards, the chateau, and its occupants without any of the stuffiness that normally afflicts the wine industry.

These are serious and hard-working folks who know how to have fun; their feet are planted firmly in France (Anne-Marie grew up in Champagne) and the soils of eastern Washington (Tom grew up in Richland). Chris serves as national sales manager, chief label designer and actual builder of the chateau; their daughter Sarah Goedhart is the assistant wine maker. The wines are consistently at the top of their class, by variety or by blend, you name the price point. And they certainly seem to understand the future. "Online wine buying is finally making sense," they say in their newsletter. "Studies show than nearly half of all premium wine in five years will be sold direct to consumer." So Hedges has partnered with Amazon to offer free shipping, alongside pricing that is equal to or better than local retailers.

MISSOULA FLOODS

Turn back the clock 15,000 years. What is today eastern Washington is a sandy desert covered in volcanic ash, bereft of organic matter, inhospitable to agriculture. Then the ice dam in Montana, on the western side of the Continental Divide, gives way, not just once but a cycle of at least two dozen cataclysmic events. Muddy floodwaters rush toward the Pacific, carving into basalt cliffs the Columbia River channels we know today. The waters back up into the Yakima Valley and deposit their nutrients; when they recede, they leave behind fertile topsoil: today's farms, orchards, and vineyards.

BRIAN CARTER Master Blender

Outside of the United States, there's hardly a winery that releases a wine made entirely from cabernet sauvignon grapes. The notion that a wine must be 100 percent pinot noir, for example, comes from Burgundy, where there simply are no other grapes around, and pinot noir by itself is nigh onto perfect. But in Bordeaux, the wilder side of cabernet sauvignon needs to be subdued with merlot, then given some backbone with cabernet franc and maybe a little perfume with petit verdot if you've got a few vines in a corner of your  vineyards. Those complex and vaunted "Bordeaux blends," much drooled over, are often nothing more than combinations of whatever your grandfather's grandfather happened to plant on the land around your farmhouse.

With the modesty of a teenage Mozart sitting at the keyboard in the court of Franz Josef, Brian Carter demonstrates his inherent understanding of a wine's components: sangiovese grapes from Dick Boushey's vineyard in the heart of the Yakima Valley; cabernet sauvignon from Upland Vineyards on Snipes Mountain; syrah from Olsen Vineyards outside of Prosser. What to do with them? He has an intuitive sense that the whole can be greater than the sum of its parts, so he blends a "SuperTuscan" called TuttoRosso, bottles a thousand cases, and sells it for $30 a bottle.

Carter also understands a fundamental principle of wine marketing: you can't push wine through the distribution pipeline. It has to get sucked out, a bottle or two at a time. The TuttoRosso might well be "worth" $100 a bottle, but the number of people who suck on $100 bottles is limited. Better by far to position it at an accessible price.

Carter does this with all his wines, all blends that allow him to select the best available grapes. In addition to the TuttoRosso SuperTuscan blend, there's a white, Oriana (viognier with roussanne topped off with a touch of riesling), Solesce (traditional Bordeaux varieties) and Le Coursier (right-bank, no cabernet sauvignon), Byzance (a southern Rhone blend), Trentenaire (mostly petit verdot) Corrida (Spanish varieties), Opulento (port-style dessert wine) and my personal favorite, Abracadabra (a "magic" blend of syrah, cabernet sauvignon, cabernet franc, sangiovese, petit verdot, grenache and malbec).

JON RIMMERMAN Seattle's Garagiste

A *garagiste*, in geek-speak, is an artisan wine maker without many vines, whose entire operation fits into a shed. The term originated in Bordeaux, on the right bank of the Gironde (Saint Emilion, Pomerol, and their satellites) where land holdings are tiny and a "château," likely as not, refers to a single-story outbuilding, or garage. The first such winery was Le Pin, all of five acres. (Lafite Rothschild, in the Médoc, is fifty times that.) In earlier generations, the owners of these small parcels would have sold their grapes to brokers, but in the 1970s a new crop of young farmers began making and aging wine for themselves, *vin de garage* as they called it, and selling it on the open market. It's a concept that has existed everywhere else in France for generations, of course, but once critics like Robert Parker began to write admiringly of the results–in snobby Bordeaux!–the term *garagiste* took on a prestige of its own.

These small-scale producers and their lush, fruit-forward wines found favor with the American public: ready for early drinking because most of the *garagistes* lacked traditional cellars for aging wine. Their yields (and production) were usually minuscule, their prices sometimes astronomical, their reputations (fed by the admiring Parker) often disproportionate to the quality of their wines, which were nonetheless snapped up by collectors.

The American garage as a symbol of creativity, with its lone occupant changing the world through nothing but ingenuity and perseverance, chewing gum and bailing wire, pervades the mythology of American startups. From Hewlett Packard to Amazon, budding entrepreneurs have shown they don't need office parks populated by MBA marketing directors or PhD statisticians to build a business.

Which leads us to Jon Rimmerman, like Parker a mid-Westerner who found that people paid attention to his wine recommendations. Rimmerman's online wine store, Garagiste.com, does $30 million a year in sales out of a nondescript frame building in south Seattle. Customers visit twice a year. On a cool October afternoon, Rimmerman is dressed in designer jeans with four-inch cuffs that reveal lace-up high-tops. He's wound a bright red scarf over a tweedy, double-breasted pin-stripe blazer. Curly hair worn long; salt & pepper beard, trimmed short. He radiates enthusiasm and confidence. In the office, half a dozen assistants are hunched over computer and laptop screens. It looks like the back-office operation of a bank.

The internet, whose users are younger, wealthier, and more tech savvy than most wine buyers nonetheless accounts for only two percent of all wine sales, even after double-digit annual growth since 2010. Shoes and clothing, which presumably have more issues about fit and style, have ten times the level of adoption. Yet even now, four out of five bottles of wine are still sold in brick-and-mortar stores like groceries and wine shops. The biggest dog is Costco, which sells over $1 billion in wine a year, more than any other retailer in the world. Costco employs over a dozen buyers, domestically and internationally, to keep its warehouse shelves stocked; wine is treated like toilet paper or flat-screen TVs, priced to move fast.

On-premise sales (restaurants, tasting rooms) are a distant second. On line? Barely a blip, one bottle in every four cases, though not for lack of effort. Trouble is, the 50 US states are like 50 foreign countries, each with byzantine regulations regarding the sale and shipment of alcohol.

Rimmerman blasts daily newsletters, which he writes himself, filled with effusive descriptions of wines that he's offering, to some 250,000 subscribers; there's a once-a-week version if you find the prose too exhausting. Examples: $30 for a 2012 SuperTuscan; $20 for a 2011 Savennières from Nicolas Joly. A "mystery" Washington red is priced at $20; an 8-year-old Fleurie from Beaujolais at $40. If you trust Rimmerman's palate, you could go broke acquiring all the bottles he recommends. (Personally, I'd go for the Savennières, a biodynamic vineyard overlooking the Loire in central France.) Rimmerman says he has tasted every wine he describes, and claims to remember every one of them. But you can't actually buy anything on the garagiste.com website; you have to send an email to Rimmerman's assistant, Nicki, to place your order and pre-pay for your wine. And then you wait, because Garagiste only ships its wines twice a year.

It can be heartbreaking to realize that a wine grower (in Sicily, in St. Émilion, in Sonoma) will sell his wine for $3 "ex winery" only to see it on the shelf at Safeway for $20 or more because of middlemen. Garagiste provides an outlet for small, independent, artisanal producers without their own established sales channels. Rimmerman offers to buy a certain number of cases, offers the wine in his newsletter, collects the money, and only then confirms his purchase from the winery. (He will distribute it to his customers months later.) All the while by-passing the sacrosanct system (and expensive) of international brokers and shippers, national importers, state-level distributors, and local retailers.

The leading online wine retailer (some $60 million a year) is Wine.com, but it sells and ships physical inventory, whereas you have to trust Garagiste to be in business six months from now. A couple of years ago, an admiring profile in the *New York Times* claimed Garagiste did $30 million in annual sales, all of it based on emails. (Then again, the same article described Howard Schultz as the "founder of Starbucks," so one has to wonder with how much skepticism the *Times* fact-checkers approached the story.) Does Rimmerman buy inventory upfront and resell it? Or does he collect from his customers and only then purchase the wine? Who's taking the credit risks? Rimmerman is mum; he dazzles with footwork.

Garagiste currently operates out of a complex of four south Seattle warehouses, and Rimmerman is more than doubling his floor space. He limits the number of people on his mailing list because he doesn't have enough wine to sell. His business model is known as wine futures: customers order and pay for the product sight-unseen, even untasted, then wait for it to arrive. Plenty of wine merchants have been tempted to abscond with the deposits, not Rimmerman, who has a "trusting and loyal relationship" with his readers.

The online competition is fierce, starting with Wine.com, Amazon, and InVino. They send email flurries to their subscribers, sometimes more than once a day, carefully crafted offers with pictures, quotes, scores. It's no longer automatically illegal to ship wine across state lines, and credit card purchases make the buying process easy.

In addition to Garagiste, two others are based in Seattle. Paul Zitarelli, a Harvard-trained mathematician, started **FULL PULL WINES** as a newsletter when his wife got into grad school at the University of Washington; he eventually opened a wine shop in Seattle's Sodo district so that his readers could buy the wines. And there's Yashar Shayan, a sommelier and UW grad, who started his online company, **IMPULSE WINES**, in 2013, primarily to showcase hard-to find Washington reds.

So far, Costco is slumbering. Ebay, too. But if either Doberman ever decides to get into online wine sales, all bets are off.

THE "ENO SOC" Seattle Wine Society

Founded in 1975, the Enological Society of the Pacific Northwest was the oldest volunteer-organized wine appreciation group in town. Rechristened the Seattle Wine Society in 2004, it continued to sponsor monthly wine dinners and an annual wine judging whose excruciating fairness was better suited to the days when Washington and Oregon combined had fewer than 100 wineries (many owned by paranoid individualists barely on speaking terms). But its leaders recruited international wine authorities as judges, and their influence helped put the Pacific Northwest on the map. Its founding board came straight out of Seattle's Blue Book (Dorothea Checkley, George Taylor, Nancy Davidson Short, Betty Eberharter), with a mission to guide its members "in viticulture, enology, and the appreciation, enjoyment, knowledge and proper usage of wine."

For over three decades, under the guidance of Dr. Gerry Warren (pictured, a clinical professor of medicine and bioengineering at the University of Washington), it did just that, providing its 3,000 members with monthly educational programs and an annual wine festival, all run by volunteers. Chapters were added in half a dozen outposts, from the Tri-Cities to Spokane. The festival became a focal point for a growing body of wine enthusiasts, not the least of them the internationally renowned judges. Over the years, they included Paul Pontallier of Chateau Margaux; the Italians Angelo Gaja and Piero Antinori; the American historian Leon Adams; writers Roy Andries de Groot and Gerald Boyd; California wine makers Joe Heitz and Warren Winiarski; UC Davis professors Maynard Amarine, Denny Webb and Ann Noble. Their palates, unfamiliar with the unique wines of the Northwest (especially in the early years) were always impressed by the quality of the top bottles; they were also unafraid to criticize flawed wines.

Today, the number of wineries in Oregon, Washington and Idaho has grown from fewer than a hundred to well over a thousand. The Wine Society's casual, chatty summer festival has morphed into the tony Auction of Washington Wines, one of the nation's biggest charity auctions. The Washington Wine Commission (which didn't even exist when the Society started) runs a two-day Wine & Food Festival; there's also a privately run Seattle Food & Wine Experience. There are smaller festivals in every valley and hillside of the wine country, and wine maker dinners at restaurants across the region. And no shortage of independent, benchmark judgings, either, from the Platinum Wine Awards run by Andy Perdue of Wine Press Northwest, to the high-profile Seattle Wine Awads (and its companion, the Oregon Wine Awards) run by sommelier Christopher Chan, who brings in a panel of top-name judges.

John Bell, an engineer who spent his career working at Boeing while he made wine in his Marysville garage, is among those who regard the Wine Society's work with fond nostalgia. Now the owner of a successful boutique winery, Willis Hall, he's also a longtime Society board member who appreciates what the Society did as a catalyst for wine education and appreciation. "We are proud of our accomplishments," Bell says. "It's the end of an era, but it was truly a bright era, wasn't it?"

WOODINVILLE 'S IMAGINARY "WINE COUNTRY"

Visiting an actual winery is about as exciting as touring a toaster factory. Nothing to see except at harvest, when they're busy (and closed to the public). A giant space filled with tanks, pipes, a lab counter, racks of barrels, stacks of cases. You have to be a fanatic to find this even remotely interesting. The scenic vineyards where grapes are grown? In eastern Washington's otherwise arid desert. So a visit to Woodinville Wine Country, half an hour from downtown Seattle, is interesting in the same way as a trip to the perfume counter at Nordstrom: you get to sniff (and swirl) a lot of brands. Almost 150 labels have set up tasting counters.

CHALEUR ESTATE Money Lends a Helping Hand

 Charles Lill was a refugee from Europe who settled in Seattle and built a prosperous business selling insurance. When the German government paid out reparations, decades ago, for property confiscated by the Nazis, Lill invested the money he received in eastern Washington vineyards and a wine-making operation in Woodinville. The venture's cofounders (along with Lill's son, Greg) were Chris Upchurch, who'd been a wine buyer for Larry's Markets, and Jay Soloff, a sommelier and wine broker. Within a short time, it became one of the top boutique wineries in the state.

Chaleur Estate Blanc, one of the DeLille Cellars labels, is probably the most serious white wine produced in Washington. It's a Bordeaux-style blend of sémillon and sauvignon blanc that stands out from the field of perfectly drinkable Washington whites by its ability to age like a great work of art: with grace and dignity.

This became evident at a retrospective tasting of Chaleur Estate whites dating back to 1996. Grapes came from Red Mountain's award-winning vineyards: Ciel du Cheval, Boushey, Klipsun and Sagemoor vineyards. Upchurch treats the grapes as if they were ingredients in a premium red wine: low crop levels (three tons to the acre for the whites, two for the reds), whole berry fermentation with native yeasts, moderate use of French oak. Most white wines get little respect (think chardonnay or pinot grigio) because they're based on high yields and quick-and-dirty winemaking. They sell at low prices because the wine makers don't make much of an effort at quality. It's a self-fulfilling prophecy.

The proof of Chaleur Estate Blanc's quality is in the glass, and here the wine writers are having a field day. Dried apricots, figs, grapefruit, gooseberies, lemon, lime, hazelnuts, grilled bread, toasted straw, flint. No question that it has a rich and silky mouthfeel, and a lingering, nutty finish. It's as good as the white Bordeaux blends it emulates (names like Haut Brion Blanc, Domaine du Chevalier, Château Smith Haut Lafitte, or Château Carbonnieux), yet it's less than half their price.

As for the reds, well, even better. A retrospective going back to 1992 showed wines that could pass for top estates in Bordeaux: elegant, complex blends that came on the market when single-variety "fruit bombs" were all the rage. Consumers weren't too sure what to make of them (pricey, understated) but restaurants understood the appeal. A wine list selling Chateau Lafite for $1,000 was happy to have a locally-produced Bordeaux blend like Chaleur Estate's Grand Ciel available for less than $500.

Then Charles Lill passed away, the 2008 recession hit, and DeLille Cellars stopped growing. It was stuck at that awkward, 12,000-case size, a boutique winery with a national reputation and a national market but unable to keep pace with demand because there was no more capital for vineyard acquisition or new equipment. The elephant in the room, Chateau Ste. Michelle, has a staff of business analysts to help allocate capital expenditures from a deep-pocketed corporate parent. An umbrella company like Precept Brands has been successful by helping wineries (Columbia, Waterbrook, half a dozen others) on track. For DeLille, without Charles Lill, the question was how to shake off the stagnation, and the surviving founders thought perhaps the time had come to sell.

And then an interesting player turned up. Bacchus Capital Management. Co-founded by Sam Bronfman, grandson of the Russian Jewish immigrant who built the Seagram Company, Bacchus provides what it calls strategic capital and "expertise" to the wine industry. It has taken ownership positions in half a dozen prestigious wineries in California (Sbragia, Madrigal) and Oregon (Panther Creek), and now it stepped in at DeLille. Bacchus installed one of its managing directors, Tom Dugan, as general manager, and moved the winery's banking to Silicon Valley Bank in Napa. One immediate result was to release Lill, Upchurch, and Soloff from the personal guarantees they'd signed on loan documents with Key Bank, which had tied up all their private assets. Even more important, the new infusion of capital allowed DeLille to buy grapes, vineyards, and equipment, and to increase its production (at the same level of quality) to over 30,000 cases. At last, there's enough wine in the pipeline to sell.

"We're going to stay terroir-driven," Upchurch assures the wine world. "Unique and competitive."

KATHRYN COLE Oregon's Biodynamic Voodoo Chronicles

In *Voodoo Vintners*, Seattle-born Kathryn Cole takes her readers on a guided tour of Oregon vineyards run by cast of Carhartt-wearing characters who make biodynamic wine. They may only farm five or six percent of the state's vineyards, but they produce an outsize share of its best wines, especially the elusive pinot noirs for which Oregon has become famous. Many of the practitioners come to the wine-grower lifestyle with what Cole calls "good genes, good fortune, good work ethic and good credit," the good credit being particularly important, in my view, in an industry with 800 competitors state-wide. So far, 68 vineyard properties in the US are Demeter-certified, 16 of them in Oregon.

So what's the point of biodynamic, or BD (as it's called)? Above all, it's a respect for the land and its connection to the cosmos. "Those who don't understand biodynamics-- and don't understand voodoo," writes Cole, "use the term in reference to the preparations: the buried cow horns, the hanging stag's bladders...they're thinking

Louisiana voodoo." But in fact it's more like Haiti's voodou, a nature-worshiping belief system, not agricultural but spiritual. Are its viticultural practitioners batshit crazy dreamers or brilliant wine makers?

Prior to the original planting of a conventional vineyard, Cole points out, earth-moving equipment uproots trees, bushes and boulders, then smooths the soil. Weeds sprout among the vines, so the grower spreads herbicide, which kills off benign cover crops that might restore nutrients to the soil. Meantime the roosting spots for birds and insects have been bulldozed, so there are no longer any owls to eat gophers or birds to eat larger insects. This calls for pesticides, which in turn curtail the aerating and phosphorus-releasing capabilities of earthworms. Fungi move in, the dirt gets rock-hard, lifeless and brittle; the farmer tills the rock-hard soil, dispersing dust and whatever organic matter was left. Without humus to store moisture and nutrients in the topsoil, the vine droops, gets sick and attracts pests, for which the conventional solution is, you guessed it, chemical fertilizers, "a steroid shot straight to the vein of the plant, pumping it up for now but setting it up for a future heart attack or stroke."

MADELEINE PUCKETTE A sommelier herself, Puckette won the "wine blogger of the year" title at the International Wine & Spirits Competition in 2013. She's also a graphic designer who brings a welcome intellectual rigor to her presentations. Her book, "Wine Folly," isn't going to make you an instant wine expert, but it will help you take a big step in the right direction: practical information (maps, serving tips) that could help your confidence in the wine shop or at the dinner table. Puckette organizes the book by grape variety (not "varietal") rather than by growing region (not "terroir"). So the next time you see a wine made from unfamiliar grapes

(like Torrontes, like Mencia), just flip open this book and you'll get a crash course.

PAUL GREGUTT is a scrupulous writer (who authored the essential textbook, *Washington Wines & Wineries*) and humble reviewer, who, like a plate umpire, does no more than call 'em as he sees 'em. Gregutt is pretty much the only game left. National bigshots from the syndicated newsletters blow into town from time to time and anoint their predictable favorites, but Gregutt's here all year long, with an impeccable perspective on the top vineyards, Even better, sez I, he's making more-than-decent wine on his own, at Waitsburg Cellars outside Walla Walla.

Chapter 28 · "CRAFT BEER" CAPITAL OF THE WORLD

So said a British beer journal, recognizing that Washington had more breweries than any other state. Two important names: Redhook (founded here, but no longer a craft beer, since it's one-third owned by the same international conglomerate that produces Budweiser) and Pike Brewing, which has kept its commitment to small-batch quality.

The key to the state's good fortune is access to three ingredients: water, wheat, and malt. Well, that plus the right people.

CHARLES & ROSE ANN FINKEL: Craft Brewers

It's been over 35 years since Charles and Rose Ann Finkel opened their Pike Pub & Brewery. It's such a fixture at the Market, you'd think it's been there forever, but there was a time, not that long ago, when fewer than half a dozen national breweries supplied the entire country with "lawnmower beer" while perhaps half a dozen artisans and idealists were brewing what they called "craft beer." It was a battle between industrial, bottom-fermented lagers and flavorful, top-fermented ales, between standardization and individuality. In the end, as we know, it was the consumers who won. Local artisan beers flourished, and some, like Redhook, even formed an unholy alliance with the big boys to get national distribution.

Into this fomenting vat of yeast and mash stepped the Finkels, who had decades of experience navigating the currents of beverage sales. Back in Oklahoma, Charles had been an early champion of Chateau Ste. Michelle wines and was hired to run the company's national sales effort. Arriving at the same time was a young marketing whiz, Paul Shipman, who became Ste. Michelle's brand manager. Later, Charles started a company called Merchant du Vin, which, despite its name, imported nothing but craft beer, while Shipman went on to run Redhook. Then the Finkels opened a shop on Western Avenue that sold home brewing supplies in addition to housing a tiny craft brewery. Over the years it grew and grew to its current location, a multi-level, gravity flow, steam-heated brewery and brew pub.

The Finkels sold the company, "retired," and embarked on bicycle trips to the food capitals of Europe and Asia, but they ended up taking the place back a decade ago, with Rose Ann as president. They hired a serious master brewer, Drew Cluley (who has since moved on to other breweries), and quickly restored Pike to prominence. The sprawling, family-friendly pub seats 300 and features a dozen or so brews on tap, a vast array of bottles and mixed drinks. Down in the brewery, several bourbon barrels stand alongside the stainless steel trappings of a craft brewery that produces 9,000 barrels a year. (At 15.5-gallons a barrel, that's about 1.5 million 12-ounce glasses or bottles of beer. Sounds like a lot, but Budweiser probably spills more every day.)

Rose Ann is one of Seattle's most prominent foodies. She and a couple of pals owned Truffles, a specialty food store in Laurelhurst; she was chief operating officer of Merchant du Vin, started Seattle's Slow Food convivium, and is a member of Les Dames d'Escoffier. Charles, in addition to his passion for craft beer and fine wine, has a remarkable talent as a graphic designer, specializing in marketing materials for breweries. He's also a writer, photographer and world traveler; his design shop website is a hoot. But his favorite stories still revolve around wine.

On vacation in California decades ago, the Finkels paid a call on the wine writer Leon Adams at his home in Sausalito. "Pay attention to the Yakima Valley," said Adams. (Shades of "Go north, young man.") Eventually, as Ste. Michelle's sales manager, Finkel found himself sorting through resumés. One was from a promising microbiologist who'd just returned from a year in Europe. "My claim to fame," Finkel says, tongue in cheek, "is that I called Bob Betz back." Betz, of course, went on to become a mainstay of the Washington wine industry, while the Finkels have become fierce advocates for local beer.

Pike Brewery was the very first to use malt from Skagit Valley. Most of their beers and ales use distiller's malt delivered in 50-pound sacks from suppliers like Briess in Chilton, Wisc. Even the specialty grains taste pretty bland, but a couple of bags, shipped from Burlington, bear the name Skagit Valley Malting, and they're quite tasty: Alba, developed at Oregon State University, and Copeland, a hybrid from the Washington State University's bread lab (headquartered in the same Bayview Industrial Park as SMV). To differentiate the beers them from their established brands like Naughtie Nellie and Kilt Lifter, Pike calls these Lo-Cales. "It's one of the most exciting things in beer," says Charles Finkel, whose spent the first two decades of his professional career in the wine world. "It's like 1965, when all we had was stuff like 'Pink White Port.'" The pale Alba has a lemon-y fragrance; it could be a sauvignon blanc. "The malt sets a foundation for the hops," is how Finkel explains it.

BEER HEAVEN: Amber Waves of Malt

Fly into Skagit County's regional airport, overlooking Padilla Bay outside Burlington, and you traverse rich, loamy farmland that grows more tulip bulbs, daffodils, red potatoes, cucumbers and vegetable seed than any county in the nation. Its two paved runways intersect at the southeast corner of a woodsy, thousand-acre swath of property known as Bayview Industrial Park, where three dozen budding enterprises lease commercial space. Food and drink for pilots, passengers, and workers comes from a brewpub on the flight line called Flyers that boasts 16 taps, including a fancy bitter brewed with English Maris Otter Malt; it's a pretty good specialty malt but hardly local, and in a state like Washington, that takes such pride in its craft breweries, that seems like a shame.

Fortunately, the promise of local salvation is out the back door and just up the road, in a windowless building where a tinker and former software exec named Wayne Carpenter runs a five-year-old outfit called Skagit Valley Malting. It's a semi-secret skunkworks (full of elaborate, patents-pending equipment) that is revolutionizing local craft brewing and craft distilling by taking advantage of the unique geography and fertile soils of western Washington, especially the grains that farmers grow as part of their crop rotation to maintain and restore the soil. Amazing grains, as it were, but they get little respect.

We have plenty of hops growing in eastern Washington's Yakima Valley, but hops are just the seasoning for beer and play no role at all in spirits. Beer's backbone, its heart and soul, is grain, malted grain specifically, and by this definition virtually no beer in Washington is truly local, at least not yet. Malt arrives at Washington's breweries and distilleries in 50-pound bags from the Midwest and from the grain fields of Canada: barley, wheat, rye, oats, millet, sorghum, triticale, and corn, sprouted so the germinating seed begins to release its sugar, then dried ("roasted") to arrest the process. Mass market breweries like Budweiser even use rice, which can be polished to release large amounts of fermentable sugar (producing cheaper alcohol); specialty brewers, on the other hand, overwhelmingly favor barley, which can be roasted to produce a wide range of colors and flavors. But of the 30,000 varieties of grain on the planet, only a dozen are used for the industrial brewing of commercial beer, let alone for distilling. It's a bit like the wine business, in that there are thousands of varieties of grapes, but only a dozen or so varieties (like cabernet sauvignon or chardonnay) readily available on the shelf.

"The entire industry is monolithic," says Carpenter, who set out to create a greater range of choices for brewers, bakers, and distillers. He's got a rapidly increasing assortment of squat silos on the property to store the grain he buys at a premium price from local farmers. Skagit Valley grain is highly prized by specialty bakers and brewers; the valley's unique climate and rich soils (marine influence without drought stress; long, dry days during harvest) are ranked among the best in the world. It seems a shame to let that natural advantage go to waste selling Skagit malt into the commodity market. "Why should the Chicago mercantile exchange set the price for our crops?" So Carpenter and his staff of engineers have built a phalanx of secret machines that cost about a million dollars each to customize the malting process for thousands of grain varieties, unlocking a world of choice and flavor for its customers. International patents are still pending, so no public access or photos allowed.

Brewers aren't the only ones looking for better raw materials. Washington's eight-year-old craft distilling industry is required by law to source at least half of its grain locally, and Skagit barley is a natural. The largest whiskey distillery west of the Mississippi, 60,000-bottle Westland Distillery is an enthusiastic adopter of Skagit Valley Malting's output, even though it's several times as expensive, $1 a pound for peated malt, and they need four pounds per bottle. But Master Distiller Matt Hofmann, a Bellarmine Prep grad who dropped out of UW to study the craft in Scotland, swears by Skagit Valley Malting and looks forward to the day (in three years or so) that his peated single malt using SVM grain reaches maturity. The term "Single Malt" has specific meaning in Scotland, referring to the distillery's location as well as the ingredients, but there's room in the world for "American Single Malt" as well. And Westland, which operates out of a facility in SoDo and matures its casks at a rack house in the cold, moist air of Hoquiam, was recently named the world's best craft distillery by Whisky Magazine.

So even with the growing pains, the wealth of locally brewed beer and locally distilled spirits will turn out to be a good thing. Local products take the accident of geography–our unique location–and turn it into a commercial advantage: beers and whiskeys that simply have more individuality, more character. They're a central element of our local identity, an integral part of our culture. Those Skagit Valley tulips can have their photogenic festival every April; the rest of the year, if Carpenter, Hofmann, and Finkel are right, we'll soon be enjoying the new flavors of Skagit Valley malt as well.

REDHOOK From Banana Beer to Budweiser

Gordon Bowker, the advertising executive and little-heralded originator of Starbucks, knew Paul Shipman from his work on the Ste. Michelle winery account. As the most junior guy in the top-heavy executive suite, Shipman had an MBA and a fancy title ("Ste. Michelle Brand Manager"), but ended up with all the crappy assignments. Bowker had an idea for a craft brewery, unheard of in those days. One banker responded by saying, "Breweries don't start up, they shut down." (Says Bowker: "That's when I knew I was on to something.")

Still, he realized that he knew nothing about actually running a brewery. So, over dinner at Adriatica, he pitched his idea to Shipman, who immediately replied, "I want to be the president of Redhook."

They launched their brewery out of a machine shop in Ballard, and it created a sensation, though not in a good way. Only 15 percent of the people who tried Redhook loved it, 85 percent couldn't stand it. *Hated* it. "Banana beer," they called it. And they were right. But the Redhook folks stood firm. Even the slightest compromise, they told detractors at the time, was the first step on a slippery slope that would lead directly to lawnmower beer. Redhook had its enthusiastic supporters, of course, the vocal minority that drank more flavorful beers from imported bottles. And they loved it on draught in Alaska, especially.

On the technical side, the problem was quickly identified as a quirky strain of yeast that had the disconcerting side effect of generating the same esters found in bananas. Within a few months, a Christmas ale called Winterhook was brewed using a new strain of yeast; this time it found near-universal favor. The Winterhook recipe was renamed "Extra Special Bitter," ESB for short, and by springtime Redhook ESB was the brewery's flagship. Today, with the brewing facilities located in Woodinville, it's Longhammer Ale.

Well, as time went on it became clear to Shipman that the key to survival was to grow, and not just to build a bigger brewery. You had to sell the stuff, and that meant muscle: Budweiser-style distribution. The deal was forged with the best of intentions, to unite Portland's Widmer Brothers with Redhook and create a Craft Beer Alliance; Hawaii's Kona Beer joined in 2010. So far, so good, but the fateful decision came when CBA sold about a third of its shares to (wait for it) Budweiser's parent company, the based-in-Belgium behemoth Anheuser-Busch InBev. Not only are the CBA brands now no longer eligible to be called "craft" breweries, Redhook is the weakest link. The solution, announced in mid-2016, is to make Redhook "more local again," by opening a new brewpub on Capitol Hill.

But even that is not to be. Latest word is that the brewing part of the operation will be transferred to Portland, and the Woodinville facility will be used to brew Pabst beer under contract.

BEER HALLS Tapping into Your Thirst

Wine bars, we've come to expect, are intimate places, cozy, where you can concentrate on what's in your glass. Beer halls, are vast, bawdy stages, full of noisy good cheer. Are we right? The original Hofbräuhaus in Munich feels like a train station, which works in context, but Americans seem to prefer smaller spaces, or at least enclaves where you're not surrounded by hundreds of fellow revelers.

There's nothing in Seattle even remotely like **REINHAUS**, a 10,000-square-foot barn of a place on Capitol Hill, a former candy factory and furniture warehouse that's been converted, at a cost of $1.5 million, into a 420-seat Bavarian Biergarten. It's the latest venture of Deming Maclilse and James Weimann, the duo behind Bastille and Poquitos. Their genius is to assemble a giant garage sale worth of genuine vintage items and salvaged pieces, whether from Paris flea markets or Mexican market towns. The inspiration was clearly the Hofbräuhaus in central Munich, nondescript outside, lavishly decorated inside, with long wooden tables and painted ceilings. The designers added Viennese chandeliers, railings salvaged from the McCaw mansion in Medina, stuffed elk heads, leather club chairs, Belgian doors, and a colossal Austrian fireplace. Three bars, two mezzanines, and five indoor bocce ball courts, each 8 by 50 feet (complete with a bocce ball concierge). One misstep: the original name, Von Trapp's. Seems someone forgot to clear it with the actual Von Trapp family, still alive and feisty on the east coast.

New to the restaurant biz are the local co-owners of **QUEEN ANNE BEER HALL,** Jana and Lubo Katrusin, natives of Slovakia and eight-year residents of Seattle. They've partnered with Lubo's brother (and his associates), longtime operators of European-style beer halls on the east coast (Brooklyn, Hoboken) and local developer Scott Shapiro (Melrose Market) to renovate an old clothing factory on Lower Queen Anne.

The 7,000-square-foot space seats over 300, plus an outdoor Biergarten. Seating is at long communal tables, custom-built by Lubo, a carpenter by trade.

Two dozen taps will feature not your ho-hum local brew but authentic brewski from Germany, Austria, Czech Republic and Slovakia. Sour beers, Hefeweizens, Dunkels, Doppeldunkel. If there's a glass custom-made for that beer, they'll try to get it. Their most treasured souvenirs come from the Pilsner Urquell brewery in Czech Republic, which, yes, is now owned by SABMiller, but, says Jana, "It's what we grew up on."

Then there's **STOUT**, a 5,700-square-foot, 180-seat hall, also on Capitol Hill, the latest venture from Paul Reder. He's an imaginative and fearless developer, whether rehabilitating old warehouse and showroom spaces or digging through abandoned mezzanines and forgotten passageways of downtown office buildings. Reder has been in the restaurant business all his life and put his signature on the two Tap House Grill / Yard House spaces in downtown Seattle. At Stout--carved from the Sunset Electric Building at 11th and Pine--Reder himself has given direction to the beer list; the menu planning is a clear case of overkill by Reder's culinary consultant, Arnold Shain of The Restaurant Group.

Almost everything on the menu can be read as a paean to bacon, but, in a nod to Capitol Hill's minority of beer-drinking vegetarians, one flatbread is described as "pasilla chile roasted cauliflower." Not ancho chilis, mind you, but pasilla, usually used only to make the mole negro of Oaxaca. And roasted cauliflower, dry and crunchy, not sweet, soft and braised. Okay, your call, but here are the garnishes: "chipotle cream, chimichurri, roasted corn, tear drop tomatoes, cotija, queso fresco, green onion, Mexican crème." Eight freaking garnishes on a $13 vegetarian flatbread. The straightforward salami version ($12) doesn't do that much better: "Mama Lil's peppers, red sauce, provolone, garlic marinated fresh mozzarella, fried capers, fresh lemon thyme." Woe betide the cook who fails to marinate the mozz in garlic!

And the Morning After Burger? A beef patty's not good enough; it's got to be blended onsite with fresh-ground bacon, then hand-pressed to within an inch of its life, grilled to the consistency of sawdust, slathered in more bacon, topped with a fried egg, and surrounded by peppery fries. Is it any wonder this overwrought style of food preparation went out of style in most Seattle restaurants two or three decades ago?

And finally the ultimate cop-out, **OPTIMISM** Brewing at the corner of Broadway and E. Union, which brews a dozen of its own beers and completely bails on the food. Husband and wife owners Troy Hakala and Gay Gilmor have an appropriately vast space but no on-site kitchen; they rely instead on a a parade of food trucks.

MONICA MARSHALL Rachel's Ginger Beer

Rachel's Ginger Beer is a Seattle phenomenon based on a British pub tradition. Like the American rural tradition of sarsaparilla ("root beer"), ginger beer is non-alcoholic, but its spiciness and affinity for citrus makes it a fine mixer for spirits like the Moscow Mule (vodka, lime) and the Dark & Stormy (dark rum, more lime). From modest beginnings in the Pike Place Market in 2013, RGB has expanded to Capitol Hill, where Marshall has teamed with Chef Monica Dimas to create a pop-up called Sunset that serves Seattle's best fried chicken sandwiches.

Chapter 29 · THE SPIRIT WORLD

Behold the cocktail, embodiment of Western Civilization. Distillation was known to Babylonian alchemists 25 centuries ago, and medieval pharmacists concocted flavored alcohols. Now the ancient technology has been enhanced by contemporary imagination, and designer drinks have graduated from patent medicine to emblems of sophistication. Not that there's anything inherently wrong with wine, beer, or cider (or even non-alcoholic soda), but a lively cocktail culture seems to be a part of every big-city environment.

KENT FLEISCHMANN Dry Fly Distilling

There was a time that no one understood the term "small batch distilling." Yes, Bigfoot still roamed the Cascades in those ancient days, seven or eight years ago, when fishing buddies Don Poffenroth and Kent Fleischmann would stand streamside along the Gallatin (yup, Montana, where a river does indeed run through it) and cast their flies in quest of rainbows and brown trout. I'm not a fisherman myself but I do know that the subtext of fishing isn't catching fish; it's about what you do before and after. In this case, the two friends were making plans to open a distillery, back in Spokane, where they both worked in marketing and brand development. No matter that it hadn't been done since Prohibition, no matter that their project wasn't even legal. And yet, the Legislature got turned around; it created a "craft distillery" category requiring 50 percent local ingredients, and the wheat farmers of the Palouse got themselves a new customer.

Today, Dry Fly is one of the top three craft distillers in the state (along with Woodinville Whiskey and Westland Distillery), and has just done something the others, so far, have not: partnered with a restaurant chain as its exclusive vodka supplier. The chain is California-based Eureka, which has an outlet at University Village, lots of burgers and other interesting fare like beet salad, osso buco riblets, and shrimp tacos. And Dry Fly vodka as the base for spicy cocktails like the Reaper.

"True craft distilling isn't profit-making," Fleischmann explains. "It's a high-overhead, low-margin business." Still, 10,000 cases a year, all of it from wheat grown in the Palouse country of eastern Washington, milled to a fine powder. From Spokane, it's shipped to 35 states and 22 countries, one batch of 576 bottles at a time.

ORLIN SORENSON & BRETT CARLILE Woodinville Whiskey

Flickering, flappering, the black & white glamor of moonshine is making a comeback.

The drink may look like a vodka martini with a twist, but it's not. It's that steakhouse staple, a Manhattan. Except that this one is clear, without any of the vanilla notes or amber color of your grandfather's bourbon, unless your grandfather happened to own a still in the hills of Kentucky or Tennessee or West Virginia during Prohibition. In which case, you'd probably understand the notion of a perfectly clear, unaged spirit called, variously, White Whiskey, White Lightning or White Dog.

Now, the woods of Woodinville are not exactly crawling with revenuers on the hunt for illicit stills. It was entirely legal for high school buddies Orlin Sorensen (left) and Brett Carlile (right) to set up shop as Woodinville Whiskey Co. in an industrial park backing on the Sammamish River. Carlile had made a career in sales, Sorensen flew Bombardier jets for Horizon but had lost the chance to fly bigger planes because he didn't have perfect eyesight. (Rather than feel sorry for himself, he started a motivational program, Rebuild Your Vision, to help others improve their vision through eye exercises.) At any rate, both men harbored a strong desire for some sort of joint commercial adventure and decided on a craft distillery, a business category authorized in Washington since 2008.

Better yet (not "better still," that would be overkill) Sorensen and Carlile had the good sense to hire a savvy consultant by the name of David Pickerell (center), who was the Master Distiller, no less, for Maker's Mark for almost 15 years. Pickerell has helped dozens of small distilleries get off the ground and loves what he sees in Woodinville. "These guys work their tails off," he says, "and they're willing to experiment. That's the strength of the small distilleries, experimenting."

Woodinville's first release, bottled while the rest of the production was aging, was White Dog. Yes, Pickerell's boys will eventually release an aged whiskey, but they're in no great hurry. Meantime, you can age your own. Seriously, they're selling age-your-own mini-barrels, a huge hit.

The federal government has a few rules about liquor labels. No flags, no living persons (without their permission), no cartoon characters. The state imposes a production limit for "craft" distillers. Dry Fly, in Spokane, was the first under the new "Craft" category, and is still the largest. In fact, the authorized production of a craft distillery was tripled, from 20,000 to 60,000 gallons by the last legislature because Dry Fly was bumping up against the upper limit.

STEVEN STONE Sound Spirits

The first legal distillery since Repeal within Seattle city limits actually opened in that no-man's-land called Interbay a month before Woodinville Whiskey. It's called Sound Spirits, and it's the dream of Boeing engineer Steven Stone. The first release was a craft vodka called Ebb+Flow, an unfiltered, single-malt distilled from Washington barley. Rather than a bland, iceberg lettuce of spirits, Ebb+Flow has a floral nose and sweet, multi-layered flavors. Coming soon: gin and more. You can legally buy two 750-ml bottles of the vodka at the distillery, $31 apiece.

MATT HOFMANN Westland

The story of Westland Distillery starts among the giant trees of Grays Harbor County on Washington's west coast, where Douglas fir, spruce, alder, cedar, and hemlock grow tall and moss-covered on Federal forestland, bathed in the cold, moist air of the Pacific Ocean. In that respect, Hoquiam and its neighboring towns, Aberdeen and Cosmopolis, are almost like the waterside communities of Scotland, but that's getting ahead of the story.

Here, at the turn of the last century, a young Stanford grad named Frank Lamb crossed paths and fell in love with the daughter of George Emerson, a sawmill manager in Hoquiam. Lamb started a company to design and manufacture logging and milling equipment, moved into paper making, and was instrumental in developing the Port of Grays Harbor; his son, David, began exporting the machines to Scandinavia, which also has abundant forests. But David's son, named Emerson Lamb, became interested in something quite different. Not yet 20, he approached a classmate from Bellarmine Preperatory Academy in Tacoma, Matt Hofmann, with a business plan to distill malt whiskey.

Hofmann dropped out of the University of Washington to sign on, and the two friends set out for Scotland before they were old enough to drink legally in the US.

They raised money from family and friends, and leased a couple of buildings in South Park to get started. They decided to make their own mash rather than purchasing from a local brewery like Elysian (as Copperworks Distillery does). Their grain would come from the Skagit Valley, their water from the Cedar River. Because they wanted a uniquely American product, a uniquely Northwest whisky, they also decided not to hire a Scottish master distiller.

Their 55-gallon casks are heavy-toast, low-char, made from American oak by the Independent Stave Company of Lebanon, Missouri. The whiskey ages for 27 months at a rack house in Hoquiam, where the air is colder and moister (which significantly reduces expensive evaporation) and extracts the sugars from the wood. The process also oxidizes the whiskey, and develops the unique esters of a mature Scotch.

Lamb has since dropped out of the venture (his family continues to be an investor) and it's Hofmann, unexpectedly, who has truly blossomed. He's on a nationwide list of 30 Tastemakers Under 30. Better still (as it were), Westland's Peated American Single Malt was named Best of Class by the American Distilling Institute.

ERIK LIEDHOLM Wildwood Spirits

Erik Liedholm grew up on Wildwood Street in East Lansing, Michigan, where his parents were on the faculty of Michigan State University. He found his way into wine and was recruited to into John Howie's fold as director of wine & spirits. "I had no real experience as a distiller," Liedholm admitted, but he did know about Kris Burglund, a biochemist at MSU who's considered the expert's expert.

Howie's new project, located at the north end of Lake Washington between Bothell and Kenmore, is Beardslee Public House, a high-class tavern and brewery that will make its own charcuterie and cheese. And, why not? Distill its own gin and vodka as well. ("Not so fast," said the Liquor Board; it took forever to negotiate assignments of space, ownership, doorways, and so on.)

Five years ago, on a trip to Portugal, Liedholm bought a nine-liter copper still and promptly made a batch of grappa from petit verdot grapes that he sourced from the Ciel du Cheval vineyard. Add homemade grappa to the Beardslee project, yes! Use the best red winter wheat from TriState Seed, yes! Ship 15,000 pounds of the wheat to Prof. Burglund, yes! Learn the elements of making beer and turning it into vodka (saccharification, fermentation and distillation), yes! Get your equipment from the master, CARL. And because vodka is essentially the tofu of the spirit world (colorless, odorless, virtually flavorless), use that vodka to make your gin. Use a dozen or more botanicals.

Wildwood's vodka is known as Stark Vatten, "strong water" in Swedish. The gin is called Kur, pronounced "cure." It's so good it will convert folks who think they don't like gin. "We think there's room at the top end, and for spirits made with Washington products," says Chef Howie. "It's a step into a whole new arena." As for Liedholm, one more exam and he added "Master Distiller" to his resumé. The opening lineup, Kur Gin and Stark Van Vatten Vodka, have both won top honors from the New York World Wine and Spirits Competition and the San Francisco World Spirits Competition, the two most recognized competitions in the spirits industry. Coming up: a second gin, and the the first two barrels of a premium bourbon line called Dark Door.

MICAH NUTT & JASON PARKER Copperworks

Micah Nutt and Jason Parker are the co-owners of Copperworks Distilling. Parker (right) is also president of the Washington Distillers Guild. Before turning to the spirit world, he was the first brewer at Pike, back in 1989. His take on the explosion of craft distilleries: "It happens–or has the potential to happen–wherever there are farms." With little barrier to entry (a beautiful copper still isn't cheap, but it's no worse than a Lamborghini or two), the niche took off, creating 15,000 jobs along the way. And that's in addition to the Washington's thriving restaurant industry, which contributes $250 million in liquor taxes to state coffers.

After several years of working on legislation, Parker has helped open up even more options for local distillers, privileges like selling at farmers markets; adding non-alcoholic mixers in the tasting room; special events and parties at the distilleries; gift cards; Internet sales and shipping ("A huge one"). All due to the craft distillers act.

The earliest products from Copperworks were vodka and gin, and (as of 2016) there's a single-malt whiskey as well. And if they ever get around to tearing down the Highway 99 viaduct, Copperworks will be right there, on Seattle's waterfront, with its gleaming copper stills ready for tourists en route to the Ferry Terminal.

GWYDION STONE Hammering Man

Marteau is French for "hammer." It's also Gwydion Stone's brand of absinthe. Stone is the founding member of an association called the Wormwood Society, whose purpose is to educate bartenders and drinkers about the magic green distillate. Not an easy task, since competitors (virtually the entire alcoholic beverage industry, not to mention zealous government bureaucrats) are more than eager to demonize absinthe, ascribing to it every evil and unfortunate medical condition known to the planet.

Never mind that real absinthe, properly made, is a thing of beauty, "like drinking an Alpine meadow," as Stone puts it.

To sweeten the absinthe, drip some ice water through a sugar cube suspended on a slotted spoon above the glass. Don't set fire to the sugar! That's a bar trick from eastern Europe designed to camouflage counterfeit absinthe. The real stuff turns milky when water is added. Absinthe used to be cheaper than wine; that's why it was so popular during the Belle Époque, at the end of the 19th century. In its early years, until craft distilleries were legalized in Washington, Stone's Marteau was distilled under contract in Switzerland. Remember, it's a distillate, not an infusion. Now close your eyes and taste the meadow.

ERIN BROPHY & MHAIRI VOELSGEN BroVo Spirits

With backgrounds in marketing and sales, Mhairi Voelsgen and Erin Brophy may not be your typical team of craft distillers, but then, their self-described "lady-made liquor" is not your usual Jack-and-Coke happy-hour drink.

When Brophy (photo) and Voelsgen decided to create their own liquor brand, they aimed at setting themselves apart from other craft distilleries by steering away from the typical vodka, gin and whiskey of their competitors. Instead, the pair created BroVo Spirits in 2014 with a focus on unique liqueurs made with ingredients local to Washington, such as Douglas fir foraged from the Glacier area of the North Cascades, or lavender grown in Ferndale.

Lower in alcohol than most other liquors, liqueurs are spirits flavored with fruit, herbs, nuts, flowers or spices, and bottled with added sugar. BroVo's varieties use the least amount of sugar possible to still classify as a liqueur, so they're light enough to be served solo on the rocks as well as in creative cocktails. Flavors include lemon balm, rose geranium, ginger, Douglas fir, and lavender. Along with their original five options, new seasonal flavors of mint and rhubarb have also been introduced; all can be purchased in select liquor stores (around $40 for a 750-ml bottle) and in restaurants around the city, including Ray's Boathouse in Ballard, El Gaucho downtown, and any of Tom Douglas' restaurants.

Mike Thiede of Ginkgo Forest Winery & Ginkgo Distillery holds the artisan distillery license for BroVo. In terms of new product development, Voelsgen and Brophy are asking their prime customers: local bartenders. Sometimes this works, sometimes not. The line of amari (Italian bitters) is a welcome addition to the city's inventory, but I found wine-based vermouths didn't offer any zing. You think this would be better: "Jammy" is a red vermouth that starts with a Merlot base, and is enhanced with cherries, hibiscus, ginger, tellicherry peppercorns, coriander seed, orange peel, lemon peel, cacao nibs, and decaf coffee beans, then sweetened with agave nectar. Too many notes, and curiously unexciting.

IN GOOD SPIRITS · Four Behind the Bar

MURRAY STENSON

Eater.com actually has a "MurrayWatch" hashtag, which tells you how closely cocktail fans follow Murray Stenson's whereabouts. Named America's best bartender in 2010 by the Tales of the Cocktail gathering in New Orleans, Stenson is sometimes referred to as "Murr the Blur," but that's a misnomer. He's fast because he's focused, that's all. He doesn't use fancy jiggers with graduations every 1/8th ounce; he knows what he's doing. When your neighborhood barkeep dips a straw into your daiquiri and tastes the drink, that's Murray's real legacy: make sure it tastes good.

When Stenson had heart surgery a couple of years ago his friends raised something like $100,000 to make sure he'd get properly treated. These days, he's no longer working five-six-seven nights a week, and he tends to move from one spot to another, hence the #MurrayWatch posts on social media. He's said to be working on a project for his own place, but in the meantime, if you introduce yourself, he'll make you a cocktail called the Last Word: gin, Chartreuse, maraschino liqueur, lime juice. His own drink: Campari soda.

JAMIE BOUDREAU

Canon, on Capitol Hill, is Seattle's best-stocked bar, with an astonishingly broad list of single-malts as well as local spirits. But only good ones; Jamie Boudreau has little tolerance for half-assed distillations. Canon, opened in 2010, is not just any bar, either, but twice recognized by the annual Tales of the Cocktail convention in New Orleans as America's best bar with the most extensive collection of spirits in the world.

Canadian-born Boudreau is always tasting new products, including bottlings from the new local distilleries. "Unfortunately," he tells me, "there is a lot more questionable product out there than there is quality." Many of the drinks on Canon's 168-page Captain's List sell for three and even four figures. That said, Boudreau is a fan of both Westland single malts and Woodinville Whiskey's bourbons, "But just because anyone and everyone can get a license doesn't mean it's going to be good. The wealth of choices? Not really."His own drinks show an exceptionally sure touch. The Vieux Carré, to name just one, is a beautifully smooth blend of cognac, rye, sweet vermouth, and bitters. The menu calls it "lush and assertive," perhaps the first time that menu-speak has been completely accurate.

JAMES MacWILLIAMS Canlis

Emerging like a mole from the canyons of Belltown, barman James MacWilliams was appointed by the Canlis family to research and resurrect the cocktail scene of the 1950s. Tiki drinks were particularly exotic so it was natural that the restaurant, in its earliest years, served them. They eventually faded from view (as did the kimono-clad waitresses) only to be revived now, modified slightly to suit current tastes for drinks that are less sweet. No extra charge for the fireworks, or the fancy garnishes.

This one's called "Yes sir, Mr. Canlis," a mixture of Gentleman Jack, pineapple, Pernod and Benedictine topped with a brûléed banana meringue. "Have a drink with us," a customer might say 50 years ago to founder Peter Canlis, no doubt assuming he'd have something simple like a rum and Coke. "My usual," Peter would signal. "Yes sir, Mr. Canlis," the waiter would say, and return ten minutes later with this elaborate cocktail. Tastes like a toasted marshmallow.old Barista magazine last year, "Professional growth is sexy and it keeps you on your toes!"

ROBERT HESS

Not a professional bartender but a software exec for Microsoft, Robert Hess nonetheless has a profound interest in cocktails and is one of the founders of the Museum of the American Cocktail in New Orleans. He used his tech skills to put together an app called Drinkboy, which produces a roster of cocktail options tailored to the bottles you happen to have on hand. He also has a show on the Small Screen Network. Above all, though, Hess was a driving force–for better, not worse–in popularizing the "craft cocktail" revolution.

STEVE & JUSTIN COX Icemen Cometh

You want something memorable for your buffet table, like an ice sculpture. A traditional Wedding Swan (so 1970s) is less than $400. But maybe you want something else. A 3-D logo? An oyster luge? A heart-shaped cup for your sorbet? A giant ice cube for the punch bowl? The Starbucks logo ($500)? Jumping salmon ($600)?

Comes as no surprise to learn that there's a father & son team, Steve and Justin Cox, who will provide any of dozens of hand-carved ice sculptures. No molds; the ice gets cloudy. Their catalog is online (creativeice.com), and if you want something custom-designed, they'll work with you. That's Steve in the picture, but young Justin does most of the carving these days, at a warehouse down in Kent that's equipped with three walk-in freezers.

Now remember, ice is heavy. No charge if you pick up, but delivery will run $50, and removal (because you've got to leave your venue pristine) will cost at least twice that much.

Chapter 30 · COFFEE & TEA

Worth a whole book of its own, the real, true, honest Starbucks saga may never be known. On the one hand, a gent who knows what really happened (but he's not talking); on the other hand, a Trump-like narcissist with corporate ADD and fabricator of reality who (so far, so far) has been incredibly fortunate.

It's hard to tell if it's premeditated villainy or just ineptitude, or if this is "crazy like a fox" ingenuity. After all, for every $1,000 worth of SBUX stock you bought at the IPO in 1992, you'd have a cool quarter million today. Uncle Howard himself is worth billions. But that doesn't make him right, just lucky.

HOMETOWN LOLITA

Dare we say this about our hometown Lolita, growing up too fast before our eyes? That she's always trying on (and tossing aside) new outfits like a petulant and moody teenager? And where does she get the money? We don't dare ask; we're afraid it might involve sneaking out the upstairs window for furtive encounters with strangers.

Only yesterday, driving up East Madison, we thought we spotted Uncle Howie sitting in the window at Healeo, the hippie health food spot, ingesting something he no doubt found nutritious, but he was gone by the time we found parking. We wanted to ask him: when did he make the decision that Starbucks should stop being a coffee company and start being a candy store?

While we're at it, we'd like to know if anyone has kept track: how many Global Concept Officers Howie has recruited, hired, trained, motivated, and sent out into the world to certain death? Do you know if they were they slaughtered or eaten alive? Have any ever returned from that Global Heart of Darkness?

But the past is prologue. First, this item from the *NY Times:*

"Starbucks is taking on the thriving market for yogurt, teaming up with French dairy powerhouse Danone to create a line of yogurts that will be sold in the coffee company's stores and in grocery stores."

Yogurt! Well, I never. What is this? Penance? No, opportunity. Danone's CEO calls it a new sales channel and says he admires Starbucks for the way it interacts with its customer base of "70 million visitors a week." (Actual number: more like 60 million a month, but still impressive.)

If you've visited a supermarket lately, you'll find far more of the cold case devoted to yogurt than to any other dairy product except milk itself. Danone is right: yogurt needs more elbow room, especially to make room for the new "Greek" styles. I might personally wish for *healthier* yogurt rather than chalky, plastic goo flavored with icky-sweet artificial blueberries, but that's just the food snob in me, wondering why so many of today's picky eaters think they can eat themselves thin.

The new Starbucks/Danone yogurts will be part of Evolution Fresh, the juice-bar concept that our Lolita picked up for a mere $30 million..

But before the yogurt gets to the stores, it's time for an update on two other product lines. First, the now-ten-year-old autumnal beverage known as PSL. Stands for Pumpkin Spice Latte. The *Wall Street Journal* describes it thus: "The pumpkin-spice sauce (note, not syrup, like most Starbucks drinks) made with cinnamon, clove and nutmeg spices, combines with steamed milk, espresso, whipped cream and a pumpkin-spice topping. But no actual pumpkin in the Pumpkin Spice Latte."

To me, it tastes like a warm pudding & pie filling, with a vague cinnamon aftertaste; no character, no vibrancy. But the drink has legions of fans and followers; I'm happy to let them have it to themselves.

Far better, if only too briefly, was Starbucks' big bet ($100 million) on La Boulange, a 122-unit chain of California bakeries created by a young Frenchman, Pascal Rigo. No more dry slices of pound cake! No more cold, greasy croissants! What Rigo figured out was how to bake croissants and sweet rolls, then freeze them so they wouldn't need preservatives. The individual pastries are reheated onsite in convection ovens. And they're pretty amazing. Wait! Stop the presses. Uncle Howard has thrown La Boulange under the bus. Dunzo. He's dumped the Frenchie for a sexier Italian, Princi. Not saying how much she cost, but you can bet it's plenty.

GORDON BOWKER No More Coffee for You!

Not many people, even longtime Seattle residents, recognize his name, but if there is one person who really should be feted as the instigator of Seattle's rise to the top of the region's (if not the country's) innovative food communities it would be this man: Gordon Bowker.

Ballard native, O'Dea grad, college dropout (San Francisco State), he was bumming around Europe when he happened to order a cappuccino at a caffè near the Trevi Fountain in Rome in the summer of 1962. It changed his life. This was not just good, it was beyond an awesome cup of coffee, this was life-changing.

Gordon returned to Seattle determined never to drink bad coffee again. He became an evangelist for better coffee, made with freshly roasted, freshly ground beans. He started making monthly runs to Vancouver, BC, to buy beans at Murchie's; in his green Alfa Romeo he brought back beans for friends and neighbors whom he had converted to the cause of better coffee. And one day he had his second epiphany: that he and his friends could (and indeed should) roast the beans themselves, in Seattle.

Thus was born Starbucks. (There's more to it than that, obviously.) The founders, Bowker and his roommates, didn't hire Howard Schultz until years later. And let him go because Schultz wanted to grow the company in a different direction.

Schultz returned to Seattle a couple of years later, rounded up a gang of investors, and bought the company from its founders. But by that time, Bowker was on to other ventures: an ad agency ("Rrrrrrrraineeeeeer Beer!"), and a brewery (Redhook).

In the meantime, Schultz returned to give Starbucks a kick in the pants. He bought out the founders; it's none of my business but I hope he paid them in stock because the value of a single share has increased 250-fold since the company's IPO.

And Bowker, for the past couple of decades, has stood deliberately apart from the crowd, believing that creativity requires a certain level of idleness. And that lack of ambition drives some people crazy. "But I didn't want a Gulfstream," he told me last year. Instead, he bought a Tesla, which he didn't keep because it was just too big.

THE MADNESS OF UNCLE HOWARD

No book about food in Seattle would be complete without at least one chapter about everybody's favorite Crazy Uncle, Howard Schultz.

Early in 2016 he announced that Starbucks would close its Teavana super-stores. Except the one at University Village. But the rest, three in Noo Yawk and one in Beverly Hills, dunzo. When Teavana opened, barely two years earlier, Schultz admitted he'd paid about $620 million for the chain, most of whose stores sell tea in bulk.

Meantime, one of Starbucks biggest suppliers, Keurig, has been sold. Just as well, perhaps. But somebody still has to provide the (wretchedly unfriendly-to-the-environment) K-Cups. "No problem, we'll go it alone," said Schultz.

The cold-pressed juice revolution Schultz was touting less than four years ago? He had Starbucks buy a company called Evolution Fresh for something like $50 million. So far, no national roll-out; just three stores.

Remember La Boulange? The French baker who had figured out how to make tasty pastries on a large scale and warm them up just when you bought them? About $100 million, if I recall correctly. G-gone. In its place, an Italian import, Princi. Seattle is on the list to get the very first one.

Remember that whey-powder drink called Vivano? Vaguely. Long-haired Italian kid, right? Remember "Race Matters"? The less said, the better. Remember Starbucks movies? Starbucks music? Remember Danone yogurts? Big push with the Frenchies, but I don't think the product even made it into the stores. Remember whatever Starbucks was calling its water?

We won't even talk about Flat White, Latte Macchiato, Starbucks wine nights, or the upscale Roastery on Capitol Hill (with pizza by Tom Douglas, no less). It's one thing to put up with the moodiness of a teenager, but this crazy corporate conduct is unprecedented.

How much longer will the SBUX board of directors put up with this schizoid, ADD-addled guy? A lot of Seattle people still haven't forgiven Uncle Howard for selling the Sonics. They're the lucky ones.

TALL GRANDE VENTI

Recognize the title? Congratulations, you're one of tens of millions of Americans who have ordered a drink at Starbucks. Why their menu should call the shortest drink a "tall," their middle drink "big" and their large one "20" makes no sense. But it's one more aspect of the scrambled brain cells that seem to run the company. Sadly, it all started out so well.

THE MAN WHO WOULD BE EDITOR

All but forgotten: a ten-year-old interview Howard Schultz gave to *USA Today* in which he said he sees Starbucks as the "editor" of American popular culture. "One of the great strengths of Starbucks is our humility," he said, with a straight face. Not satisfied with being America's most frequented brand and its top pusher of caffeine, he wants to be our cultural pimp as well.

TEAVANA Whatever Soothes Your Spirit

 In 2004, a lanky, young software salesman named Charlie Cain wandered into a tiny tea shop on the outskirts of Bonn, Germany. What he saw there made an indelible impression: 300 different leaf teas for sale! Cain had just read Howard Schultz's "One Cup at a Time," in which Schultz recounts *his* coffee epiphany as he watched Italians drinking espresso ("This could be a real business!"). Now it was tea, "my Howard Schultz moment," Cain said at the opening of Seattle's new Teavana store at University Village. He said goodbye to software, hello to tea, and eventually joined Starbucks.

Tea is the world's second-most consumed beverage, after water. And it's not as if Starbucks had never heard of tea; after all, the company was originally called Starbucks Coffee Tea & Spices, and sold two dozen loose-leaf teas at its first stores before turning to the dark-roasted side and emphasizing coffee.

Well, what goes around comes around. Starbucks paid over $600 million to buy the Teavana chain (over 300 retail outlets, all in malls, no seating).

"With Evolution Fresh, Starbucks got into juice; with La Boulange, we got into baked goods –food of all sort, really," Cain says. "And now, again, tea." But this time, the tea will have its own, separate locations. It's a different mind-set, after all. Coffee is seen as an energy drink, tea as a relaxing beverage. Even the name, Teavana, suggests Asian mysticism.

Just as a wine aficionado can wax on (and on and on) about grape varieties, single vineyards, and legendary vintages of *vitis vinifera*, a devotee of tea can cite literally hundreds of varieties of *camellia sinensis* leaves (white, green, oolong, black), and their methods of "withering" (steaming, pan-firing, shaking, bruising, rolling, drying, oxidizing). Then there tea-like drinks that don't contain *Camillia sinensis*, like prepared are herbal infusions, rooibos (red teas), and the green-powdered matés.

But now, Starbucks is doing a deal that will change everything, a deal with Budweiser. The parent company of Bud, Anheuser-Busch InBev will produce, bottle, and distribute a ready-to-drink line of Teavana. The move will help Starbucks broaden its reach beyond coffee. And it will help Budweiser use the excess capacity at its breweries (and beer volumes have been falling). It will also give Budweiser's network of more than 500 distributors and 300,000 retail sales points a nonalcoholic beverage to sell.

Ready-to-drink tea is one of the fastest-growing beverage categories (consumption was up 6 percent last year) according to the Beverage Marketing Corp. An amazing opportunity, said Budweiser's chief executive.

EVOLUTION FRESH Still Evolving

Evolution Fresh, the juice bar concept that Starbucks launched in 2012, is on the ropes. "We have the opportunity to change people's lives and to change trajectory of nutrition for the future generations," the company tweeted. Muddled grammar aside, it sounds awfully self-important, wouldn't you say?

Wasn't it Schultz himself who reminded us, in the title of his first book, about the virtues of humility, that you build a company "one cup at a time"? That book, by the way, was a rewriting-of-history memoir published in 1997, after Howard had returned, triumphant, from his short-lived exile. He'd been tossed out of Seattle's best-loved coffee brand by the founders, having wrangled Starbucks from a local chain to a worldwide player, but returned to purchase the company.

In his second book, titled "Onward: How Starbucks Fought for its Life Without Losing Its Soul," Schultz cites the impressive statistics: 16,000 stores, $10 billion in revenues, 200,000 employees, and, most impressive of all, 60 million customer visits a month. By virtually every measure, the Starbucks mermaid is a huge success, the world's most frequented brand, so why does she continue to behave like a petulant teenager, constantly trying on new outfits, desperate for approval, afraid she is unloved?

Down at the SoDo headquarters, the suits are never satisfied. It's their job to be hungry, to look for new opportunities, new markets. Most recently, Starbucks introduced a blonde roast, finally acknowledging that not everyone enjoys the strong, bitter flavor of a Full City Roast. They're finally opening shops in India. At the company's annual meeting one year, the emphasis was on healthier snacks in the stores, and on the acquisition of a premium coffee machine called the Clover. The company shut down for a full day to "retrain" team members in the finer points of coffee-making and customer service. Few people remember that the Vivano, introduced in 2008, was a banana smoothie with protein powder. More recently, there was a big dustup about single-serve coffee machines made by Keurig.

And, what with Starbucks canned "refresher" drinks making their way into grocery stores, the company was clearly aware of something called the cold-crafted juice category. It's worth some $3.5 billion and growing. Even a small piece of that was enough for a San Bernardino, Calif., company called Evolution Fresh, but Starbucks sniffed around the company and smelled a new conquest. It bought Evolution Fresh for a paltry $30 million last November. You get the feeling that Starbucks was just waiting to pounce: they banged out the first store, complete with graphics, equipment, new products, staff training in under four months. (TV's "Restaurant Impossible" pretends to do this in three days; don't believe it.)

Calories, fat grams, protein, fiber, and sodium content are given for every item on the menu, albeit in teensy type. There's an abundance of W symbols for items that contain no wheat, and a profusion of V symbols for vegan.

Starbucks insists this isn't about pandering to a faddish crowd of self-diagnosed gluten-intolerant young moms. "It's a trend," Arthur Rubinfeld told me. He's the Starbucks President for Global Store Development who put this whole concept together.

Cynicism aside, Starbucks has been a key element in a cultural shift in American cities. In the space of a generation, coffee shops have become what bars, taverns, diners and private clubs once provided: a third place, between home and work, neutral territory where people can gather. Do the SoDo Suits know something we don't? Is coffee itself no longer the catnip it once was? If Evolution Fresh provides an alternative to caffeine, then Starbucks will succeed with this transformative concept. If not, well, no harm done.

When Starbucks removed its name from its logo, it was, Schultz said, so that future ventures wouldn't necessarily be tied to coffee. Ironically, Evolution Fresh carries no Starbucks branding or logos whatsoever. This may be playing it safe. If the concept tanks, it would be far easier to sell off or shut down without the Starbucks baggage. What's more significant is that Starbucks is moving away from a reliance simply on coffee-based experiences (romantically ducking into an Italian caffè in Milan or Torino) and wading instead into that vast market the Italians call *benessere:* health and wellness. It's worth a cool $50 billion a year.

This is way more than spas and massages. At its worst, its nothing more than catering to the whims of distracted, 30-somethings with self-inflicted eating disorders and food allergies. At its best, however, health-and-wellness is a defense against the stress of modern life. If Evolution Fresh can get us there, can "change the trajectory of nutrition," then more power to the Mermaid.

But here's the downside, and it's grim: That $8 serving of cold-pressed juice generates over three pounds of pulp. Waste pulp. Pulp you now have to dispose of. And don't think that, just because it's vegetable matter, that it's easy to compost. By the way, 100 million 16-ounce servings of cold-pressed juice produced close to 200,000 tons of pulp waste. Wet and heavy waste. Terrible for landfills. Okay for composters, except that it generates methane rather than carbon dioxide.

LOIS PIERRIS B&O Espresso

Lots of people opened coffee shops in Seattle over the years, but none with a background as eclectic as Lois Pierris. An artist with wanderlust, a true Sixties hippie, she went from raising a family in a brownstone in Brooklyn to designing clothes, from taking photo safaris in Africa to living on a nude beach on the Mediterranean island of Corfu, eventually settling in Seattle and opening the B&O Espresso on Capitol Hill. For a quarter century, she opened a string of bars, restaurants and clothing stores (Pony Ristorante, the original Serafina, among others). In 2003 she sold or closed her business ventures and began spending most of her time in Africa.

ALI GHAMBARI Sexy Persians

It started with a single shop, at First & Cherry, where Ali Ghambari took over a pizza parlor. Today, his Cherry Street Coffee House is a chain of five stores, decorated with Persian caligraphy, domes, and arches. The Belltown store includes a fountain. Ghambari, born in Persia, has lived in Seattle since 1979 and is married to an Americn. His daughter, Laila, grew up in the coffee business; she was named the best barista in the United States in 2014.

PAUL ODOM Fonte

Even though, in 1992, Starbucks had been around for a while, the specialty coffee business was still in its infancy. Paul Odom's family owned the local Coca Cola franchise, but it was the caffeinated (rather than carbonated) route that interested young Odom. He hired a Master Roaster named Steve Smith and set out to conquer high-end chefs and restaurants. Then came a retail outlet and a café-bistro-wine bar on First Avenue, backing into the Four Seasons Hotel. He was even going to move to New York, before thinking the better of it. Breakfast, lunch, and Happy Hour, more than enough to keep Odom busy.

MARSHA GLAZIÈRE Landscape of Coffee

When Marsha Glazière returned to Washington after a six-year "artistic sabbatical" on the coast of Florida, she found herself unhappy in the stressful, crowded urban center of Seattle, so she moved to a calmer, quieter place. Not to hippy-dippy North Bend or Duvall or Whidbey but to the blue-collar community of Tacoma.

Landscapes, architectural abstractions, horses became her subjects. Then she branched out. Over a three-year period, she began seeking out, photographing, and committing to canvas a series of artisanal coffee shops around Puget Sound, visiting over 200 in all and selecting 120 for her book, *Eclectic Coffee Spots in Puget Sound*.

While coffee shops have always been part of modern urban environments (and over 50 of the shops that made the cut are in Seattle proper), Glazière's research turned up dozens of off-the-beaten-track spots: La Crema Coffee & Roastery in La Conner; Useless Bay Coffee Co. on Whidbey Island; the Mandolin Cafe in Tacoma. Sometimes Glazière records the past; the Old Silverdeli Coffee Shop in Silverdale was painted before it became a hair salon.

This isn't a rigidly organized guidebook; Glazière shuffles photographs, paintings, recipes and musings according to her own rules, but it's a fine addition to anyone's collection of the region's most charming cultural institutions and icons.

Chapter 31 · IT'S THE WATERS

With all the outrage over Nestle's line of waters (Aqua Panna, Arrowhead, Perrier, Poland Spring, San Pellegrino, etc.), all basically tap water in non-recyclable PET bottles, shipped cross-country at great environmental cost), it seems barely worth mentioning that Starbucks owns a bottled water brand of its own, Ethos. The gimmick is that SBUX supposedly shares the profits from the sale of Ethos in order to send fresh, safe drinking water to places in the world that don't have it. What a wretched, guilt-inducing marketing tactic! One giant crocodile tear is all you get from me.

SHARELLE KLAUS Dry Soda

We Americans spend more money on soda than on real food. And it gets worse when you include flavored waters, energy drinks, and fruit juices, not to mention coffee and tea, and leaving aside beer, wine and spirits. We are a nation built on liquids enhanced with artificial flavors and sweeteners, and we're getting bulkier every day.

Into this fray, in 2005, stepped a Tacoma woman, Sharelle Klaus. A foodie, yes, but primarily a high-tech consultant with four little kids. She set out, very deliberately, to create a new category of "natural" carbonated beverages (water, cane sugar, natural flavoring, and phosphoric acid) that would pair with food; she named her brand Dry Soda .

At the time, there were basically three flavors of canned fizzy drinks: cola, lemon-lime, and root beer. So Klaus thought about it for a while and came up with four candidates: Kumquat, Lavender, Rhubarb and Lemongrass. (She would soon add Vanilla and Juniper Berry, drop the Kumquat when it turned out that not many people knew what a kumquat was; she substituted Blood Orange.) Each flavor required a lot of experimental formulation in her kitchen, a thousand batches each, Klaus says.

She's grateful for early guidance from a food scientist and a beverage industry consultant. Turnstile Design Studio of Ballard, back then a startup as well, did the appealing logo. Dry's flavors are developed in association with a company in California;

the bottling is handled by contractors; the closest is an outfit in Portland. "Building a beverage brand is very expensive," Klaus acknowledges, so, in addition to its own sales team, Dry Soda has hired a savvy, $2 billion national food broker, Acosta, to make sure Dry gets onto the right grocery shelves and into the right restaurants (like the French Laundry).

There's an air of Energizer Bunny around Klaus, now in her 40s. On the day she was named one of Seattle's 15 Women of Influence by *Puget Sound Business Journal*, she was launching a new flavor of soda, Wild Lime (think 7-Up on steroids) at Dry's headquarters in Pioneer Square, then hopped the red-eye to South Carolina to launch a new venture with Urban Outfitters.

Dry Soda today is sold in over 100 Seattle restaurants, 600 nationwide, but on-premise is only 15 percent of their business. There are nine mainline flavors, plus two seasonal: Malali Watermelon (smooth, juicy, cool), Serrano Pepper (spicy, bright, savory). The Fuji Apple Dry Sparkling was named 2016 Editor's Pick for best new product by *Gourmet Retailer*. Sales are up 50 percent over last year, and have hit a total of 40 million bottles.

Klaus is not alone in this niche. For one, there's **JONES SOSDA**, best-known for a flavor (since retired) called Turkey & Gravy. Jones's one-time CFO is now on Dry's board of directors. Jones was never an upscale brand, and has even given up on cane sugar. It also launched and then canceled a line of carbonated waters called **GABA**; and (at the last minute) backed out of a deal to sell itself to a California rival, Reed's.

KEVIN KLOCK Singing in the Rain

You've got to give Doug MacLean credit. Credit for head-shaking foresight. In 2004, the health and fitness enthusiast put a bet on bottling and selling water. Imagine! Water in the Pacific Northwest! Why would anyone pay money for the pure stuff that comes out of a tap? But of course they did. And sales grew to something like $50 million a year. Not enough to satisfy the owners of the privately-held company though. So they added flavored water, sparkling water, and iced tea to the lineup, and sales soared. With **SPARKLKING ICE**, The new CEO, Kevin Klock, found himself on a wild ride in the rushing torrent of flavored and sparkling beverages . By late 2015, the Japanese brewery Asahi was said to be interested in an acquisition for nearly half a billion dollars. (False alarm, it turned out.) By mid-2016, Sparkling Ice was the leader in the category of "alternatives to diet soda," with 3% fruit juice and a low calorie count. Wall Street was proving to be thirsty for this sort of product, right along with consumers.

Chapter 32 · MOTHER'S MILK

DARIGOLD

This farmer-owned cooperative, almost a century old, is one of Washington's largest private companies, with $2 billion in annual sales. Some 450 members of the Northwest Dairy Association in five states contribute milk from their farms. Darigold has a great slogan, too, although it's no longer used in public all that much: "They had pitchforks. They had pride. They had no days off."

In addition to the usual (milk, butter, cream, yogurt, cottage cheese, there's a chocolate-milk drink called Re-Fuel, as well as a handsome magazine called Fresh.

SMITH BROTHERS

Talk about nostalgia. Is there any figure more idealized, in a past that never was, than the milkman on his rounds? Smart white uniform, black bowtie? Smith Brothers have been the custodians of this image for decades, offering a guarantee of freshness to the customers on its routes. Delivery charge is a buck and change if your order is under $10; less than it would cost you to drive to the Mini Mart. Plus they

deliver eggs, bagels, cookies, muffins, Beecher's cheese, chocolate milk, Stumptown Coffee, not to mention hard-boiled eggs, pasta and sauces from Cucina Fresca, crackers from La Panzanella, goodies from Sahale Snacks, Oberto beef jerky, Chobani yogurt, and baby carrots in plastic bags. Well, you get the idea.

Clearing the Table

Whose Turn to Clean Up?

Chapter 33 · DELIVERANCE
The Gleaners

We are not talking here about Bite Squad, Munchery, or Lish. We are not talking about UberEats bringing you a sandwich at work or Blue Apron dropping off a box of goodies at your condo. Rather, these are the folks who will save us from ourselves.

ARMEN STEPANIAN The Guru of Recycling

Forty years ago, if you lived in Seattle, you'd drag your clunky metal garbage cans out to the curb once a week to be emptied into a big, noisy truck. There were no curbside containers for recyclable materials, let alone wheels on garbage cans, not to mention the notion that stuff you no longer wanted or needed could be "recycled." Well, all that changed when Armen Napolean Stepanian, a New York transplant who'd worked as a carpenter and actor, came to town and settled in Fremont. He founded the food bank, he started the Fremont Public Association, he developed low-income housing, and, in 1973, he created a booth for the fledgling Fremont Fair that invited neighbors to drop off their aluminum, tin, and old newspapers that he would sell to junk dealers. By the following year he was offering curbside recycling services to 65 homes, making his monthly rounds in a white Chevy van, helped by a handful of teenage miscreants who'd been ordered to do community service. He soon had 500 customers.

Then he wrote a widely-publicized open letter to President Carter arguing that recycling saved energy ("The energy saved by recycling is the most critical of all," he wrote). By 1988 his concept had become the national model for municipally sponsored recycling programs. The SeaDruNar program showed it could also be profitable. Within a decade, 40 percent of Seattle's garbage was being recycled; Mayor Greg Nickels bumped the target to 60 percent; the new target is 70.

Today, at 84, Stepanian remains the honorary major of Fremont, but he says gentrification has made his old city too expensive, and some years ago he retired to Ocean Shores.

ENCORE RESTAURANT SUPPLY

 Half of all restaurants fail in the first year, a high price to pay for ignorance, lack of business skills, and the willingness of unscrupulous outfits like Groupon to prey on the unprepared. Nobody opens a restaurant planning to fail, nobody likes to see a lovely space and its yummy menu go dark. But when a restaurant does go out of business, owing money to the landlord, to its suppliers, its employees, and the tax man, there are signs, and the one that says "Closed for Remodeling" is rarely the only one. It can also be a sidewalk full of kitchen equipment, fixtures, and furniture. Somebody has to pick up the pieces, and in Seattle one of the dealers who recycles the used stuff is Encore Restaurant Supply.

The showroom on First Avenue South is a jumble of freezers, refrigerators, stainless steel tables, chairs, slicers, choppers, beverage dispensers, dishwashers, coffee makers. The guy behind the counter keeping an eye on the customers knows where everything is stashed and is more than happy to walk you to its hiding place. Professional quality equipment for a home kitchen: a lot of buyers are yuppies. There's a repair shop in the back, where a couple of guys with metal cutters and soldering guns fix up the stuff that comes in off the truck. And then there's the truck itself, which company owner Tim Gilday pilots through neighborhoods near and far with a checkbook and a nose for misfortune. Remodeling? Closing? Moving? Selling what, exactly? Metal is valuable, copper particularly. His offer is fair, much less than the purchase price (obviously, even if the item was recently purchased from Encore). Into the truck it goes.

Gilday refuses to be called a scavenger; business is best when people need equipment to remodel or open new spots. Open on a shoestring, maybe, but *open*. "People buy stuff, even if it's only hotel pans because they're expanding, when times are good."

THE WISErg HARVESTER: Food Waste In, Fertilizer Out

It looks like an overgrown ice machine at a chain hotel, with a big green tank attached. It's called the WISErg Harvester, and it may save the world.

The Harvester eats food scraps and turns them into a soup of nutrients. Everything is monitored, so the system knows when the tank needs to be emptied; back at the main plant, the soup (or slurry) is converted into fertilizer. This isn't a gadget for home use; it's for supermarkets (overripe fruit, spoiled vegetables) and restaurants (fish bones, beef bones, food scraps, and so on), as much as two tons of food waste a day for large commercial installations.

The machine is neither a composter (producing greenhouse gases as a byproduct of anaerobic digestion) nor a compactor (requiring additional energy) but a new process entirely, invented here in Seattle by a couple of Microsofties, Larry LeSueur and Jose Luego. Customers can buy or lease; installation can be inside or outdoors. And that's just the "garbage in" part of the equation. The end product is a completely organic fertilizer that can be applied to farmland as well as home gardens. One day, soon, these devices will be everywhere. For now, they're being rolled out as quickly as the fledgling company's finances will allow.

KEURIG'S DISPOSAL PROBLEM

Keurig's single-cup coffee maker is the preferred tool for many who want their morning cup of joe with as little effort as possible. It's quick and easy to use, and if you're more interested in the caffeine than the taste of the coffee, it produces a fine beverage. Of course, it requires K-cups, little pods of coffee contained in plastic, which produce a fair amount of waste. For the Keurig user who feels guilty about its environmental impact, good news has arrived. A roastery in Ontario, Canada, is selling 100 percent compostable PurPods that fully disappear in a compost site in less than three months.

The pods, sold by Club Coffee, are made out of coffee chaff, a natural byproduct of the bean-roasting process. It's a step in the right direction for environmentally conscious coffee drinkers, although they aren't perfect: they require more energy to make and more space in shipping than traditional pods. What's move, some municipal composting programs won't accept them for fear that old-fashioned, non-compostable coffee pods might slip through the cracks.

JASON WILSON Coffee Flour

The problem with coffee may be that we're looking at it wrong. Those plastic K-cups, those aluminum Nespresso pods, they're a PR nightmare, sure, but that's not where attention should be paid. Rather, it's the coffee plant itself.

Enter Jason Wilson, whom we've seen earlier in these pages as the chef at a roaringly successful steakhouse in downtown Seattle. But before he hooked up with the team behind Miller's Guild, he made his bones as an imaginative chef at his own place, Crush, on East Madison, where his multi-course menus took center stage. In that same century-old house, he is now exec chef for a business called Coffee Flour, which was spun off from Nathan Myhrvold's Intellectual Ventures. Dan Belliveau, who'd been director of technical services at Starbucks, was convinced that the pulp left over from harvesting coffee "cherries" could be used for something more interesting than fertilizer: high in iron, anti-oxidants, and fiber, it was also easy to recapture at the source, rather than allowing it to rot. So now we have coffee flour as a viable commercial product, with Wilson designing recipes.

MISCHIEF & KRAINICK Spending the Grain Again

If you think it's wasteful to "throw away" uneaten food or otherwise unused edibles, if you've ever wondered what happens to all those perfect plums and plump tomatoes when they start to deteriorate, you'll get a kick out of this.

One of the most "wasteful" sectors turns out to be the beverage industry. Brewers and distillers buy tons of grain and use huge amounts of water to produce beer and liquor. If the water's contaminated, they can't just divert it into a river; and once the grain is "spent," it can't be reused. (Yes, craft breweries send the grain across town to craft distilleries, but that just postpones the ultimate problem of disposal.)

So here's what happens at Fremont's Mischief Distillery, according to co-founder Patty Bishop, and to tell the story we're going to introduce third-generation land-owners

Mike and Leann Krainick of Enumclaw. Their 2,700-acre farm, in the shadow of Mount Rainier, produces a variety of grains; its barns and pastures are also home to 1,200 head of dairy cattle. The Krainicks are innovators, winners of the King County small rural business of the year award. For example, they package their cow manure in cubic-foot bags for sale to home gardeners looking for natural and organic soil amendment (lawns, flower beds, potting mix). The name? Scarecrow's Pride. Price: $5 a bag.

So these folks come into town and pick up all of Mischief's spent grain, 12 tons a year. Krainick also picks up from Fremont Brewing, Hale's Ales, and other distilleries. Some of that grain supplements the feed for their Holsteins; they also have a composting unit that allows them to process it, bag it up, and send it right back into the fields. "Krainick alone diverts four million pounds a month from the landfill," Bishop reports.

ALTERNATIVES TO LANDFILL

We've got plenty of food, just in the wrong places. America actually has plenty to eat ... we just waste a huge amount of it.

Angelo Pellegrini, a generation ago, exhorted people to Grown Your Own, in your own back yard. There are lots programs to teach people to grow food at home, and a Food Forest on Beacon Hill to let people pick fruit. 21 Acres in Woodinville teaches gardeners. Supply side is covered, it would seem. But there's still a vast sea of food that goes unused. Perishables.

The canned & bottled stuff, running close to or past its sell-by date, has a well-established network of "distressed food" channels to unload these items; three retail Grocery Outlet supermarkets in Seattle alone.

Chapter 34 · GRAVEYARD

What happens when we turn on the tap? What happens when we take out the garbage?

DOWN THE DRAIN

No question, it's the least glamorous and most misunderstood municipal utility. Flip the switch and the light comes on; that's what City Light does. Turn on the tap and water comes out; that's "Seattle Public Utilities." And the same people who bring you the water also flush it away so they get to charge you twice. Seattle maintains nearly 2,000 miles of pipes for incoming municipal water, connecting to nearly 200,000 individual users (households, businesses). There are 18,000 fire hydrants in Seattle, in case your kitchen or roof starts to go up in flames. When something goes wrong, it could be any of 20,000 water valves the city is expected to maintain.

Water (treated, sanitary, water) isn't free, but it's a heck of a lot less expensive than the bottled stuff. A cubic foot of water, to use the common standard for utilities, CCF, costs just over five bucks in Seattle (twice that much in Gotham). And what do you get for this? Well, for starters, you get 750 gallons of fresh water. A gallon of water is 128 fluid ounces, or 8 of those plastic pint bottles of Dasani or Crystal Geyser. For one dollar, you can fill up 150 one-gallon jugs of perfectly drinkable tap water.

If you pee and poop an average number of times, you'd flush maybe 10 gallons a day. Take a shower, two gallons per minute. Wash the dishes? Six gallons. Laundry? Up to 25 gallons per load. Add it up, the average household uses more than 100 gallons per person per day, but that's still well under a buck per person per day. (Just don't go watering the lawn; the supply isn't unlimited.)

What about the waste water? To wash away the sewage, Seattle maintains 1,400 miles of pipes. Biggest problem: keeping them free from FOG (fat, oil, grease). There's a separate line item on your utility bill for "drainage," based on the property's square footage. As for garbage and recycling, well, recycling is free for Seattle residents. The target is to recycle 70 percent of Seattle's solid waste by 2025; we've made it to 60 percent already. (Thanks, Armen Stepanian!) The smelly stuff that gets hauled away, "garbage," gets collected curbside weekly and charged monthly, about a buck a day for a typical, 32-gallon can.

Now, when it comes time to treat Seattle's waste water, the county takes over. King County Metro maintains 400 miles of sewage pipes and 47 pumping stations to serve a population of close to two million. It runs three large treatment plants processing close to 200 million gallons of sewage a day (West Point, at the tip of Discovery Park; South Plant, in Renton; and Brightwater, near Woodinville) and a host of smaller facilities. It's an unglamorous but essential skeleton for Seattle, what differentiates "us" from third-world countries.

TO DUST AND LAWN MULCH WE SHALL RETURN

As we've seen, public utilities, whether supervised by the city, the county, or private enterprises (because there's a lot of money in trash, you can imagine), rely on an infrastructure. Part of that is the predictable system of collecting and emptying those cans, those recycle bins, those dumpsters. Garbage trucks these days are powerful, sophisticated behemoths that compact their smelly loads and keep them contained as they make their rounds. When they're full (maybe carrying as much as ten tons of trash), they head off to the dump or to the transfer station. You can take your own junk to the transfer station, of course; it's $30 per trip (for garbage), $20 for clean yard waste. If it's all recyclable, free!

Side note: retailers can provide study plastic bags if they want, but no more flimsy, single-use bags; and they're required to charge at least a nickel for paper grocery bags. As a result of this "revolution" (fought tooth and nail by the chemical industry, which manufactured the flimsy bags, but welcomed by everyone else), we've now seen a huge increase in reusable cloth and polypropylene shopping bags.

Seattle Public Utilities and King County Metro farm out the trash collection to a variety of private contractors. In the good old days, you knew the names of the local families involved (Banchero, Razore, Morelli), and the names of the corporate entities (Seattle Disposal, Rabanco, Northwest Waste, Emerald Services). Then things got complicated. Allied Waste and Waste Management were big national outfits. And who or what are Republic Services? Cleanscapes? Cedar Grove? What is Recology?

The good news is that Cedar Grove is, in fact, the Banchero family. (Jerry Banchero, a distant cousin and a meat man, operated one of the first wine shops in town, Mondo's World, in the Rainier Valley.) Firmly in charge is J. Stephan Banchero III, a UW grad who last year created Cedar Grove Organics Recycling. That's a new division responsible for hauling food waste and organic material from some of the most iconic local companies and venues (Boeing, Amazon, Safeco and CenturyLink, the Space Needle, Columbia

Center, Pagliacci Pizza, Ivar's . Garbage, he once told an interviewer, is "his" thing, the way other professionals might view the law or journalism.

Today, the entire Cedar Grove operation is the principal composting undertaking in King and Snohomish Counties, and diverts 350,000 tons of organic waste away from landfills each year. In 2016 alone, Cedar Grove Organics Recycling will collect more than 85,000 tons of material from its customers; material that before the company's inception in 2007 would have been sent to landfills.

Cedar Grove plays a critical role in the Puget Sound's recycling infrastructure and sustainability efforts with its processing facilities in Maple Valley and Everett. One result everyone can appreciate: bags of nutrient-rich compost and lawn mulch sold to businesses, governments and residents. Headquarters are alongside Boeing Field in Georgetown, while the compost is produced at the suburban facilities (open only to permitted vehicles). If you should meander along the Maple Valley highway, there's a traffic light but not even a street sign for the turnoff; just follow the dump trucks. And sure, you can pick up compost and landscape mulch, but Cedar Grove will deliver to your driveway for the same price.

Adjacent to the Cedar Grove facility is the only actual landfill in King County, the 920-acre Cedar Hills Regional Landfill. Owned by King County and operated by its Solid Waste Division; it receives over 800,000 tons of solid waste a year, mostly from trucks shuttling waste from eight transfer stations around the county. .

Feeding Back

Professional assessments of Seattle's restaurant industry.

Chapter 35 · THE BIG PICTURE

The business of restaurants is not synonymous with the restaurant business, or even the hospitality business. And an organization like the Washington Restaurant Association exists to help its dues-paying members make more money, a mission that overlaps with but is not identical to the expectations of the folks who walk in the door expecting dinner, also known as "guests."

ANTHONY ANTON The Business of Restaurants

No one understands the balancing act between profit and hospitality better than Anthony Anton, the CEO of the restaurant industry's trade association. Anton roams the corridors of the Legislature as well as the aisles of trade shows. Can't stay in business if you don't have happy customers; can't stay in business if you don't make money.

Most important of all, it seems, (even more than standardized ingredients and reliable delivery) is POS equipment, also known as Point of Sale. Here are some of the non-food categories from which exhibitors could choose at the most recent Food Service trade show: from aluminum foil and beverage dispensers, to water purifiers, pest control. Takes a lot to run a restaurant beyond canned pizza sauce and dish-washing equipment, dontcha know. Oh, and we're not even talking about outfits like OpenTable.com that offer a soup-to-nuts takeover of the hospitality side of the business.

Another way to understand the challenges facing the restaurant industry is to look at the rundown of lectures.

Twenty "top food trends," as presented by the folks who know best (tip: not the editors of glossy magazines). Top of the list, yet again, is "Local." In second place, alas, is "Chef-Driven," a catch-all that covers every sin in the book. Numbers 3 and 4, more local. You have to crawl down to 14 to get "artisan butchery," which could produce anything from a pork chop to a loin of rabbit. And all the way to the bottom, Number 20, to see street food and food trucks. (Note to the WRA: you're not listening hard enough. Street food does not mean a hot-dog cart.)

Anton himself spoke on "Forging a New Restaurant Model in 2016." As he explained it, "New ways of doing business take into account not just restaurant operations but the political reality as well." And that political reality is multifaceted. The push for a $15 minimum wage, the concurrent pressure on owners to abandon the notion that servers can be paid by customer tips, and, not entirely unrelated to those issues, the increasing shortage of labor. Used to be, you could round up dozens of reasonably qualified bussers and even line cooks with a single Craigslist ad. No more.

Where have all the usual suspects gone? Many (especially the legions of undocumented, mostly Hispanic, workers upon whom the industry depends) have taken advantage of improving economic conditions in their home countries. Others, voicing concerns about immigration crackdowns, have simply returned to Mexico and other Latin American nations. Plus the crackdown on phony and profiteering culinary "academies" that take a full year, cost tens of thousands of simoleons, and dump their "graduates" into the fish pond of a market for minimum wage jobs. The sad fact is all the TV glamorizing of a career in the kitchen has not translated into a stable, long-term supply of labor.

And now the issue of scheduling. In a gig economy, where it seems half the workforce is "on contract," managers of all stripes and in all industries are saying they can't run their departments, their assembly lines, their cafes, their catering operations, their kitchens if they have to "predict," two weeks out, how many people they'll need. So they rely on that old standby, "on-call" employees. As for the dangling workers, when their cellphones ring, these hapless students, single moms, and assorted minimum-wage slaves must decide if they want to pick up a shift (Childcare? Missed class? No sleep? No matter.) For what? Peanuts. One group wants anything they can get, another needs more notice, the boss just wants the shift covered.

FORKING PROFESSIONALS

It began life as Seattle Chefs Collaborative, an occasional meet-up of industry professionals (chefs, sommeliers, and a gaggle of suppliers (not table linens but fishing-boat owners, osytermen, farmers) presided over by Zach Lyons, who knew everybody because he spent seven years as executive director of the statewide association of farmers markets. To give you an idea, almost every person in these pages would be welcomed. The Chefs Collaborative morphed into an organization called FORKS (Fields, Oceans, Ranches, Kitchens, Stewards) and an annual event referred to as F2C2 (Farmer-Fisher-Chef Connection). Lyons, currently a wholesale manager with Alvarez Organic Farms, remains an uncompromising advocate of purity and high standards in the local food chain.

DINNER BY APP

First, our friends at Urbanspoon sold off their Rezbook business, sold it to their arch-nemesis OpenTable! C'mon, Urbanspoon! Surely you remember why you started Rezbook in the first place, because OpenTable is a hated, predatory service that once required restaurants to "rent" their hardware and use their proprietary software, that it might seem all warm and fuzzy until the bill came at the end of the month and the restaurant would find, g-gulp, that those hundreds in membership dues and reservation fees (about $10 for a four-top) added up to a hefty chunk of change.

And it's not just unsophisticated mom & pop restaurants that begrudge OpenTable (but fear that dropping the service will cost them business); top-tier dinner houses are also resentful because OpenTable's business model depends on taking the restaurant itself (any restaurant) *out of the customer relationship*. It's OpenTable that's calling the shots, with loyalty points and newsletters and the lure of special deals for customers who use its service to make reservations. So OpenTable is constantly adding value for the consumers who use the site to make reservations (accounts that provide user data to the restaurants as well). The consumer gets to see local restaurants by cuisine, by neighborhood, by price point, by popularity. And the restaurants? Well, they have to be there, don't they? On the same screen as their rivals. So it just makes sense, doesn't it?

Almost every restaurant uses its own computers these days, running plug-in, point-of-sale software to enter orders and ring up checks, so there's no revenue stream anymore from renting dedicated terminals; instead, reservation services like OpenTable charges monthly fees to be displayed on the participating restaurants home pages. That's about two-thirds of OpenTable's revenue stream, in fact.

Last year, OpenTable shelled out a relatively paltry $10 million for a social-media app called Foodspotting. The draw was several million images of restaurant dishes taken by diners and displayed alongside the restaurant's listing. Not what the restaurants wanted to show, but what (often photo-challenged) eaters actually saw. Restaurants were not pleased, but Foodspotting was the least of their worries.

What happened was that Priceline—the discount ticketing and hotel reservation company—bought OpenTable for a whopping $2.6 billion, an $800 million premium over its share price, and mind-boggling for a company whose profits last year were about $50 million. Calling William "The Negotiator" Shatner: are you sure you can't do better?

In practice, OpenTable is a crutch for restaurants that don't understand the hospitality business. It's part of a trend toward "disintermediation," which takes responsibility for hospitality away from the restaurant and gives it to a Big Data outfit. In return for a hefty fee or commission, OpenTable then sells the diner's butt back to the restaurant where he or she wanted to go in the first place, but now the restaurant has just forfeited its $20 margin. This is a more sophisticated scam than Groupon (because neither party is aware of its cost), but a scam nonetheless.

It's just another dance move in the decline of actual, person-to-person hospitality. Going out for dinner has become a digital commodity, and more of a drain on restaurant resources (with steep commissions and fees that come right off the bottom line) than increasing the minimum wage.

Every major restaurant nonetheless feels compelled to use OpenTable, from tiny neighborhood spots like Bistro Turkuaz in Madrona to chronically empty joints like (the late) Fumaça in Belltown. Prestigious houses like Canlis and the Space Needle are on the list. Almost 500 in Seattle alone.

But wait, there's more. The latest apps are end-runs around OpenTable. Gary Vaynerchuk, who became famous for his over-the-top online wine reviews, launched an app called Resy that lists and sells reservations at hard-to-book restaurants. The more demand, the higher the price. He sees restaurant reservations as a commodity similar to Uber's "congestion pricing." And if a foursome has actually paid upfront for the table, it's doubtful they'll cancel at the last minute, or fail to show up, notorious problems in New York City and Los Angeles. Resy is approaching a stratospheric IPO in a field that's suddenly crowded with competitors like Zurvu, Killer Rezzy, Shout, even Yelp.

In the *New York Times*, Julia Moskin acknowledges that, for many restaurants, "charging patrons for reservations feels like touching the third rail."

One solution is the Alinea model, as it's known in the industry: selling tickets to dinner as if it were a Broadway show. Specific table, specific time and date. Non-refundable. Alinea, the Chicago hotspot, is actually licensing the software. Sounds simple enough, but it's no protection against scalpers buying up every ticket in sight and hawking them on Craigslist. Cheaper at 5 PM, by the way.

And as if that weren't enough, you've now got a whole online industry of "restaurant food" apps that deliver dinner to your door. The latest, whose arrival in Seattle later this year was announced in June, is called Munchery.com, and the venture capitalists couldn't throw money at it fast enough. Restaurant-quality dinners, they promise, cooked by actual chefs in local restaurant kitchens, delivered to your door chilled, ready to heat up in environmentally correct containers. The drivers will text you when they're close by. I haven't tried it (it's only available in San Francisco at this point), but it looks suspiciously like airline food. Upscale, business class airline food, but still.

Another new outfit called BiteSquad sends your order to a Samsung tablet that's mounted in the kitchens of participating restaurants, at which point the cooks are forced to prioritize between the online order and the impatient customers in the dining room. A less complicated site called GrubHub also sends orders to nearby restaurants. Of course, you could also just phone the restaurant and put in an order to be picked up later.

I should point out here that no restaurant cook wants to do this. No extra money; in fact, the restaurant makes less on these orders than on a dine-in or even a call-ahead & take-out. They charge less because they have to, in order to get listed by Munchery or Bite Squad. But the whole point of the online services is that the customer doesn't have to become personally involved. (the online testimonials include quotes like "I didn't have to talk to anybody!") Indeed, you don't have to deal with whichever harried server happens to be near the phone, or with a bored or inexperienced host. So what to do? Log onto another service, Blue Apron, which simply delivers you all the groceries for a meal that, g-gulp, you have to cook yourself.

And if you're too lazy even for that, how about TheGatheredTable.com, another startup (this one with financing from Howard Schultz, no less) that lets families plan a week's worth of meals based on stuff they like to eat and what's already on hand. One assumes this is for people who barely know how to open their fridge or cupboard and look inside. Why anyone considers this a good idea is beyond me.

A THOUSAND POINTS OF SALE

If you own a restaurant, there's a lot to worry about. Before you or your cooks draw that first streak of gastrique onto the plate for your artisanal, hand-grown, chanterelle-crusted poussin; before those cooks were recruited and taught how to prepare your carefully-guarded recipes; before you train your bussers and wait-staff; before you extend your contract with New System Laundry, Auto-Chlor, Sysco, Charlie's Produce, Corfini Gourmet, and DinerWare not to mention your social media consultant, your customer still has to walk into the door.

Because butts in seats is still the name of the game.

Running a restaurant is intense, akin to driving a high-performance race car: nothing to worry about (it seems) when all is running smoothly, but white-knuckle terrifying when you're doing over 100 mph half a lap from the pits and you hear a funny noise. With so much to go wrong, and it's understandable that many owners want to reduce the risk of utter disaster. Hence the reliance point-of-sale devices known as POS. Heartland 500-lb gorilla, swallowed Digital Dining late last year. Other vendors include Auphan, Oregon POS, Mynt POS, Focus POS, Maitre D POS, and NBS.

At its simplest, it's the screen where servers punch in orders, and a black box in the kitchen prints the ticket. Later, another printer in the dining room produces the bill, and the server swipes the customer's credit card to pay. Cash, ahem, is supposed to go into the till, not the server's apron pocket. In theory, the all-knowing POS tells owners which dishes are the most popular, how many hours the dishwasher and bussers worked, and how many lobsters the new server sold. The lady who comes in once a month or so to do your books insists on knowing how many hours the dishwashers and bussers worked, how much the servers pocketed in tips, and how big a check to send to Olympia for the sales tax collected and to the IRS for payroll deductions.

Play it right and you can jigger the system to tell you when it's time to order more flour (because it knows how much pasta you've used), when to call the liquor rep for refills. An uptick in sales also translates to more table linens, more glassware pushed through the dish machine, and so on. Savvy operators like Terresa Davis look at these numbers every day, but most owners just wing it. They're "restaurateurs," they tell themselves. They're not accountants, they're hosts. Yeah, but restaurants can leak cash like a sieve, but the ones that are still in business after a couple of years have someone on staff whose most important job is watching the till.

JENNIFER TAM Restaurant Navigator

There are over 1,500 restaurants in Seattle, and, from her office on the 57th floor of the Municipal Tower, Jennifer Tam has her pulse--or at least the perspective of city's Office of Economic Development--on all of them.

Tam, officially Seattle's "Restaurant Advocate," grew up on the Oregon coast in a restaurant family who had immigrated from China. "We would close the restaurant, clean everything, and turn out the lights. Then we would eat." In the dark.

Her job right now is to help turn *on* the lights so aspiring restaurant owners (as well as existing operators hoping to move or expand) don't get lost in the dark corridors of the urban bureaucracy. Tam is both interpreter and facilitator for the ambitious and the brave who want to throw themselves into the restaurant business, letting them know about leasing contracts, permitting (health, construction, remodeling), human resources requirements, and so on. A daunting task, those 17 permits.

There really is a "GrowSeattle" website, and "restaurant success" is a real mission for the City. And though there's a desk and phone for Tam at OED, she's usually found walking Seattle neighborhoods with clients. In the 18 months she's been on the job, Tam has worked on projects all over town. The "Only in Seattle" initiative isn't hers, but restaurants are an integral part of Seattle neighborhood vitality, so she's part of the team that's helping restaurants in the International District, to name just one. Opening, closing, moving, relocating, expanding from mobile to brick & mortar, each situation (Super Six in Columbia City, Hurry Curry in South Lake Union) is different and requires different doors to open.

Before she moved to 700 Fifth Avenue she worked in the Rainier Valley as a business case manager, and before that, she spent time in India with village-level "micro-entrepreneurs." Is she a bureaucrat herself? Yes, and no, she admits. Bureaucracy is all about process rather than innovation, but, she claims, "Process is nuanced in each city, or even in different municipal departments." From developing a business plan to scouting locations, from getting permits (a nightmare) to stocking the larder, Tam is a sort of midwife, or as she puts it, "the navigator."

"I enjoy bringing everyone to the table," she says. "Everybody loves food."

Chapter 36 · WILL WRITE FOR FOOD

We are not talking about self-described food bloggers who fill their hollow lives with instagrams of oatmeal and ham sandwiches. We are most definitely not talking about the sad and unloved who recount their slights (unfilled water glasses in particular) on Yelp. There is, one would hope, a higher barrier to food criticism than access to a keyboard. So yes, there is the internet, but there are still books as well.

What is today described as Seattle's lively food culture was fortunate to have, in its infancy, a voice that was at once wise, ambitious, and critical. "A Gourmet's Notebook," published reviews in the 1970s by a gang of Madrona neighbors, who took as their model a newsletter in San Francisco filled with long, occasionally pedantic, critiques of local restaurants. Eventually the Notebook became Northwest Best Places, and, when the time came for its demise in 2013, supplanted by easily updated online reviews, it went quietly into that good night.

DAVID BREWSTER The Man Who Loved Words

In the long, dimly lit days before Google was born, we saw the world through a glass, darkly. There were vaults of printed tomes called libraries, there were archives, city directories, gazetteers, card catalogs, and microfiche files. And in every community, every neighborhood, there was a wise person who knew how things actually worked, knew who was who, what was what. Like the guy in shirtsleeves and eye-shade at a metropolitan newspaper's City Desk, in other words. Almost always oldsters, male or female, they sat behind counters at cigar shops and news stands, at lunch counters and taverns, behind a desk in an office or on a bench in a park. Not gossips who traded in rumor but living repositories of local history. The ambitious ones would have turned to politics or real estate, the less practical would have found jobs in academia.

David Brewster is Seattle's own version of Google: a keen intelligence, wide-ranging curiosity, a love of literature, respect for artists, and boundless energy. When he came to Seattle half a century ago (from the wilds of New Jersey and New Haven) it was to teach at the University of Washington and to write for the Seattle *Times*. Instead, he ended up at King Broadcasting, helping the son of founder Dorothy Bullitt run a progressive magazine. Heady times! And, on the side, running a newsletter called *A Gourmet's Notebook*. His support for thoughtful food writing is a relatively small part of his legacy, but we are undeniably a better city for it.

Brewster had a knack for knowing what people were up to, and after the magazine tanked, he applied this gift to the assignment desk at KING TV. And from there to the first of his lasting contributions to Seattle's culture; he launched a weekly newspaper. Around the country, similar votes of confidence in the rising popularity of urban living (*Village Voice, Boston Phoenix, Chicago Reader, SF Bay Guardian*). *Seattle Weekly* was hip, irreverent, a thorn in the side of traditional newspapers, and Brewster was the consummate editor; he knew more about every story than his writers; he knew more about the politicians, the artists, the restaurants. He had me writing about wine and food because I had just returned from two years of living in France; he had a fine palate of his own but gave me wide latitude to write what I wanted. One thing he spotted, early-on, was the need for more information about restaurants and food. He called the first book produced by his writers (and published by Madrona Press) "Seattle's Best Places," which evolved into Northwest Best Places., which became the centerpiece of a company called Sasquatch Press, today the premier publisher of food-related titles (not to mention travel, history, and so on) in the Northwest.

Eventually, the Weekly was sold to New York investment bankers who were gobbling up the old urban weeklies and repackaging them as upscale suburban "shoppers," and Brewster moved on to another form of civic discourse: the old-fashioned lecture hall. Where? In a downtown landmark, of course: Town Hall, a century-old Christian Science church topped with a Romanesque dome. In addition to the Grand Hall, which seated almost 1,000, the building also offered a lower-level performance space.

But journalism called again, and Brewster was persuaded to start an online public affairs magazine called Crosscut, which reunited some of the old Weekly gang (those who were still active, at any rate) and showcased the prodigious talents of Brewster's successor as the city's conscience, Knute Berger. For Brewster, it was another multi-year run at the edge of the spotlight, and no one begrudged him his retirement when he turned over the Crosscut reins.

But then, like an unstoppable whirlwind, Brewster launched yet another venture, a membership library inside the downtown YMCA. Brewster calls it Folio: The Seattle Athenaeum. Unlike politicians who want to build roads or bridges or tunnels or transit systems, Brewster (no less influential than any politician) wants to mold Seattle's civic life. Berger again: "Not Seattle's body as much as its mind and spirit." An ark for books, with Brewster as Noah, the timeless man who knows everything, including the best place to have lunch.

BOOKS ABOUT WHAT WE EAT

Cookbooks are the largest-selling category published in the United States, everything from "The Meatlovers BBQ Guide" to "365 Ways to Cook Carrots." Agents who specialize in cookbooks maintain websites with detailed instructions for authors eager to navigate the shoals of mainstream publishing. And, hey, it can be done. Among the local celebrity authors, Kathy Casey's recipes are published by Chronicle Books, Ethan Stowell has Ten Speed Press, Braiden Rex-Johnson has John Wiley, Kurt Dammeier lined up Clarkson Potter for his first book.

No surprise that Seattle should have its own store for cookbooks, called Book Larder, on the northern slopes of Fremont. It's the outgrowth of a series of lectures (started by the much-loved Kim Ricketts) curated by bibliophile Lara Hamilton.

CYNTHIA NIMS Cooking the Oyster

Cynthia Nims, a disciplined and prolific author, is an energizer bunny of recipe writing (books about mushrooms, salmon, game-night snacks). Now she has turned her attention to oysters. By her count, *Oysters* (from Sasquatch Books) is the ninth or tenth food title she's written under her own name. A graduate of La Varenne in Paris, she also moonlights as a translator and tour guide for Nathan Myhrvold's *Modernist Cuisine* gang. The Oyster book includes tips for the skittish (suggestions for mignonettes, granités and relishes) as well as breading and saucing suggestions for fried, baked, and battered bivalves. A real hunger for this title!

RENEE ERICKSON Menus and Stories

On page 163 of this magical book is a recipe for Pacific Octopus Salad. You have to be willing to step out of your normal pattern of food shopping, and to find a fishmonger willing to think outside the box. Braise the large parts in aromatics and wine, or cook the smaller bits in olive oil. It's not scary if you follow instructions. But by now you know that you can trust Renee Erickson, Seattle's iconic chef. PS: You can buy octopus (fresh or frozen) at the Pike Place Market.

LISA DUPAR Fried Chicken & Champagne

Lisa Dupar grew up in Atlanta, started cooking at home because her mother wasn't interested, and entered an apprenticeship at the Peachtree Plaza hotel after high school. She made her way to Zurich and cooked in European hotels, and, in 1984, landed in Seattle at the Palm Court, the first female chef at a Westin Hotel property.

She left the hotel biz to open hero wn place, Southern Accents, as well as a catering company to provide stylish, high-quality food for private events in the growing market on Seattle's east side. Six years ago she and her husband, Jonathan Zimmer, opened Pomegranate Bistro in Redmond, an intimate spot adjacent to the spacious catering kitchen. When Barack Obama comes to town for a fund-raising dinner, she's in the kitchen.

Yes, there's a yummy recipe for comfort-food fried chicken in the book (saltine crackers do the trick for the crust) but her favorite sophisticated recipe is for Barolo osso buco (there's a source for veal demi-glace if you're not making your own). The book is filled with handwritten observations and kitchen tips ("Mash Notes"), as well as vignettes and charming photographs of eastern Washington wine makers. What comes through, above all, are Dupar's culinary intelligence and generous spirit.

BECKY SELENGUT Tales of Fish & Forests

Seattle chef Becky Selengut is one of the people who will save Western Civilization (alongside fellow Seattleites Langdon Cook, Jon Rowley and Kate McDermott). She knows the difference not just between good and evil (too easy), but, when it comes to seafood, between good and not-good-enough.

Selengut's first book, *Good Fish*, came down squarely on the side of the animals. "We humans," she writes, "eat too much fish," To be clear, she means we eat too much of the *same kinds* of fish. But this is a cookbook, and a very elegant one at that, so you know there's going to be a lot of informative (and politically correct) instruction, accompanied by Clare Barboza's evocative photos. Most importantly: seafood is like produce, and you should only buy what's in season. That may not always mean "fresh," because salmon and tuna might well be better frozen. Farmed salmon, imported shrimp and bluefin tuna are on Selengut's no-no list.

She points out that shellfish, especially local mussels and clams, should come with a state-issued tag that tells the consumer where and when they were harvested. If the retailer can't provide the tag, don't buy.

The well-organized recipes include wine recommendations by Selengut's wife, sommelier (and restaurant GM) April Pogue. There's also a useful list of seafood at risk of mercury contamination. Selengut's strong suits are mouthfuls: seasonality and sustainability. Easy concepts to grasp, not always simple to execute.

Her second book, *Shroom*, is another terrific cookbook dedicated to the fungal fruit of the forest floor: mushrooms.

TIBERIO SIMONE The Man Who Loved Women

Loving women, loving their bodies, a passion long-celebrated, has fallen into disfavor, what with sordid sex scandals at home and abroad. But there is nothing shameful about Tiberio Simone's delight in the human form (in all its forms).

He's a chef, first and foremost, with a business called La Figa Catering. Literally, the fig. Metaphorically, symbolically, and in Italian slang, it's what you think it is. "Bella figa" is the highest compliment a man can pay a woman, Tiberio writes.

"And since when is that a bad thing?" he asks in his book, also called La Figa, subtitled Visions of Food and Form, which features some 40 short essays about food, 20 recipes, and artful photographs by Matt Freedman of models covered in food (cucumbers, berries, zucchini, radishes).

"Our need for food and sex goes way beyond pleasure: we wouldn't exist without them," Tiberio writes. And, just as vegetables come in assorted shapes and sizes, so do the models, young and old, skinny and full-figured, all shades of the rainbow.

TAMARA MURPHY Connecting to the Earth

Sometimes we forget how good simple things can be," Tamara Murphy writes in her wondrous book, "Tender," which also serves as the manifesto for her restaurant on Capitol Hill, Terra Plata. The book gives away a "secret" (actually a well-known truth) that only a few ingredients are necessary to cook and eat well, that what grows together goes together, and that "pure deliciousness" comes from real food.

With that mantra, Murphy encapsulates a philosophy and a way of life: paying attention, making good choices, handling the earth's bounty gently, one meal at a time.

"Perfect foods--fruits and vegetables--come out of the ground and not out of a box or can," she writes. Earth-to-plate, in other words, with careful and caring intervention in the kitchen.

This is not "minimalist," "modernist," or "chef-driven" food. Rather, it is selfless, without ego, almost self-effacing in its refusal to show off fancy techniques or bizarre ingredients. Murphy's resumé includes both a James Beard award and an Iron Chef appearance, but she's too self-aware and introspective for the life of a media hog.

Her cookbook, Tender, is published by a non-traditional publishing company called ShinShinChez, which offered her a collaborative approach to publishing, marketing and community development.

"Our planet needs some crucial nurturing," Murphy writes. We were put on the planet knowing how to take care of ourselves, Murphy believes. "But there's been a big disconnect."

"Support the people who take care of the planet," Murphy says, and she's not just talking about professional chefs. "When you do, you feel better. And you'll be a better cook."

LESLIE MACKIE Macrina's Goddess

As a young baker from Portland, Mackie got her start at Gwen Caldwell Bassetti's Grand Central Bakery. She started Macrina, in Belltown 20 years ago, and her second cookbook, "More From Macrina," has now come out. Among the changes since the first volume was published: Mackie turned over control of the company to the local foursome that owns Pagliacci Pizza and DiLaurenti's, and moved into a new production facility in a century-old building in SoDo.

The best part of the book is its lack of pretension. Want bread with deeper flavors? Roast your seeds and nuts. Want to keep your cupcakes firm, yet moist? Mackie suggests Xantham gum, an ingredient (made from fermented corn syrup) that most cookbooks are afraid to mention, let alone recommend. Want an artisan bread you can make without kneading the dough? Mackie tweaks the famous *New York Times* recipe from 2006 by adding ½ cup of rye flour.

"Leslie Mackie is the goddess of bakers in Seattle," says none other than Tom Douglas.

MICHAEL NATKIN Plugged in Vegetarian

It wouldn't be Seattle if there were not also an earnest, unadorned vegetarian cookbook to put all those passive-aggressive diners and self-centered fusspots to shame. This is where Michael Natkin comes in. His blog, Herbivoracious.com, may be a tongue-twister, but he comes by his enthusiasm honestly: he quit his software job at Adobe after 12 years to concentrate on cooking and photography, but not before he spent months working in professional kitchens.

And how can a reader resist a Spanish lentil and mushroom stew? It's not all tofu: pappardelle with eggplant ragu and fresh ricotta comes right from the Old Country. Natkin celebrates the "golden age" of readily available organic produce and ethnic ingredients: Mexican, Indian, Korean, Middle Eastern. Not to mention World Spice Merchants in the Pike Place Market, and Chef Shop in Interbay.

And, as befits a book by a blogger, "Herbivoracious" is also available in an "enhanced e-book edition," with two dozen videos featuring Natkin touring ethnic markets, introducing ingredients and showing how to choose them, and preparing recipes from the book. The e-book will offers social media functionality for sharing recipes, photos, and video on Facebook, Twitter, and blogs.

LANGDON COOK Hunter of Mushrooms

Langdon Cook is trim, with wiry russet hair and bright blue eyes. He grew up in the wealthy enclave of Greenwich, Conn., prepped at Phillips Exeter, graduated from Middlebury in Vermont. An MFA from U-Dub and a post as book editor at Amazon.com followed, a genteel, Cheever-ish career path if ever there was one. Then he came to realize that his job at Amazon wasn't really to edit books but to "sell things," so when his wife won a fellowship that involved living "off the grid" in southern Oregon, he jumped at the chance. "I'd always liked the outdoors," he says

of this experience, not realizing how it would change his life completely.

Without running water or electricity, Lang (as everyone calls him) learned to live off the fat of the land, and in the half dozen years since he and his wife returned from their isolated sojourn, he's become one of our foremost foragers. He began writing essays about ferns and mushrooms, birds and berries, and, after many rewrites, collected them into a book, *Fat of the Land*, published by an offshoot of Mountaineers Books. Encouraged to start a blog to publicize the book, Lang found himself increasingly admired by sedentary foodies whose foraging expeditions were limited to farmers markets. "I'm surprised by the foodie angle," says the outdoorsy Lang. It turned out that the more he foraged, the more he would cook, so the book also included recipes.

Next project: a guide to North America's regional wild foods, from morels in Michigan to ramps in West Virginia. So off they go, Cook the writer and forager, accompanied by a devoted mushroom picker named Doug Carnell. They are tracking down lobster mushrooms, growing in the forest shade, big and bright red. "With each new discovery, I am filled with immense pleasure. It's like being a kid again, on a treasure hunt in the woods."

The Mushroom Hunters, introduces us to new characters. In addition to Carnell, there are professionals like Jeremy Faber of Foraged & Found Edibles, and Cook's friend, restaurateur Matt Dillon of Sitka & Spruce and half a dozen other ventures. Cook is the guy you want at your side if you so much as set foot into the natural world, though you realize that even in a city park or vacant lot he'd find plenty of interesting stuff to eat.

So what's the subtitle all about? Turns out that "On the Trail of an Underground America" doesn't really refer to the shrooms but to the pickers, "...the men and women–many of them immigrants from war-torn countries, migrant workers, or refugees from the Old Economy–who bring wild mushrooms to market."

To write the book, Cook embedded himself "...in the itinerant subculture of wild mushroom harvesters, a traveling, carnivalesque, mostly hidden confederacy of treasure-seekers that follows the 'mushroom trail' year-round, picking and selling the fungi that land on exclusive restaurant plates around the country." The book takes place over the course of several mushroom seasons and follows the triumphs and failures of a few characters, including an ex-logger trying to pay his bills and stay out of trouble; a restaurant cook turned mushroom broker trying to build a business; and a celebrated chef who picks wild mushrooms on the side to keep in touch with the land.

As always, it's Cook's story-telling skill that keep you reading. Here he is in the Willamette Valley:

"I went to the Oregon Truffle Festival to eat, of course, but I also went to meet the truffle people, these passionate, determined, sometimes loony people who all had one thing in common: a taste for a wild food that no one has ever been able to fully or properly describe, a taste that has driven some to the edge, or beyond the edge, of madness. I myself had never experienced this loss of control. As much as I loved fungi, I still thought of myself as a relatively sane person."

Well, of course Cook succumbs to truffles. You will, too.

GREG ATKINSON Bainbridge Island Forager

Greg Atkinson began his culinary career as a dishwasher in the college cafeteria and quickly worked his way up to chef. He also wrote a column for the *Journal of San Juan Island*, and originally published *In Season*, his first book of recipes and essays, in 1997, when the concept of a culinary memoir was pretty much unknown. Atkinson won the Distinguished Writing Award from the James Beard Foundation in 2001, and today, of course, personal essays are a component of most good food writing.

From the San Juans, Atkinson was summoned to Seattle, where he spent seven years as executive chef at Canlis, then transitioned smoothly into a teaching job at Seattle Community College and, a couple of seasons ago, finally opened his own place, Marché, on Bainbridge Island.

Meantime, Sasquatch Books has reissued *In Season*, replete with familiar recipes: risotto, roast chicken, strawberry sorbet. In spring, there is lamb, there are spot prawns; in summer, you pick berries and roast a whole salmon; in fall, you hunt for chanterelles and pick apples; in winter, there are oysters galore.

"In the woods, finding mushrooms, my very soul is refreshed," writes Atkinson. His style is lyrical and inviting; the recipes have the familiar sense of place, of family, of comforting smells, of light. Reading the book, you feel as if you're sitting in a pool of sunshine, waiting for dinner to come out of the oven.

BLAINE WETZEL & JOE RAY Lummi Island Foragers

Blaine Wetzel, a native of Olympia, has come a long way. After spending a year and a half in the kitchen at Noma, in Copenhagen, he decided it was time to return to his home state and open a restaurant of his own. As it happened, the owners of a resort on remote Lummi Island, off the coast of Bellingham in northern Puget Sound, were looking for a chef, and (as restaurant owners do these days) put an ad on Craigslist. In one of those fortuitous coincidences, Wetzel was hired. He soon found a plot of land on the island where he planted a garden to supply the restaurant with produce. Three years later we are seeing reviews like these: "brilliant

restaurant, producing the type of magic that can be created only when a well-trained, creative chef finds the perfect spot from which to source the freshest and finest of ingredients"; "several of the vegetable dishes will stay with me forever"; and "his hot-smoked, Lummi Island reef net caught salmon might be the best thing I ate all year." His co-author is Joe Ray, winner of travel writing and photography awards . Ray spent a year on the island to chronicle Wetzel's culinary ventures. Geoduck is on the menu, alongside locally foraged mushrooms. You might raise your eyebrows at a broth of roasted madrona bark, but Wetzel and Ray assures us it's a natural digestive and "lovely to drink after a main course of rich lamb or deer."

JILL LIGHTNER Edible Seattle

Edible Seattle, the local bi-monthly franchise, was launched in 2008 under publisher Alex Corcoran, an East Coast transplant who had owned Edible Rhody, with veteran Seattle food writer Jill Lightner providing editorial direction. (Note: I contributed a series of wine column to the magazine.)

Edible Seattle: the Cookbook, edited by Lightner, gets a tone-deaf blurb from its New York publisher: "an adventurous, ingredient-driven destination for gastronomes," but they're just writing ad copy. Lightner sets the tone from the first sentence of her introduction: "Seattle is the biggest small town in the country," where it sometimes seems that everybody knows everybody, especially in the food community. We're also a city of nerds, she points out. Farmers and food artisans are retired scientists, software geeks, medics. Chemical engineers make cider, nurses make cheese.

The book is filled with mouthwatering recipes (Kate McDermott's peach pie), tips from high-profile chefs like Jerry Traunfeld (Poppy), Brian Gojdics (Tutta Bella), Mark Bodinet (Copperleaf), Holly Smith (Cafe Juanita), and Lisa Dupar (Pomegranate).

LEORA BLOOM Food Artisans

Which brings us to the fascinating profiles of local food artisans. Many of them fly below the celebrity radar: Amy Grondin of FV Duna; Wade Bennett of Rockridge Orchards; cheesemaker Rhonda Gothberg; the Vojkovich family at Skagit River Ranch. James Hall, who runs the shigoku oyster beds for Taylor Shellfish gets a profile, as do René Featherstone and Lena Lentz Hardt, who grow whole grains in Marlin, a hamlet in Central Washington; and Georgie Smith of Willowood Farms, who grows heirloom beans on Whidbey Island.

That Seattle's "food scene" would be much poorer without these farm families, fishing boats, and chefs committed to using local ingredients was the impetus for Leora Bloom's book, "Washington Food Artisans."

Bloom, a baker who trained in Paris and contributes to the *Seattle Times*, had never written a book, but told me, "I could have written a whole book about any one of the 17." There's great pleasure in meeting Bloom's subjects. One fascinating profile is about Mary and Duncan MacDonald of Turnbow Flat Farm on the Palouse. Duncan was a free spirit, a Doctor of Jurisprudence, a ski bum, a Microsoftie. Then he tasted Mary's farm-fresh eggs. "This is real food," he realized, and virtually overnight turned himself into a pig farmer.

MODERNIST CUISINE

You can't write about cookbooks in this day and age without mentioning these ambitious and infinitely detailed if overwrought, volumes. The brilliant computer genius (former Chief Technology Officer at Microsoft) and patent troll Nathan Myhrvold (now CEO of Intellectual Ventures) also has a keen interest in cooking, and has the wherewithal to finance a fully equipped research kitchen and food laboratory. Here he employs a staff of earnest culinarians to (literally) dissect recipes and photograph the results. Five volumes, well over $500 for the boxed set. All that sous-vide stuff, all those foams, all those tweezers, blame Dr. Myhrvold. On the other hand, true believers in science over instinct will want the whole set, or at least the simplified, single-volume version.

Chapter 37 · STROKE MY KEYBOARD

Seattle has a thing for food-related websites. UrbanSpoon.com, ChefShop.com, Sur La Table.com, Foodista.com, Barn2Door.com, CowTipping.com, to name just a few. And the granddaddy, Allrecipes.com, launched here in 1997.

ALLRECIPES.COM

Recipe sites are said to be the fourth-most frequented internet category, after porn, search, and social media. (Cookbooks are the best-selling category of books, too.) Allrecipes got its start because Tim Hunt, an early web entrepreneur, wanted a better cookie recipe; the result was a site called Cookierecipe.com. with what was then a most unusual content model: crowdsourcing. Before long, he and his colleagues, Dan Shepherd, Carl Lipo, Mark Madsen, Michael Pfeffer, and David Quinn, had added Cakerecipe.com, Breadrecipes.com and so on, eventually rolling them all into one, Allrecipes.com.

That was 20 years ago. The company became part of Readers Digest in 2006, and was acquired in 2012 for $175 million by powerhouse publisher Meredith (*Better Homes & Gardens*, and a stable of related food, family, home, and lifestyle magazines).

With 1.5 billion site visits a year, Allrecipes is the internet's leading online resource for information about food and cooking, focused not on the frou-frou but on the basics of getting the family's dinner on the table. Readers have contributed 250,000 recipes to the site. (By comparison, the *New York Times* has 17,000.) It ranks in the top 500 websites worldwide, and, boy, do they know what the world is about to have for dinner. At the Seattle headquarters opposite Westlake Center, you can track the activity on 19 Allrceipes websites in 13 languages in 24 countries. The international sites are administered from Seattle, thanks to the polyglot pool of native speakers lured here by the tech industry.

The most downloaded recipe in the US: meatloaf (200,000 times a month). In France, leg of lamb. In India, chicken kebab. More generally: less processed food, more fruit and vegetables. More South American and Japanese recipes. Less meat, but more pies (but using store-bought crusts). For all that, more frequent shopping trips to local bakeries, farmers markets, fruit stands, wine shops, butchers. Now, you could say that these are self-fulfilling prophecies, that cooks with the inclination to look up recipes are more savvy than most, and that trends like "eating healthier" are nothing new. But it's hard to argue with the data provided by hundreds of millions of visits, and that sort of information is like catnip to companies targeting the world's kitchens, and the $300 billion spent on food (and kitchen gadgets) by Allrecipes users. Ad revenues have doubled in the three years since Meredith took over, by the way.

But the Internet is changing. In an age of Facebook and Twitter, of iPads, broadband, and wi-fi, a simple bulletin board is no longer enough to draw and hold onto readers. Meredith, which has revived a dozen legacy magazines, understands all too well the need to retool in order to reengage its audience, both in print and online. Two years ago they launched a print version of Allrecipes, and then they essentially reinvented the website itself, leaving behind the content-heavy bulletin board in favor of a more engaging (and visually attractive) social community where the star is the user.

This shift didn't come easily, but the investment is worth it, according to Stan Pavlovsky, who runs Allrecipes for Meredith Publishing. "We build the technology," he says of his Seattle staff (some 225 in editorial, tech, marketing, ad sales), "but the cooks build the brand."

FOODISTA.COM

You want to tinker with that recipe you found online? Go right ahead. Anyone can edit Foodista.com. It's also a comprehensive directory that links ingredients, techniques, tools and pictures.

Foodista was the brainchild of three veterans of Amazon.com, Barnaby Dorfman (CEO), Sheri Wetherell (VP Editorial) and Colin Saunders (CTO). Dorfman, who'd also worked at Internet Movie Database, realized that people looking for information about movies, say, tend to use the web, but that people are still inclined to use cookbooks when it comes to recipes. Existing sites, Wetherell realized, weren't particularly user-friendly, and anything but "interactive."

So the founders came up with a different model. Their physical space is a collaborative loft in lower Queen Anne. There's no giant server platform; they use Amazon Web Services. Privately owned with no outside funding. And if the Wikipedia model of collaboration is any guide, they've got a million foodies ready to turn the wonders of cloud computing into the Next Big Thing.

Dorfman (Wetherell's husband) and Saunders have gone on to other ventures,0 Wetherell has stayed, with a daily newsletter to over 30,000 subscribers, and monthly site visits over 1.1 million.

ZOMATO GOES STALE

The restaurant review app Zomato.com is retrenching in its battle with Yelp. Zomato's predecessor, Urbanspoon.com, got its start in Seattle eight years ago as a restaurant directory app launched by tech entrepreneurs Ethan Lowry and Adam Doppelt. Within a couple of years they sold the business to IAC Interactive, a growing empire of crowd-sourced sites under the aegis of social-media wizard Barry Diller, and moved into more spacious quarters on Eastlake Avenue. Then Urbanspoon was been gobbled up for a second time, and the new owner, Zomato, decided to swallow hard and discontinue the name.

The buyers were a pair of internet entrepreneurs from India, Deepinder Goyal and a colleague from the New Delhi office of private equity firm Bain & Co., who had launched Zomato at about the same time that Urbanspoon got off the ground in Seattle. Within a few years, Zomato established itself as the leading presence in restaurant search in some 20 countries outside the US.

When they looked at North America, though, they saw a hornet's nest of competing apps. Urbanspoon, by then the oldest, had started small (and local: just Seattle) but soon became part of a $3 billion global communications and entertainment empire, IAC Interactive. And there were soon plenty of competitors in the niche of crowd-sourced restaurant searches: Zagat, OpenTable, Foodspotting, GrubHub, TripAdvisor, and many, many more. Plus a loose cannon, Yelp, that also promised to deliver whatever dish your tummy growled for via its Eat24 affiliate.

The Urbanspoon app had one trick: it would locate and identify nearby restaurants. Just shake your iPhone and you'd get a roster of taco stands, or pizza parlors, or burger bars. It used the iPhone's geolocation function overlaid with restaurant addresses, a novelty at the time. Food bloggers were encouraged to link their posts and photos to the Urbanspoon listing, readers could add their own comments. It was a groundbreaking marriage of tech and taste.

IAC installed professional management, which guided the company towards successful geographic expansion (Canada, the UK) and a venture into restaurant reservations, known as Rezbook, as well. "We want to build out the restaurant experience," former CEO Keela Robison explained from her headquarters offices on

Lake Union. "Not just for our existing users, with, for example, more explanations of menu terms" and maps to locate restaurants inside malls and airports. Urban knife and fork, in other words.

But competition in the niche sector of mobile restaurant search proved to be fierce. Yelp moved aggressively into online reviews, protected by court decisions that permitted anonymous posts. Foursquare built its business model on "finding nearby friends." Google started running reader reviews, as TripAdvisor had already been doing for some time. Groupon, as always, muddied the waters by allowing cheapskate diners to complain about poor service. Outflanked by behemoth Priceline, which bought rival Open Table for $2.6 billion, Urbanspoon finally sold its struggling Rezbook operation in 2013.

Still, with 30 million unique site visitors a month, Urbanspoon remained a takeover target. The first-and-fastest pursuer was Zomato, whose CEO, Deepinder Goyal, saw Urbanspoon as a golden opportunity to get into the US market and came from India armed with a a very big check. After five months of tinkering with a new site design for Urbanspoon that didn't meet expectations, Goyal gave the order to pull the plug. There will be some adjustments to make sure ratings remain consistent after the content migrates to Zomato, but one thing that's gone for good is the "shake to search" feature. Nearby restaurant locations still show up, but you no longer have to twitch your wrist.

Sad ending to all this.

Alas, the sauce curdled. Zomato shut down its US operations and sent the two dozen workers in its Seattle office into the street. The Dallas headquarters will also be closed.

Meantime, the Zomato.com website is advertising three dozen open positions, virtually of them in India.

FEXY MEDIA

You know that mysterious blob in the fridge? First, it starts to get moldy, and then you have a nightmare that it starts to grow and one day it will grab you and eats you? Nah, won't happen to you, right, because you keep a close eye on your fridge. Well, hah! Here's a totally under-the-radar company called Fexy Media.

The Fexy triumvirate consists of Lisa Sharples, who spent almost six years as president of Allrecipes.com; her husband Cliff, a former exec with Home Away; and Ben Sternberg, an investment adviser who previously held a top role at Cheezburger. They've raised $6 million from investors for their venture; the company is based in an office park on Mercer Island.

The trio started as Teneology in late 2014 with the goal of creating a digital media company with a portfolio of food-focused brands popular with the 21-49 female demographic. Their most recent acquisition is a 13-year-old cooking blog called Simply Recipes, led by Elise Bauer, which offers suggestions for millennials who want to cook at home, from scratch.

"We are very deliberate about our acquisition strategy as we build a complementary portfolio of food-focused brands," said Cliff Sharples. And what are the others? Serious Eats, Roadfood, The Food Lab, and Relish, as well as a consulting division to advise other companies on tactics to reach their target demographic.

ONLINE FOOD LINES Eater, SeattleDining

It's not just that we are what we eat, we're also more and more what we read about eating, what we're tweeting and instagramming and blogging about what we're eating.

Nobody understands this better than Eater.com, a national group of websites that focus with uncommon fervor on the food at local bistros, the peeps in restaurant kitchens, and the ever-shifting patterns of who's cooking up what. Who's in, who's out, who's planning a new spot. All the inside-baseball stuff that used to be fodder for press agent emails finally finds a voice, thanks to Eater, which relies on a small group of part-timers in Seattle and an astute cadre of editors at the national level (part of Vox.com) to feed ideas and a consistent style. Let it be admitted that this writer, too, regularly picks up the keyboard and fires off tips and sightings to the Mothership. Adam Callaghan plays the role of Captain Picard, with Megan Hill as his current Sulu.

Connie Adams, a PR veteran, and her business partner, Tom Mehren, have been publishing SeattleDining.com since 1999. (I write a monthly review for the site.) Mehren also publishes a motorcycle magazine, Sound Rider. SeattleDining also produces an annual fund-raising event, Cooking With Class.

Chapter 38 · SHOW & TELL
Classes & Tours

I'm as dismayed as anyone that the Food Channel has degenerated into a network of ads for industrial dreck masquerading as edible food, and that so many chefs are wasting their talents dumping ingredients into mixing machines for the TV cameras. On the positive side, the number of Americans interested in preparing food (as opposed to opening a box) seems to be growing, and so are the number of classes designed for home cooks. Along with that, Seattle's reputation as a foodie hotspot means that more visitors want to sample the local culinary scene.

TSELANI RICHMOND Chopping Your Way to Better Health

We'll leave for another day the argument that Walmart's business model has done great harm to the nation's independent businesses, especially in small towns. For the moment, let's applaud them for taking a stand in favor of sustainability and health. ("Force of Nature," published by HarperBusiness, describes the "green-washing" of Walmart).

Which brings us to Tselani Richmond, a Paris-trained, Portland-based chef. She was hired a few years back by Jonathan Hensley, the then-rotund CEO of Regence Blue Shield, to help develop a program that would encourage better eating by his policy-holders. "We didn't want to be a company that just looked after sick people," Hensley explains, in what has become a mantra for HMO executives.

Tse (pronounced "Say") was perfect. Telegenic and down-to-earth, she travels the Northwest giving hands-on cooking classes and shooting how-to-cook videos. Students learn how to hold an onion for safe and easy slicing (make a "claw" with your left hand to keep the onion steady and guide the knife), how to sauté mushrooms (no oil, no salt), how to sear a steak (hot pan, hot oil, no peeking for two minutes, don't crowd the meat, let it rest for ten minutes before cutting), how to make vinaigrette (tablespoon of mustard, tablespoon of vinegar, add pinches of salt & pepper before drizzling in oil, then whisk vigorously).

Buy fresh, buy seasonal, they're watchwords for Chef Tse, as they should be for anyone who wants to eat healthy food. Better still: avoid buying food in boxes, bags or cans. They're full of unhealthy chemical preservatives. (As for that staple of American home cooking, frozen peas? Quite possibly from China.) Here's another advantage of "real food." It's actually harder to eat. So-called "easy-to-eat" boxed food, with its artificially creamy texture, makes it all-too-easy to overeat. You feel full with a meal of real food because you have to chew!

KATHLEEN FLINN Sharpening Your Knives

At the QFC on Broadway one day some years ago, Kat Flinn stood behind a woman with a shopping cart full of boxed industrial cans and boxes ("edible, food-like substances") like Hamburger Helper and Dino Bites, complain about the price of chicken breasts. Trying to be helpful, Flinn pointed out that whole chickens were on sale for 99 cents a pound. "But I wouldn't know what to do with a whole chicken," the woman said.

From that moment of epiphany, that most housewives really have very little idea how to actually cook, Flinn embarked on what has become her calling. To write her manifesto, "The Kitchen Counter Cooking School," she recruited a group of nine women (the lone man to volunteer dropped out), and, in the privacy of their own kitchens, gave them ten weeks of cooking lessons...and a lifetime of confidence in their own abilities.

The universe doesn't need another restaurant chef, Flinn believes, so much as it needs people who can teach others how to cook. "Cooking on TV is like a magic show," she says. She knows better, having trained at Le Cordon Bleu in Paris.

One revelation for Flinn herself: "Season to taste" as a recipe instruction is useless, since most of her students have no idea what the dish was supposed to taste like in the first place, and don't trust themselves to know. So the back of her book includes a helpful "cheat sheet" of flavor profiles: French is "butter, shallots, onions, celery." Italian is "garlic, onions, basil, prosciutto, parmesan ..." Tex-Mex is "cumin, chili powder ... " North African is "mint, lemon, saffron, turmeric ..." Not a magic show.

DIANE LAVONNE Market Kitchen

Diane Lavonne grew up in Minnesota, where her grandparents had a dairy farm. She worked in the healthcare industry for several Fortune 500 companies, then started a catering business. In addition to hosting events for many local companies and foundations, her Market Kitchen has hosted international visitors (Korean journalistsm Brazilian agri-business folks, Italian cookbook writers). She teaches free classes for the Market Foundation, pairings of libations and food, classes hosted by other chefs from pastry to sushi, and tours of Pike Place Market whose vendors comprise part of an extended family of which Diane has been a part for over 30 years.

WAYNE JOHNSON Fare Start

Think of him as the Sage of South Lake Union. He is Wayne Johnson, the newly appointed executive chef at FareStart. A fixture at major Seattle restaurants like Andaluca and Ray's Boathouse, Johnson has long had an interest in culinary education as a path out of poverty. It's a 16-week program at FareStart, Each day, up to 200 people come into the restaurant for lunch to enjoy delicacies such as goat cheese bruschetta, curry lamb cannelloni and green tea crème brûlée. Founded more than 20 years ago to help the homeless, FareStart recently partnered with the Washington State Department of Corrections to also help people coming out of prison.

BRIDGET CHARTERS Hot Stove Society

When Tom Douglas and his lieutenants went looking for new ventures, they didn't stop at restaurants. The block-long project along Sixth Avenue does include one eatery, Tanaka San, but also encompasses a coffee-&-juice meeting place called Assembly Hall; and a deli called Home Remedy, that also houses a flower shop. They already had an event space (Palace Ballroom), and several smaller projects in the works (including a pizzeria at the new Starbucks Roastery on Capitol Hill), but then they thought about the Hotel Andra, at 4th & Virginia, where they were already operating a dining room called Lola.

There was unused space on the mezzanine level of the hotel; T-Doug turned it into a Scandinavian bar called Lök. And the banquet rooms behind those balcony doors? Well, that became a year-round, mainstream cooking school, the Hot Stove Society.

Yes, there were other culinary centers around town, some operating as chains (Le Cordon Bleu, Art Institute), some as offshoots of community colleges for people who wanted professional, vocational training (South Seattle, Central, Bellevue, Renton, etc.). And from time to time, restaurant chefs have offered cooking classes to their fans, and cookware stores like Sur La Table (and the late, lamented Dish It Up) have also offered hands-on classes. But Hot Stove Society was designed for serious amateurs rather than line-cooks-in-training. (In that regard, the model was more like Blue Ribbon on Lake Union or Diane's Market Kitchen on Post Alley.)

To run his program, Douglas and his CEO, Pamela Hinckley, recruited Bridget Charters, one of the Art Institute's top instructors. "Her energy, passion and professional past guarantees that we are going to have a rocking good time while learning new skills," Hinckley said last year.

As for Charters, she started at Gonzaga, moved to San Francisco, and returned to Seattle to work in TV production with Italian chef Nick Stellino. She continues to work for food festivals around the country (New York, South Beach, Aspen) while managing Hot Stove Society's full schedule.

The good news is that the dozen Tom Douglas restaurants and catering divisions have plenty of culinary talent, so it's easy to slot in an on-staff *pastaiolo* like Herschell Taghap, or even a celebrity guest chef like Armandino Batali or Thierry Rautureau. What the downtown location offers as well is that all-American corporate event known as "team building." Nothing like getting your hands on some hamburger to strengthen those bonds with co-workers.

MAXIME BILET Imagine Food

He's Maxime Bilet, a Frenchman, for what it's worth, and a fine writer and cook. She's Erica Chriss, the CEO of his new company, Imagine Food, and she's in charge of moving Maxime into the private sector. He's the author of Modernist Cuisine, you see, the seminal tome (four volumes, $250) produced by Nathan Myrhvold's Intellectual Ventures in 2014. The question on everyone's mind, now, is whether he can stand alone in his custom-built kitchen and event space at the foot of Denny.

ANGELA SHEN Savor Seattle Tours

Angela Shen arrived in Seattle with her husband a decade ago, with an MBA from the Wharton School and a stint in brand management with Quaker Oats. But it was hubby who had the job and Angela who had no network of personal or professional connections to fall back on. Still, off she went to chat up vendors at the Pike Place Market, then return with out-of-town visitors (as well as locals) on a two-hour Food & Culture tour. Her watchword was FLOSS: Fresh, local, organic, seasonal and sustainable. She's been branching out, too, adding Capitol Hill to the map, adding chocolate to the tour topics, adding a three-day San Juan Islands tour, and, most recently, adding a four-course, four-restaurant "progressive dinner" downtown.

Savor Seattle also provides the staffing for local food tours offered by a prestigious international bus company, Tauck Tours. Among Shen's earliest backers: Tom Douglas (who asked if she needed office space), and Kurt Dammeier (who would gladly joint-venture with Savor Seattle should the opportunity arise). Shen maintains a wide-eyed sense of wonder at how far the company has come.

Shen's latest offering is called the Seattle Dinner Soirée; for under $100 you get a four-course (and four-drink) dine-around at four restaurants. On a recent evening, we started with an aperitif and first course at Loulay; a plate of mussels and a sauvignon blanc at Market Hall; a fine piece of wild Alaska salmon and a glass of Oregon pinot noir at Blueacre; and a slice of chocolate almond cake and a nightcap at Tanakasan. Shen works with close to 50 restaurants, and they appreciate her reputation for punctuality; guests are served as soon as they're seated (though never rushed).

MICHAEL ROGERS Show Me Seattle

Seattle Food Tours was the original name given to tours of local gastronomic hotspots in the Pike Place Market, Belltown, and Capitol Hill. Owner Michael Rogers, originally from Louisiana, started the company in 2007 and would lead "epicurean walking tours" of Capitol Hill. More recently he added general-interest programs, aboard a minibus, and rebranded the entire company as Show Me Seattle.

LIZ McCUNE Eat Seattle

Want a corporate team-building exercise? How about cooking together? Liz McCune's company is up for that assignment, alongside traditional walking tours through the Pike Place Market (Wednesday through Sunday at 10). Or, if you're hungry for more, a shopping trip with a chef, followed by a cooking class and a three-course meal.

McCune got her start at the Cordon Bleu in Paris, traveled through Spain and Italy with her husband, and returned to Seattle with the idea of recreating the sense of adventure and exploration she'd experienced visiting the markets of Europe.

21 ACRES

That's Chef Dina Phelps teaching a knife skills class at 21 Acres, the culinary education and agricultural center in Woodinville. Classes are given throughout the year in "Growing, Eating, Living" for professionals and devoted eaters alike. Ambitious vegetable gardener? There's a class for you. Beekeeping? Yup. Plants for winter color? Check. Solar home design? Got that, too. All this takes place in the grandly named Center for Local Food and Sustainable Living.

Chapter 39 · APPLAUSE LINES

If you go through life believing the world is a dangerous place where bad people will rob and cheat you, you're right. On the other hand, if you go through life believing in the goodness of mankind, you're right, too. Depends on your outlook. The best part of writing a book like this is realizing that in Seattle at least the good guys outnumber the bad, that we are home to more lambs than wolves.

The battle, in our time, is not between good and evil, or rich and poor; it is between those who look no further than the present and those who believe we must act as stewards of the planet's resources.

JONATHAN KUMAR Doer of Good Deeds

Say hello, won't you, to Jonathan Kumar, 27 years old and recently settled at the intersection of Cap Hill and Madison Valley. He's originally from Michigan, where he earned a degree in Informatics and Economics; his mission in Seattle is to nibble away at two of urban America's biggest problems: feeding the hungry and housing the homeless. With encouragement from investors in Ann Arbor, he developed an app, FoodCircles, that lets generous diners make charitable contributions that translate directly into meals for the hungry. Unfortunately, it hasn't been a particularly easy sell, though not for want of trying. Better success with the non-profit beneficiaries, notably the Union Gospel Mission.

The other half of Kumar's mission is to provide services like laundry, groceries, clothing, and transportation to the homeless and forlorn folk who ask for spare change on street corners. Donors who sign up receive a "beacon" (a fob the size of a quarter) which they can activate to transfer funds (a dollar or more) to needy individuals. More online at vimeo.com; search for GiveSafe.

Similarly, a program called "The Pledge" distributes stickers to neighborhood businesses offering bathrooms and other personal services to homeless people.

DENIS HAYES Udder Truth-Teller

 The country's largest private philanthropy, the Bill & Melinda Gates Foundation, which gave away two billion dollars last year, is based in Seattle, but it's not the only one. There's a tradition in American public life of family philanthropy (the Ford Foundation, the Carnegie Endowment), and many of this region's First Families have followed that tradition to pass along their legacy. Not the least of these is the Bullitt Foundation, guardian of the fortune accumulated by lumber baron Stimson Bullitt in the early 20th century and enhanced with the sale of King Broadcasting.

Today, from its award-winning headquarters on Seattle's Capitol Hill (the country's "greenest" building), the Bullitt Foundation leads the nation in environmental responsibility. Its chief executive is Denis Hayes, who decades ago spent a post-college summer as an intern with King Broadcasting in Portland. Then, working on environmental issues with Wisconsin Sen. Gaylord Nelson, his assignment was to launch an ambitious nationwide concept called Earth Day, which he did, on April 22nd, 1970. Hayes went on to expand Earth Day to 180 countries, and eventually returned to Seattle and the fold of the Bullitt Foundation.

His latest book, "Cowed," written with his wife, attorney and educator Gail Boyer Hayes, bewails the increasing reliance on bovines to provide the planet with protein, almost 100 million cows in the US alone, one for every three humans. Feeding all those cows (so they will eventually feed us) requires vast resources. Some 100 million acres of corn alone. Unfathomable volumes of water, vast amounts of antibiotics. Much wringing of hands, along with predictable calls to eat less beef.

The worst part of our national reliance on beef may well be its energy inefficiency. Hayes points out that "finishing" cattle on corn, rather than grass, is ten times more costly. And corn, unfortunately, gives cows indigestion and gas.

But, surprise! We could break the "bovine industrial complex" by shifting away from cows to bison, for example. They range free, don't need a lot of human attention, drink less water, plow through snow on their own, don't need costly supplements, and don't trample their grazing grounds. Almost wiped out by hunters who shot them for sport and took only their pelts, bison are making a comeback; a few commercial herds are supplying meat (healthier than beef, by the way) to upscale markets. It's a tough sell, since bison runs into the established bulwark of the politically powerful cattle industry, an industry that has passed so-called "ag-gag" legislation in 13 states that prohibits criticism of feed lots or cattle pens.

It should be pointed out that "Cowed" is not a screed against meat. Rather, it ends with a note of thanks: "For ten thousand years, you've given us meat and milk, pulled our plows, and pulled your weight in helping make Western civilization possible.

BILL MARLER Food Safety Advocate

The modern world is filled with people who gratefully and ravenously eat anything. In fact, much of history is fundamentally a search for secure sources of food. Governments may well declare "food safety" among their primary missions, yet some of their citizens will nonetheless sicken and die.

The US government did not always regulate food safety. During the Spanish-American war, unscrupulous purveyors sent "meat" laced with borax, formaldehyde and copper sulfate to the troops on the front lines. Similar preservatives were common in civilian food as well. It wasn't until the second half of the 19th Century that there were reliable tests for arsenic. Even so, in 1937 a Tennessee company called Masengill, produced a drug called Elixir Sulfanilamide to combat streptococcal infections. The active ingredient was dissolved in a raspberry-flavored diethylene glycol, sold without a prescription. Dozens of people, many of them children, died. In the ensuing public outrage, the US Food & Drug Administration came into existence.

Bill Marler is a smiling gent with a unique law practice: on behalf of the victims of food poisoning, he sues companies that sell unsafe food. And he wins. Marler first came to public attention in 1993 with the infamous Jack in the Box outbreak of E. Coli which sicked hundreds who had eaten undercooked burger patties. Marler represented the most seriously injured survivor in a landmark $15.6 million settlement with the company. Since then, he has filed lawsuits against dozens of food companies (from Chili's and Chi-Chi's, to KFC and McDonald's), winning over $600,000,000 for victims of food borne illnesses. Still, it was not until a second E.coli outbreak, in spinach, that US food safety laws were overhauled.

Much about food safety is misunderstood. The madness of King George III was probably due to arsenic poisoning. As described in a book called "Death in the Pot," ingesting moldy grain could produce manifestations ascribed to witchcraft. Indeed the fungus known as *Claviceps purpurea*, which we call ergot, produces hallucinogenic consequences described as St. Vitus Fire. Outbreaks of mass hysteria, wherever they were recorded, could have been nothing more than ergot poisoning. As recently as 1951, in Pont-St.-Esprit in southern France, the village baker used flour contaminated with ergot to make his baguettes. They called it *le pain maudit:* it killed four and sickened hundreds. In 1985, a quantity of Austrian wine was found to be adulterated with diethylene glycol (antifreeze). The following year, methanol was discovered in wines from Piedmont; 25 people died. In 1998, 80 people died in Kenya after drinking methanol-laced whiskey. In Estonia, in 2001, 67 died after drinking vodka laced with methanol. In Spain that same year, thousands were sicked and nearly 2,000 people died after consuming contaminated rapeseed oil.

Political poisonings abound. A woman named Ma Anand Sheela, deputy to the infamous Bagwan Shree Rajneesh, hatched a plan to contaminate the residents of eastern Oregon with salmorendena she ordered through the mail; two Wasco County commissioners were sickened. In 2004, a candidate for the presidency of Ukraine, Viktor Yushchenko, was fed a near-fatal level of dioxin at a dinner meeting with security agents in Kiev; he was badly disfigured but recovered. A Russian dissident, Alexander Litvinenko, was not so fortunate; in London in 2006 he drank a cup of tea that a KGB agent had laced with radioactive polonium and perished.

Back in Seattle, Marler is the recipient of the Outstanding Lawyer Award from the King County Bar Association. More to the point, he travels and lectures widely on food safety, and donates to industry groups for the promotion of food safety.

It's worth mentioning that you won't find Marler on the "raw milk" side of the longstanding debate over the safety of unpasteurized dairy products. "A much higher risk of contamination with harmful bacteria," he says, and says parents shouldn't give unpasteurized milk to their kids. The list of potentially life-threatening diseases is scary: e.coli infection can lead to hemlytic ureic syndrome, camylobacter to Guillaime Barre Syndrome, salmonella can lead to Reactive Arthritis, listeria can cause pregnant women to miscarry. Keeps him busy, researching, litigating, and writing marlerblog.com, one of the most fascinating food chronicles in Seattle.

MARTIN BARRETT Good in Every Glass

Wine, nectar of the gods, is what the elites drink, an expensive indulgence for snobs. Martin Barrett has heard it all. He's a wine guy, former owner of Cana's Feast in Oregon, now living in Seattle and running inner-city social welfare programs.

Over a glass of wine one evening with his longtime friend Monte Regier--a human resources manager who'd just returned from a stint on a hospital ship in Liberia--the talk turned to the contrast between Africa's grinding poverty and America's pockets of poverty in a land of abundance. Barrett realized that for a dollar a day he could feed a hungry kid. Not in some distant land but here at home, where he knew well that there are too many hungry kids. "This glass of wine," he said, "could feed a kid."

269

And so was born the concept of Sozo (a Greek word that suggests rescue), a unique project that shares the revenue from local wine sales with local food banks.

Barrett understood that Sozo had to start with excellent wines, "but the last thing the industry needs at this point is another new winery." Yet, there's a lot of good juice out there, languishing, begging for a good home. Tasting tank samples around Woodinville that seemed to have some potential, Barrett and Regier discovered the talents of Cheryl Barber Jones, the former wine maker for Chateau Ste. Michelle, now a freelance consultant. She began working her "magic," blending stray lots so that the sum was greater than its parts.

In its first year, Sozo released six or seven wines, whites like riesling and pinot gris; reds like pinot noir, tempranillo, a Rhone blend, a Bordeaux blend, in addition to special bottlings for the Rotary Club. So far, so good. In fact, the Rhone blend was named best of class at the Los Angeles International Wine & Spirits Competition last year and the Bordeaux blend won a gold medal; priced at $120, it sold out.

"Cheryl's crafted some amazing wines," Barrett says. So the "cause" is a bonus. There's a number in the lower right hand corner of the wine label, the number of food bank meals that the sale of the bottle will generate. Not a guilt-inducing "instead of" admonition thatyou could have made a donation instead of buying the bottle, but a satisfying "in addition to." Five meals for the riesling, 25 for the Bordeaux.

The biggest supporters have been local restaurants, over 70 at last count, from swanky spots like Canlis to neighborhood eateries like Magnolia's Mondello. There's no mention on the list that there's anything special about the wines, but each restaurant names its own charity (Canlis picked the None Will Perish foundation; Mondello named the Ballard Food Bank). Sozo writes the check, and the restaurant mails it to the beneficiary.

So far, the Sozo project has generated over half a million meals for hungry kids., and has expanded its "product line" to include coffee and chocolate. It also partners with a dozen companies that are looking for ways to connect to the community. "People who work in the private sector think we're crazy to be giving away our profits. Yet the idealists in the non-profit world probably didn't have the discipline and analytical skills to make this happen." Barrett says. "With Sozo, we seem to have created the best of both worlds."

And now that Sozo has moved into 40 states, Barrett is finding that his best market is corporate gift boxes, often in partnership with Mercedes Benz dealerships.

RICK STEVES Good in Every Loaf

Globetrotting TV hosts are nothing new today, but Rick Steves created the franchise three decades ago. Open, trusting, and generous, he started with a tiny travel agency in the northern suburb of Edmonds, where he sold back packs, Eurail passes, and his own guidebooks ("Europe Through the Back Door"). And he ceaseless promotes his charity of choice, Bread for the World, "a collective Christian voice" that lobbies for policies to end hunger around the world; the new Global Food Security Act is an example of their work.

4KURT DAMMEIER Food Purist

The first chapter in Kurt Dammeier's new book, *Pure Food*, is titled "A history of industrial food in America" and it outlines his mission, to teach people the dangers of factory-processed and artificially refined ingredients. "Gatorade is the new cigarette, and cigarettes were already the worst product in history," he says in a TED Talk that's going viral on the Internet. "Our food system is polluted," he maintains, citing cancer and diabetes. "First it makes you sick, and then it kills you." Drinking a bottle of vitamin water is like eating two and a half Krispy Kreme donuts; drinking one bottle of Gatorade is the equivalent of eating 13 cubes of sugar. And the worst part: helicopter parents who try to show their love by giving their kids Gatorade at sports events.

"Read food labels," Dammeier implores his listeners. "Vote with your dollars for a better food system." Certainly Dammeier has, donating a goodly chunk of his company revenues to the Beecher's Pure Foods Kids Foundation. The message of the foundation (better-informed choices for healthier eating) reaches 15,000 kids a year, mostly 4th and 5th graders, through two and a half hour workshops that end with kids cooking their own vegetarian chili. So far, 90,000 kids in Seattle and New York City have been through the program.

Dammeier didn't start his investment career in the food business but he did put monty into Pyramid Breweries, and then bought Pasta & Co. (OK, Amazon, too.) When the Seattle Garden Store in the Market closed down he stepped in to cobble together a deal. He had his retail location but no product. He wanted to make a cheese named for his grandfather, a gent surnamed Beecher. He hired Brad Sinko, whose family business, Bandon Cheese, had just been snatched up by Tillamook. Together they found Green

Acres Farm, a dairy in Duvall; Dammeier bought and leased them a herd of Jersey cows. While they waited for their inventory to mature, they sold cheese curds at the Market.

Today the offices of Sugar Mountain are in the heart of South Lake Union, at Westlake and Blanchard. It's Bike-to-Work week for everyone at the company. Dammeier lives on Mercer Island, and he's no slouch. Having pedaled his own machine, a fat-tired, disc-brake Cirrus "specialized" commuter bike across the I-90 bridge, he lopes around the offices on Westlake in shorts and canvas lace-ups. "We hire a lot of people," he tells a visitor, "but we no longer offer amenities like parking or bus passes." Instead, he hires people–non-tech people–who already live in South Lake Union. The last 20 people to join his company walk to work.

And now comes Dammeier's second cookbook, another beautifully detailed volume of "threaded" recipes so you can reuse the leftovers from the weekend roast for healthy snacks during the week. Its pages are covered with hand-scribbled notes, and there are different colors of ribbons so a reader can keep track of more than one cooking project at a time. But it's also a manifesto. Once Dammeier was making money, he turned his thoughts to challenging the addictive products of Big Food. The answer was providing kids the tools they need to make better decisions about what to eat. But "No one was doing the kind of work we had in mind," So he started the Foundation.

"So that's what we set out to do here at Sugar Mountain -- change the way people eat by showing them how delicious food is in its natural state...without any unnecessary additives or processing." Seattle cannot ask for more, cannot ask for better.

Chapter 40 · PITCHFORKS

Comes time to say what we really think. Seattle has a reputation for being passive-aggressive, for being too nice. So here we go, we're calling out the bad guys, the assholes, the crooks, the charlatans. Sorry if you think there aren't quite enough, especially considering how many good guys got into the book; feel free to nominate additional villains.

SEATTLE SO WHITE

Why does the food in so many Seattle restaurants taste the same? One possibility: because so many of the cooks come from similar backgrounds, and they're cooking for people pretty much like themselves. Very few women, almost no people of color.

FRANKENFISH AquAdvantage Salmon

Is this the future of food? A genetically engineered super-salmon from an outfit called AquaBounty. Unlike other farmed Atlantic salmon, Super-Salm carries a gene from an eel-like creature called the ocean pout that allows it to grow to marketable size in half the time it takes a regular Chinook to reach maturity, 18 months instead of three years.

The Food & Drug Administration says it's safe. Sales have been okayed pending approval of a new label. And then, who knows what else? Faster-growing pigs, beef resistant to mad-cow disease, and so on.

This ocean pout character (one ugly fish, by the way) has a remarkable ability to live in near-freezing water. Natural antifreeze in its veins. It doesn't go dormant. That's the ticket to Super-Salm's rapid growth. AquaBounty says it will take great precautions to prevent SuperSalms from escaping the North Atlantic hatcheries; you wouldn't want them to mate with "regular" wild salmon, would you?

VOTING WITH YOUR FORK

A lot of companies are trying to fake it; scores of packaged food products claim to produce better health. Pure poppycock. Eating Activa yogurt doesn't eliminate indigestion; drinking Pom Wonderful doesn't "cheat death." These health claims are simply part of Big Food's campaign to sell more stuff, from "healthy" breakfast cereal to "healthy" mac & cheese. It works because the audience is gullible. "The majority of American consumers really believe in the concept that certain foods provide benefits that go beyond basic nutrition or reduce the risk of disease," says a spokesman for the International Food Information Council, an outfit financed by (you guessed it) the food industry itself. Just as many American consumers have often been persuaded to vote against their best interests, they can almost as easily be persuaded to eat against their best interests by an army of hucksters and charlatans. Tax cuts for the rich may be iniquitous economics, but eating Quaker Oats for a healthy heart is no less pernicious medicine.

RESTAURANT REVIEWS Bylined Yet Anonymous

I've been guilty myself of stealth reviews, swooping in on some unsuspecting owner or chef without calling ahead, without warning. I don't do it often because it doesn't actually work very well. I don't wear a disguise, I don't use a fake name. And by now, after decades of doing this, my mug (and my hat) are fairly well known around town, so I often get spotted by waiters, bussers, sous-chefs, hosts. I don't know how the other guys do it, but I usually (not always) make a reservation to let them know I'm coming. Unlike a few other freelancers and bloggers I don't ask for freebies; I don't have a corporate expense account and I don't forget to tip the wait staff. So sometimes I'll read a review in a local publication and I'm embarrassed. Not because I disagree with a reviewer's opinion but with the disconnect between words written (often quite generous) and the final grade (stingy to the point of avarice).

It pains me to write this in such a public forum, but it needs to be said, and to an audience of more than one specific person. Look, I get it if you're just saying that you went to a restaurant several times and were served "many underwhelming or poorly executed dishes." Clams too salty? Salmon too dry? Crumbs not removed? Fine, do what everyone does in that situation, if you're required to publish a review: give the place two stars and move on. But don't, for heaven's sake, complain about the concept of "land-based, seasonally driven foods" and "artisan cooking techniques" because that, frankly, is what everyone is doing (it's called running a restaurant kitchen).

You cannot gush over handmade tortillas at one spot (made with "nixtamalized, genetically diverse, landrace corn grown on small Mexican farms") and artfully plated "beef short ribs draped in silky green chile and avocado salsa" at another, and then spit in the face of two of Seattle's hardest-working restaurateurs because they don't remove your dirty silverware fast enough. I know you know the owners. Were they haughty? Lazy? Frazzled? Or were you out to prove a point? That you're not always a Provi-Two-Shoes?

"The star ratings are assigned by me," the author wrote back. "They take into account food, service and ambiance, though the food component probably carries the most weight. The star ratings are a measure of my enthusiasm for the establishment and they reflect how well the restaurant delivers what they promise the customer--which is why a pub or a pizzeria might earn three stars and a more ambitious fine-dining venue might merit less." In the print edition, this explanation of the star ratings: One star means "Adequate."

After years of no four-star reviews, you suddenly bestowed two (Bateau and Canlis). After years of no one-star reviews, you suddenly launched three (Orfeo, Dunbar Room, Bookstore Bar). Where's the editor who might ask you, ever so politely, whether you really want to go nuclear on these three specific establishments (two of them are in hotels, so their dining rooms are subject to an entirely different set of issues), but one of them, after all, belongs to people whom you know. You, of all people, should know better than to skewer them with the one-star sword. "Room to grow," you say? There's a place for petulant, irresponsible, ill-considered reviews like that; it's called Yelp.

RESTAURANT REVIEWS Anonymous

Yelp is now in its mid-teens (you know what a handful kids are at that age) and a ubiquitous feature of American life, all the more important because we're eating out more than ever. The stats are impressive: over 130 million unique visitors a month in the US alone, 57 million reviews. Yelp itself isn't the arbiter but the forum where the merits of an establishment are laid out, played out, flayed out by hordes of (some would say) liars, beggars, tramps, and thieves, or expertly dissected by a swarm of (what others might call) discerning critics. Either way, Yelp provides a platform from which to view and admire the train wreck.

Yes, there are algorithms written by Yelp engineers that flag reviews suspected of being hit jobs by competitors or blow jobs by paid fluffers. On any given day, some 40,000 reviews are held up or removed by Yelp staffers, due to the unfathomable algorithms or to flags from customers or business owners.

Katy Hewitson Romdall came to Seattle eight years ago fresh out of college (U Mass, Boston) for a job in tech, fiercely determined to take full advantage of her newly adopted city. It was a propitious time. Various guidebook-style websites (Citysearch, Urbanspoon, TripAdvisor) were adding user comments to their directory listings, with Yelp users in particular taking passive-aggressive advantage of their anonymity to complain about the slightest perceived insult to their self-centered sense of entitlement. (Waitresses who don't refill water glasses are targets of particularly vengeful bolts of wrath.) In 2009 she became the public face of Yelp in Seattle, the one whose job description is "community engagement," not sales (definitely not) but liaison with consumers and business owners, sponsor of public and private events, and author of a newsletter with some 650,000 readers.

The irony is that it's no longer enough for a restaurant owner to serve a killer carbonara or an artisan to fashion unique leather goods; they have to learn a whole new set of skills to fight back against social media. Friends can't be too fawning lest they get screened out by Yelp's inscrutable algorithms. You have to guard against sabotage from competitors; even your own customers can turn on you at any moment.

Hewitson-Romdall hears the frustrations, and is reminded of her own family's commercial ventures. (Her older brother is following in dad's footsteps as a pharmacist.) "I would never do anything to hurt small business owners," she says. Yet Yelp continues to pretend that it's simply a platform for free speech. In July, 2016, it sued a business owner who warned visitors to its website against posting critical reviews on Yelp. But the underlying legal issue remains unresolved: whether Yelp can held responsible for inaccurate (or malicious) posts by the people who read the site.

GOODBYE, GOOD RIDDANCE

Boeing's Long Goodbye

Circling back to our earlier story about the relationship between Boeing and the Pike Place Market, remember that it was Joe Desimone, a truck farmer, who persuaded Bill Boeing to keep his airplane company in Seattle by selling him the land for an airport along the Duwamish. The result was that Boeing stayed, grew, and prospered in Seattle, and so did Seattle itself, with tens of thousands of manufacturing and engineering jobs. By and large, Boeing people weren't sophisticated eaters, but they did have to be fed, and that fact created and nurtured today's supply network of farms. In the late 1990s, Phil Condit, who had a reputation as something of a playboy, took over as Boeing's CEO, and he grew tired of bumping into his ex-wife at social events. Seattle was too small a town, so the company invented a story about needing to have its headquarters at a greater distance from its manufacturing facilities and moved itself to Chicago. Right.

Schultz's Dribbling Goodbye

There once was a basketball team in Seattle, a men's professional team called the Seattle Supersonics. In 1979, they even won the NBA championship. The team's founder and original owner, Sam Schulman, had sold the team to billboard magnate Barry Ackerly, who passed it on, in 2001, to a local group headed by Howard Schultz. For Uncle Howard, the Sonics were a pet that he loved for about a year. The pet did not love him back, neither did the city and state; neither did the fans. Five years later, Schultz bailed; he sold the team for $350 million to a Kansas City investment group, and when the Legislature refused to support construction of a new arena in Renton ($500 million would have been the price tag), the team was moved to Oklahoma.

Along the way, the new Sonics owners broke their lease at KeyArena in Seattle and paid a $45 million penalty . Not nearly enough, fans said, but they reserved their most bitter barbs for Schultz and his legal maneuvers. ESPN's Frank Hughes called him "angry, bitter and maddeningly defiant, like a petulant child who decided to take his toy and go home. Only, in this case, he quite obviously threw his toy down a drainage ditch and stalked home while boldly misrepresenting the truth, telling everybody they could still play with the toy.." Today, ten years after the Sonics left town, there is neither a new basketball team, nor a new stadium. Ask around Seattle: rightly or wrongly, fans blame Schultz.

And even if you're no fan of professional sports, you'll find plenty of evidence of Schultz's pathological behavior in the ever-shifting landscape of candy and coffee at Starbucks stores.

Tim's Crunchy Goodbye

When the Frito-Lay folks made us forget what thick-cut chips tasted like. Tim Kennedy remembered, and 30 years ago he and his family started making small batches of extra-crunchy potato chips. Within two years they were named "best in Seattle," and went on to win national recognition. Tim's started expanding into different flavors, almost two dozen over the years, but always sold in the signature red-and-white striped bag.

Today Tim's Snacks (they also produce popcorn) is a unit of Pinnacle Foods, a giant company that oversees a string of frozen and shelf-stable grocery-store products with annual sales of $2.5 billion that is itself part of the Blackstone Group private equity portfolio. Nalley's is there as well, tucked under the Birdseye label. How'd it get there?

If It's Nalley's, It's Gone Too

Back in 1903, a 13-year-old Croatian immigrant named Marcus Narancic arrived in New York with 15 cents in his pocket. He couldn't speak a word of English. He took several jobs: in a steel mill, as a meat packer, and finally in a hotel kitchen where he moved from kitchen flunky to pantry boy to fry cook. He became a chef on the Milwaukie Railroad's "Olympian," their train from Chicago to Tacoma, and ended up working at the Bonneville Hotel in Tacoma. The culinary rage at the time, on the east coast at least, were sliced potatoes, deep-fried "Sararatoga Chips," which young Marcus learned how to make, using the potatoes that grew out his back door in the Puyallup Valley. In 1918, Marcus Narancic rented a storeroom behind his apartment for $5 a month and began selling his chips from a basket, door-to-door, to households and grocery stores.

Marcus soon began adding other food products: pickles (from cucumbers also grown in the Puyallup Valley), then beans for chili, then salad dressings, and so on. He changed his name to Nalley and his company built a factory in the canyon off State Route 16, "Nalley Valley." The factory grew and grew until it became one of Tacoma's largest employers.

Marcus Nalley died in 1962. Today there are over 1,300 food products under the Nalley label, ranging from pickles to canned foods to salad dressing and peanut butter. Canned chili is the biggest seller although Nalley's itself is no more. In 2011, it passed into the hands of a large corporation (Agrilink, which was acquired by Dean Foods) and the Tacoma facility was abandoned. Then another, larger still, named Pinnacle, which was buying up "iconic" American brands like Duncan Hines, Birds Eye, and Mrs. Butterworth's.

Pinnacle Foods, in turn, had been acquired in 2007 by a private equity outfit, Blackstone Group, with very deep pockets (close to $100 billion, mostly technology and life sciences). Food? Well, sort of an anomaly, it turned out.

So this is what happens when your jar of pickles, your bag of chips, or your can of chili loses its independence. You can't really blame anyone. It's not as if Marcus Nalley intended to betray the trust you put in him or his family; it wasn't a deliberate betrayal, at any rate. Nalley's was once an icon of local food, and then? Then it wasn't. It ceased to be. Long before it closed the plant in South Tacoma, long before the pickles started coming from India, long before its slow, sad decline as a regional brand, Nalley's became infected with the cancer of ambition, a cancer that required transfusions of money from banks and investors. It wasn't failure that infected the company; on the contrary, it was success. The Nalley's that survives today, in an obscure corner of a giant holding company, didn't lose its way because it was trying to survive hard times; rather, it sold its soul because it was lured toward the dazzling light of success.

And the Steer She Rode In On

Not what you expect to see taped in the window, when what you want is a couple of grass-fed pork chops for dinner: "Due to circumstances beyond our control, we are closed until further notice." With that notice, Bill the Butcher shuttered all six of its Seattle shops.

Chew on this: the meat biz is a trillion-dollar industry that employs half a million people in the US alone. It is decentralized, with tens of thousands of farms, finishing lots, processors, and distributors. "Grass-fed" beef is maybe one percent of that, but it's a growing segment, and this is where we find the stylish and upbeat J'Amy Owens, a guru of retail who created the first Starbucks stores for Howard Schultz, then went on to found The Retail Group (which developed the Laptop Lane concept for airports).For a time she had a close personal relationship with William von Scheidau, a charismatic meat man who ran a shop called Bill the Butcher. When their affair broke up, she fought off a breach-of-contract lawsuit and retained the butcher shop name and concept, which eventually become a six-unit chain in Seattle with plans to open new markets in Oregon.

As it happened, the planned expansion into the Portland area never took place. And plans to take over her Montana-based meat supplier, Great Northern Cattle Company, never happened either.

The end came swiftly enough. Employees and suppliers weren't paid for several weeks. BTB's normally active social media campaign went silent. But there had been signs even before then. Sunny Kobe Cook, the founder of Sleep Country USA, posted on her personal blog that BTB's chief executive, J'Amy Owens, had stiffed her on a $50,000 personal loan; the *Seattle Times* had reprinted Cook's frustrated posts. Lots of dirty linen, the kind that doesn't usually get aired, but BTB--very rare for such a small enterprise--was publicly traded: the information had to be public. And this scrutiny allowed a rare glimpse into what happens when an under-capitalized business hits the rocks. And when the promoter of an old-fashioned concept (your friendly neighborhood butcher) empties the till and pulls an old-fashioned vanishing act. Not within the current meaning of Grab-n-Go.

GROUPON: Daily Deals for Cheapskates, Poison for Owners

What does Groupon have in common with Tippr, LivingSocial, Amazon Local, TravelZoo, BuyWithMe, Goldstar, and Retrevo? Well, it's the 900-lb gorilla, for one thing; it literally owns the "daily deal" market. This is not a good idea to begin with, but, worse, Groupon seriously thinks of itself as "the operating system of local commerce."

It's not hard to imagine that a website founded on the principle of "lowest possible price" got a foothold in the tough economic times that followed the financial crisis of 2008. (Parenthetical note: Walmart, for years, used "lowest price" as its slogan, but even Walmart has changed. The company now says it helps customers save money so they can "live better." Even their own employees, no doubt, who qualify for food stamps.) For a nation of uncertain consumers, in 2008, a "good deal" seemed like something worth seeking out; nobody wants a "bad deal," and nobody wants to spend more than they have to, even if it's just for a hot dog.

Suddenly, daily deals began to flood email inboxes around the country as hapless retailers fell for the argument that the only reason they had empty tables or empty aisles or empty tanning beds was that their prices were too high. Lazik eye surgery? Too expensive. Half off? Well, maybe. (More likely, maybe not.)

Groupon festers, like a tenacious, evil weed. It has survived where others have rotted away or failed completely. Its stock, which flew high in early, post-IPO days, tanked quickly once greedy investors realized that every person in the USA would have to do $1,500 worth of business with Groupon in the course of a lifetime to sustain the company's insane valuation. Even now, Groupon runs 40,000 deals every day and claims 43 million "subscribers" who delete their annoying emails.

But they're so confident, these SOBs. They've got well over 100 people working in Seattle alone, 11,000 worldwide. They call on merchants and offer the moon: quick cash and the promise of a full house. A horde of cheapskates descends, rides roughshod over the place, tips badly or not at all, and leaves for ever. Understand that, business owners: Groupon customers *never* come back. Ever.

Savvy restaurateurs used to stand in front of the door and offer passers by a $20 bill to come in and try the food, and make up their investment on the course of future visits. Now they realize that they lose ten bucks on every Groupon customer but those customers have no incentive to come back because they're only interested in the next deal. Rather than lose again, those owners should be standing at the door offering the Groupon diner $20 if they *don't* come in. Cost is the same.

Please don't whine to me about owners being business people with freedom of choice. No one holds a gun to anybody's head in this business. You will never find Terresa Davis of Blueacre Seafood, for example, offering a Groupon deal. But she's the exception; she's done the math. She knows there's no magic bullet. But the 40,000 owners who put up deals every day on Groupon? Can they all be suckers in a giant bunco game? Well, yeah.

Finally, Finally, the End. We Mean It, It's Over.

The End may not come in our lifetimes, but it will almost surely come in the next century or two.

Some 800 miles west of the Cascade mountain range, several hundred miles at sea, runs the Cascadia subduction zone. When the "Big One" hits, when the fault line cracks, drops, and rebounds, the resulting tsunami, a wave 100 feet high and 700 miles wide, will wash across the Pacific coast within 15 minutes and obliterate everything west of Interstate 5 between northern California and the Canadian border.

The west coast of Vancouver Island will be worst-hit. Seattle will have some protection while the waters wash across the San Juans and funnel through Puget Sound between Port Townsend and Whidbey Island to the north, and up the Chehalis River valley toward Olympia on the south. Salt water would inundate the fields and farmlands, poisoning the soil for a generation; only the immutable oysters would survive.

FEMA, the agency in charge of disaster planning, says 40,000 people could drown and seven million more could be left homeless. The Alaska Way viaduct, should any of it remain standing at that point, would be obliterated, along with the Space Needle and most of downtown Seattle. Clearly, very little of what's in this book would be left unscathed. The residents of hilltop communities might make it unscathed, and the farmers of eastern Washington, but the economy of the Pacific Northwest would collapse, and we will all be forked, once and for all

CONCLUSION

In the course of these pages, we've chronicled the progress of food from the fields farms, and waters where it was harvested and watched it closely as it moved from markets to kitchens to plates, and, ultimately, to the trash. That's life. Along the way we've met people from Seattle's past and present who have played important roles in that process. The stories in this book may seem skeptical, cynical, and critical, even occasionally snarky and sarcastic, but they are not intentionally nasty.

Most of those historic and iconic figures have contributed in creative and laudable fashion. Some of their stories are familiar, others haven't been fully told before. Wally Opdycke, who started Ste. Michelle; Gordon Bowker, whose epiphany at a café in Rome led to the creation of Starbucks; Jerilyn Brusseau, who baked the first Cinnabon; Maria Coassin, who to this day bakes Christmas panettone in downtown Seattle; Jay Friedman, a sex lecturer who became an expert on Asian food; Jon Rowley, a one-time fisherman who taught Seattle about salmon, oysters, and peaches; Armandino Batali, who took up the craft of salumi-making after retiring from a career at Boeing; Kurt Beecher Dammeier, who is leading us all to a new appreciation for pure food.

But there are always a few bad actors, and in the food biz, most of the bad stuff involves money. Take Howard Schultz, whose inability to tell the truth about the origins of Starbucks, and whose lack of long-term focus are nothing short of maddening. J'Amy Owens pulled an old-fashioned till-tap, but Comvest Partners did far worse, bankrupting a family company, Haggen, with $200 million in real estate assets for no apparent reason, other than the greed of its private-equity partners.

Now, not all private equity buyouts are bad. For the owners of Metropolitan Markets, Endeavour Capital offered a clean exit strategy. For the founders of DeLille Cellars, Bacchus Capital got the winery moving again. But we know that it's often greed, not idealism, that drives businesses to lower costs, increase revenues, or maximize profits (none of which are necessarily bad things), greed that creates a dismal workplace, ruins products that were once attractive, and drives away customers. Distant MBAs in suits play with companies as if they were matchbox cars. And while short-sighted owners complain about "regulation," far-sighted owners embrace change and take care of their employees as well as their customers.

Sure, food needs to look attractive on the plate, but c'mon, chef: does your banker honestly believe your guests want their plates garnished with petals of violets? Then by keep those tweezers handy, because I'll fight you with my fork.

INDEX

13 Coins	95
21 Acres	265
5-Spot	111
A Boat A Whale & A Walrus	246
Acres of Clams	144
Adams, Connie	259
Agrodolce	119
Albertson's	49
Allen, Paul	13
Allrecipes.com	255
Amazon	89
Amazon Prime	175
Anderson, Jeremy & Josh	95
Anderson, Stuart	171
Annheuser-Busch InBev	201
Anthony's Pier 66	161
Anthony's Restaurants	144
Antinori, Piero	193
Anton, Anthony	237
Apples	28
Applied Fizzics	84
Aqua by El Gaucho	161
AquAdvantage Salmon	274
Art of the Table	121
Atkinson, Greg	167, 252
Atlas Foods	111
Auction of Washington Wines	183
Azteca	112
B&O Espresso	220
Bacchus Capital Management	195
Bagley, Terry	41
Bakke, Kent	82
Ballard Bees	61
Banchero, Stephan III	234
Banh, Eric & Sophie	129, 153
Bantle, Louis	181
Bar Cantinetta	115
Bar Cotto	101
Bar del Corso	142
Bar Ferd'nand	105
Bar Melusine	143
Bar Sajor	105
Bar Vacilando	122
Barbeau, Monique	116
Bardinelli, Luciano	94
Barn2Door	33-34
Barolo	124

Baron, Christophe	187
Barrett, Martin	269
Baseler, Ted	183
Bassetti, Gwen	249
Bastille (Café)	108
Batali, Armandino	67
Bateau	143, 148
Baty, Dan	184
Bavarian Meats	68
Bayless, Alec	180
Beardslee Public House	207
Beecher's Cheese	70
Beeliner Diner	111
Beer Halls	202
Behnke, Renee	55
Belickis, William	125
Bergeron, Victor ("Trader Vic")	98
Betz, Bob & Cathy	185
Bezos, Jeff	89, 116
Bieler, Charles	187
Biesold family	42
Big Mario Pizza	140
Bigelow, Fran	81
Bill the Butcher	280
Billet, Maxime	263
Billow, Charlie	41
Biodynamic winemaking	195-6
Bite of Seattle	168
Black Angus steakhouses	171
Black Bottle	122
Bloom, Leora	254
Blueacre	145
Boat Street Cafe	143
Boat Street Pickles	62
Bodinet, Mark	114, 163
Boeing	39, 277
Boiroux, Jacques	49
Book Larder	243
Boudreau, Jamie	211
Bowen, Ray	41
Bowker, Gordon	116, 201, 214
Brasserie Pittsbourg	92
Brazilian steakhouses	149
Bread for the World	271
Breiman, Roy	163
Brewster, David	243
Breyley, Denise	33
Brindley, Erin	172
Britt's Pickles	62

Brooke, James 44
Brophy, Erin 209
Brottman, Jeff 89
BroVo Spirits 209
Brown, Stephen 57
Browne, Andrew 184
Brusseau, Jerilyn 75
Budweiser (Teavana deal) 217
Burger, David 25
Burgess, Joey 107
Butcher's Table 147

Cactus 112
Cafe Flora 115
Cafe Juanita 167
Cafe Nordo 172
Cafe Presse 117
Caffe Vita 140
Cake Spy 81
Calf & Kid 73
Callaghan, Adam 259
Canlis (restaurant) 95, 97, 211
Canlis family 97
Canlis salad 97
Carlile, Brett 205
Carpenter, Wayne 199
Carter, Brian 189
Casas-Breaux, Marco 149
Cascadia subduction zone 282
Casey, Kathy 116
Cedar Grove 233
Cedarbrook Lodge 114, 164
Centerplate 100
Centioli, Gill 54
Chaleur Estate 194
Charlie's Produce 40-41
Charters, Bridget 262
Chateau Ste. Michelle 182, 183
Chef'n 84
Cherry St. Coffee House 220
Chinoise 137
Chow Foods 111
Cicero, Providence 146
Cinnabon 75
Cinque Terre 124
Circadia 125
Claridge, Merissa Firnstahl 110
Climenhage, Richard 62
Clore, Walter 179
Club apples 28
Coassin, Maria 76
Coaston, Leslie, Laurie 121

Cole, Kathryn 195
Collins, Shirley 55
Columbia River locks 31
Columbia Winery 184
Comet Tavern 140
Comvest Parners 50-51
Cone, Adam 141
Consolidated Restaurants 161
Cook, Langdon 250
Cook, Sunny Kobe 280
Cookbooks 245
Copperleaf 164
Copperworks Distilling 208
Corfini Gourmet 44
Cosleycone, Aaron 141
Costco 42, 89
Country Breakfast (Snqoualmie) 165
Cowed (book) 267
Cox, Steven & Justin 212
Craft Beer Alliance 201
Cramer, Kirby 181
Creative Ice 212
Crowd Cow 153
Cupcake Royale 78
Curtis, Chris 53
Cutters 109, 159

Dale, Chad 143
Dammeier, Kurt Beecher 70, 147, 271
Daniel's Broiler 148
Darigold 224
Davenport, Dana 81
Davis, Kevin & Terresa 145
del Corso, Jerry 142
Delancey Pizza 141
DeLaurenti's 54
DeLille Cellars 194
Derschang, Linda 112
Desimone, Joe 38-9, 277
Dewey, Bill 19
Diane's Market Kitchen 262
Dick's Burgers 170
Dilettante Chocolate 81
Dillon, Matt 105, 113
Dimas, Monica 203
Dinah's Cheese 24-5, 73
Dinner Theater 172, 173
Dino's Pizza 141
Don the Beachcomber 98
Doppelt, Adam 257
Dorfman, Barnaby 256

Douglas, Tom (T-Doug)   14, 100, 102, 173
Drohman, Jim   117
Dry Fly Distillery   204
Dry Soda   222
Duke's Chowder House   146
Dupar, Lisa   246
Durbin, Brian   122

Easton, Mike   118
Eat Seattle tours   265
Eater.com   259
Edgewater Hotel   161
Edible Seattle (book)   253
El Gaucho   95, 148
Elliott's Oyster House   161
Eltana Bagels   57
Emerick, Scott   151
Encore Restaurant Supply   228
Endolyne Joe   111
Enza Cucina Siciliana   116
Erickson, Renee   143, 246
Ernest Loves Agnes   107
Evolution Fresh   218-19

F2C2   238
Fardeen, Aakhil   174
Fare Start   262
Farmers Markets   52-53
Farmstr   33-34
Fat of the Land   251
Female Farmer Project   27
Fexy Media   258
Fields Oceans Ranches Kitchens   238
Finkel, Charles   181
Finkel, Charles & Rose Ann   197
Firefly Kitchens   62
Firnstahl, Tim   109-110
Fleischmann, Ken   204
Flinn, Kathleen   261
Flying Squirrel Pizza   142
Focus Brands   76
Fonte   220
Food Artisans (book)   254
Food Channel   113
Food Forest   22
Food Safety   268
Food-Related Websites   255
Foodista, com   256
FORKS   238
Four Fish (book)   12
Fran's Chocolate   81

Frank, Wiley & PK   133
Fried Chicken & Champagne   246
Friedman, Ben   106
Friedman, Jay   127-8
Frog Hollow Farm   29
Fugere, Joe   139
Full Circle Farms   26
Fuller's   116
FX McRory's   109

Gai's Bakery   54
Gaja, Angelo   193
Garagiste   190
Garvey, Mike   181
Gelatiamo   76
Gelato   77, 78
General Porpoise   143
Ghambari, Ali   220
Gibson, Karen   112
Gilday, Tim   228
Gillis, Brad   106
Gilmor, Gay   203
Give Safe   266
Glaziere, Marsha   221
Goedhart, Sarah   188
Golden Beetle   119
Goldfinch Tavern   147
Good Fish   247
Gordon, Daisely   113
Gore, Bruce   14
Gould, Budd   144
Goyal, Deepinder   257
Graham, Michaela   169
Grand Central Bakery   249
Grapes, value as a crop   52-53
Greenberg, Paul   12
Grocerants   176
Groupon   168, 281
Guild Seattle   107, 140

Haggen   51-52
Haglund, Ivar   144
Hakala, Troy   203
Hall, Jody (Bite of Seattle)   168
Hall, Jody (Cupcake Royale)   78
Halverson, Terry   29, 48-50
Hamilton, Lara   245
Hanauer, Jerry, Nick, Adrian   142
Hardy, Jeremy   111
Harris, Marian   66
Harvest Vine   115

Hayes, Denis 267
Heathman Hotel Kirkland 164
Heavy Restaurant Group 112
Hedges, Tom & Anne-Marie 188
Heitzeberg, Joe 153
Hellner, Eric 150
Henderson, Josh 103
Herbfarm 162
Herbivoracious 250
Hess, Robert 212
Hewitson, Katy 276
Hinckley, Pamela 102
Hines, Maria 119
Hipkiss, Mark 150
Historic Seattle Restaurants 91
Hofmann, Matt 206
Hofstatter, Lynn, Max 68
Holcomb, David 84
Hollywood Tavern 103
Homegrown (Sandwich shops) 106
Hot Stove Society 262
Howell, Makini 113
Howie, John 106, 150, 159, 207
Hunt Club 164
Huxley-Wallace Collective 103

Il Corvo 118
Il Gabbiano 118
Il Terrazzo Carmine 96
Imagine Food 263
In Season (book) 252
Infierno 151, 152
Ipanema 149
Isernio, Frank 69
Ivar's Acres of Clams 144

Jake O'Shaughnessey's 109
James, Miles 69
Jitterbug 111
John Howie Steak 150
Johnson, Wayne 113.262
Jones, Grant 59-60
Jordan, Edouardo 69, 113-5

Kanlis, Nikolas 97
Kashiba, Shiro 40, 123, 134, 160
Katrusin, Ludo & Jana 202
Keener, Jay 152
Keff, Chris 95
Kennedy, Tim 66, 278
Keurig 229

Kingen, Jerry 158
Kingfish Cafe 121
Kissel, François 92
Klaus, Sharelle 222
Klock, Kevin 223
Kmitta, Mariah 136
Komen, Rich 109
Kosseff, Jake 125
Krainick, Mike & Leann 231
Kukuruza Popcorn 59-60
Kumar, Jonathan 266
Kupers, Karl 32
Kurovsky, Larry 112
Kurtwood Farms 24-5, 73

La Ferme Aux Anes 146
La Figa (book) 248
La Marzocco espresso 82
La Panzanella 65
La Vita è Bella 116
Lagana pasta 100
Lajeunesse, Jason 107
Lake, David 184
Lam's Seafood Market 46
Lamb, Emerson 206
Landscape of Coffee (book) 221
Lark 124
Larry's Markets 48
Latham, Geoff 43
Lavigne, Sheri 73
Lavonne, Diane 262
Le Petit Cochon 121
Le Pichet 117
Leighton, Brennon 187
Lengenberg, Uli 69
Lev, Howard 62
Levy, Peter 111
Lichtenberger, Ray 160
Liedholm, Eric 207
Lightner, Jill 253
Lill, Charles & Greg 194
Linda's Tavern 112
Linker, Chris 122
Lish 174
Little Uncle 133
Lost Lake 140
Loulay 115
Lowry, Ethan 153, 257
Luc 115
Ludvigsen, Wayne 14, 41-42
Lummi Island 252

Luster, Corky 61
Lyden, George 71-2
Lyons, Zach 238

Mackay, Chad 148
Mackay, Paul 95
Mackie, Leslie 249
Maclean, Doug 223
Macleod's Pub 108
Maclise, Deming 108, 202
Macrina Bakery 249
MacWilliams, James 211
Mad Pizza 142
Maggie's Bluff 109
Maiocco, Janelle 33
Mama Lil's Peppers 62
Marché (Bainbridge Island) 167
Marine Hardware 101
Market Sketchbook 40
Marler, Bill 268
Marshall, Monica 203
Marteau Absinthe 209
Marx Foods 44
Marx, Justin 44
Mashiko 135
McConnell, Mike 107, 138
McCormick & Schmick 111
McCune, Liz 265
McDermott, Kate 80
McDonald, Par 54
McHugh, Mick 109-110
McKinney, Larrry, Mark, Dave 48
McTigue, Dorene Centioli 54
Mehren, Tom 259
Meinert, Dave 107
Melang, Zak 108
Melina, Mamma 124
Menghe, Umberto 96
Meredith Publishing 256
Merlino, Angelo 42
Metropolitan Grill 95, 150
Metropolitan Market 29, 48-50
Michael Rogers 264
Michaelenko, Nina 149
Miller, Jeff 25-26
Miller's Guild 152
Mioposto 112
Mischief distillery 230
Missoula Floods 188
Mistral Kitchen 125
Mocha Café 81

Modernist Cuisine (book) 254
Moen, Albert 85
Moldboard Plow 34
Mondello 116
Monteillet Fromagerie 74
Moodie, Donna 113
Moriguchi, Tomio 45
Moscrip, Duke 146
Mount Townsend Creamery 74
Mulkern, Audra 27
Murphy, Tamara 248
Music, Debra 79
Myhrvold, Nasthan 254

Nalley's 66, 278
Narancic, Marcus 278
Natkin, Michael 250
NAWICO 183
Nella 85
Neumark, John 125
Nguyen, Thoa 137
Nicky USA 43
Nims, Cynthia 246
Noroeste 103
Novello, Nick 104
Novilho 149
Novotny, Naomi 63
Nutt, Micah 208
O'Brien, Julie 62
Oberto, Art 69
Oceanaire 145
Oddfellows 112
Odom, Paul 220
Oh Boy! Oberto 69
Old Chaser Farm 105
Oleson, Jessie 81
Omigod Peach Pie 80
Opdycke, Wally 181, 183
Open Table 239
Opper Melang Restaurants 108
Opper, Nathan 108
Optimism Brewing 203
Orfeo 145
Orondo Ruby cherries 30
Owens, Earl 95
Oyster Bill Whitbeck 21
Oyster Wines 20
Oysters 18-21
Oysters (cookbook) 246

P Patches 26
PACCAR 65
Pacific Coast Feather 142
Pacific Food Importers (PFI) 47
Pagliacci Pizza 54
Palisade 109, 159
Palomino 109, 159
Palouse wheat 31, 52
Panettone 76
Parker, Jason 208
Parrat, Gerard 63
Pasciuto, Ciro 65
Pasta & Co. 147
Pavlovsky, Stan 256
Peach-O-Rama 29
Pecos Pit 159
Pellegrini, Angelo 23
Pence Orchards 29
Perdue, Andy 193
Perry, Julien 176
Peterson Company 47
Pettit, Brandon 141
Pham, Yenvy 126
Phelps, Dina 265
Pho Bac 126
Pickerell, David 205
Pierris, Lois 220
Pigott, Mark 65
Pike Brewing 197
Pike Place Market 38-40
Pinkaow, Mark & Picha 132
Pinnacle Foods 279
Place, Dominique 63
Podgorski, Terry 172
Poffenroth, Don 204
Pogetti, John 93
Poquitos 108
Port Chatham Salmon 64
Portlock Smoked Salmon 64
POS (Point of Sale) Systems 241
Poulet Bleu 58, 163
Poulet Galore 103
Precept Brands 184
Price, Jeremy 143
Pure Food (book) 271
Purple Cafe & Wine Bar 112

Quality Athletics 103
Queen Anne Beer Hall 202
Quillasascut Farm 74

Rachel's Ginger Beer 203
Rainier Beer (TV commercial) 214
Ranniger, "Wild Bill" 146
Rautureau, Thierry 115
Ray, Joe 252
Ray's Boathouse 41, 146, 160
Red Cow 147
Red Mountain 188
Red Robin burger chain 159
Reder, Paul 202
Redhook beer 201
Regence Blue Shield 261
Reinhaus 108
Reservation apps 240
Restaurant Reviews 274
Restaurants Unlimited (RUI) 109, 159
Rheinhaus 202
Rhodes, Dick 48
Richmond, BC 22, 53
Richmond, Tselani 260
Ricketts, Whitney & Kim 245
Ridgeway, Lyla 68
Rimmerman, Jon 190
Rione XIII 101
Rivera, Eric 104
Rocher, Perfecte 119-20
Rogano, Pino 69
Ronspies, Derek & Dunstin 120-21
Rosella 47
Rosellini, Victor 93
Rover's 115
Rowley, Jon 11, 20, 29
RSI (Restaurant Services Inc.) 110
Rubinfeld, Arthur 218
Russell, Francia 100

Sahale Snackers 64
Saito, Hajime 135
Salish Lodge 165
Salmon 11 –17
Salmon in the Trees (book) 17
Salmon, Copper River 11
Salmon, Keta 16
Salmon, Skuna Bay 16
Salmon, Yukon 15
Salt Works 63
Salty's on Alki 158
Salumi Cured Meats 67
Sanctis, Edmond 64
Savor Seattle Tours 264
Sazerac 145

Scheehser, Brian 164
Schroeter, Josh 64
Schultz, Howard 89, 116, 215, 277
Schwartz, Lindsay 148
Sea and Smoke 252
Seastar 106
Seattle Caviar 63
Seattle Chefs Collaborative 238
Seattle Chocolate 81
Seattle Public Utilities 232
Seattle Underground Market 169
Seattle Wine Society 192
SeattleDining.com 259
SeattleSoWhite 273
Selengut, Becky 247
Settebello 94
Seven Beef 151
Sharks 17
Sharples, Lisa & Cliff 258
Shen, Angela 264
Shepherd's Grain 32
Sherrow, Dale & Betsy 63
Shipman, Paul 201
Shiro (Memoir) 134
Shoup, Allen 181, 182
Show Me Seattle Tours 264
Shrimp, burrowing 19
Shroom (book) 247
Silverman, Al 168
Simone, Tiberio 248
Sinegal, Jim 89
Sinko, Brad 71
Sitka & Spruce 105
Six Seven 161
Skagit Valley Malting 198, 199-200
Skillet 103, 104
Sky City 158
Smart Catch 13
Smeraldo, Carmine 96
Smith 112
Smith Brothers Dairy 224
Smith, Charles 186
Smith, Holly 167
Smithco Meats 152
Snack Partners 66
Snoqualmie Falls 165
Sodo Wines 269
Sorenson, Orlin 205
Sorrentino, Enza 116
Sound Spirits 206
Southpaw Pizza 124

Space Needle (restaurant) 158
Spady, Dick 170
Sparkling Ice 223
Sprouting Farm 106
Staple & Fancy Mercantile 101
Starbucks 89, 213-17
Starks, Riley 58
Steelhead Diner 145
Steinbrueck, Victor 39-40
Stemilt 28
Stenson, Murray 210
Stepanian, Armen 227
Steves, Rick 271
Stewardship Partners 25
Stone, Gwydion 209
Stone, Steve 206
Stoneburner 108
Stout 202
Stowell, Ethan 14
Stowell, Ethan & Angela 100-101
Stowell, Kent 100
Stratton, Jason 123
Sugar Mountain 147
Sugar Mountain Foundation 271
Sun Capital 109, 159
Sundstrom, John 124
Sur La Table 55
Sushi Chinoise 137
Sushi Kashiba 135

Talking Rain 223
Tallulah's 112
Tam, Jennifer 242
Tanaka, Eric (ET) 102
Tarsan I Jane 119-20
Tavolata 101
Taylor, Bill 18-21
Teatro ZinZanni 173
Teavana 217
Terra Plata 248
Thai Curry Simple 132
The Innkeeper 122
The Whale Wins 143
Theo Chocolate 79
Thompson, Jean 81
Tilth (restaurant) 119
Tim's Cascade Chips 66, 278
Timmermeister, Kurt 24, 73
Torrefazzione Coffee 54
Transcontinental Railroad 7
Traunfeld, Jerry 113, 163

Trellis	164
Trenor, Casson	135
Triple Door	77, 130
Triple-B Corp (Charlie's)	41
Truffles	198
Tutta Bella	139
UberEats	175
Uli's Famous Sausages	69
Upchurch, Chris	194
Urbanspoon.com	257
US Corps of Engineers	31
Uwajimaya	45
Van Dyck, Carrie	163
Varchetta, Salvo, Leo, Roberto	124
Vellotti Fine Foods	47
Vellotti, Mario	140
Verdi, Pasqualina	54
Vescovi, Brian	142
Via Tribunali	107, 138
Voelsgen, Mhairi	209
Voilà! Bistro	116
von Scheidau, William	280
Von's 1000 Spirits	110
Voodoo Vintners	195-9
VPN Vera Pizza Napolitana	138, 9

Wallace, Evan	83
Walrus & Carpenter	143
Wann Yen Shaved Ice	132
Ward, Jim & Elaine	95
Warren, Dr. Gerry	192
Washington Cherries	30
Weber, Chris	163
Weimann, James	108, 202
Westland Distillery	206
Westward	103
Wetherell, Sheri.	256
Wetzel, Blaine	252
Whinney, Joe	79
Whitbeck, Bill ("Oyster Bill")	21
White Moustache tours	265
Whole Foods Markets	33
Widmer beer	201
Wild Ginger	77, 130
Wildwood Spirits	207
Williams, Brady	98
Willie Green's Farm	25-26
Wilridge Winery	115
Wilson, Jason	152, 230
Windjammer	146
Wiserg Harvester	229
Wizenberg, Molly	141
Wohlers, Ray	160
Woodbourne, Lloyd	184
Woodinville Wine Country	193
Woodiville Whiskey	205
World Pizza	141
WSU Extension Programs	27
Yelp	8, 275
Yoder, Rick & Ann	77, 78, 130
Zaine, Alia	119-20
Zimmerman, Bill & Lola	162
Zimmerman, Ron	162
Zomato	257
Zoske, Mark	63

CREDITS

Portions of this book have appeared, often in different form, in print and online, in Seattle Business, Crosscut, Pacific Publishing's neighborhood newspapers, Seattle Dining, Eater, Cornichon, Belltown Messenger, Delicious City, Edible Seattle, and Home Grown Seattle.

Photographs of Luciano Bardinelli (p. 94), Ivar Haglund (p. 144), François Kissel (p. 92), Angelo Pellegrini (p. 23), Victor Rosellini (p. 93) , Carmine Smeraldo (p. 96), Victor Steinbrueck (p. 39), Pasqualina Verdi (p. 54) all © by Bob Peterson and used with his kind permission. BobPeterson.com

Photograph of Mark & Brian Canlis (p.97) courtesy of Canlis
Photograph of Dr. Walter Clore (p. 179) courtesy of the Clore Center
Photograph of Armen Stepanian (p. 227) by K. Lindsay for Fremocentrist.com.
Photograph of Bill Marler (p. 268) courtesy of Marler Clark LLC
Photograph of Denis Hayes (p. 267) courtesy of Lisa Boyer
Photo of Kent Bakke (p. 82) courtesy of La Marzocco
Photo of Kevin & Terresa Davis (p. 145) courtesy of Orfeo
Photo os Tim Kennedy (p. 276) courtesy Tim's Cascade Chips
Photo of Deepinder Goyal (p 217) courtesy of Zomato
Photo of Jonathan Kumar (p. 266) courtesy of Jonathan Kumar
Photo of Audra Mulkern (p 227) courtesy of Julin Li
Drawing of Denise Breyley (page 66) courtesy of Whole Foods Market

Remaining photographs by the author.

ABOUT THE AUTHOR

Ronald Holden has lived and worked in Seattle for 40 years as a reporter and editor for print, broadcast and online media. A graduate of Yale, he served as a news producer at King Broadcasting. As *Seattle Weekly's* executive editor he created its first restaurant pages. With Glenda Holden he wrote five early guidebooks to the Pacific Northwest, among them the award-winning "Northwest Wine Country." For 15 years he also operated a luxury wine-touring company, France In Your Glass. In 2011 he won the coveted Collio Prize for his international wine writing.

Holden contributes regularly to a variety of regional publications, including Seattle Business, City Living, Seattle Dining, and Crosscut. His personal journal about food, wine, and travel, Cornichon.org, was named one of the ten best food blogs on the Internet by About.com. Seattle Spin singled out Cornichon for "Best coverage of the local restaurant scene." In 2014 he published "HOME GROWN SEATTLE."

Made in the USA
San Bernardino, CA
09 September 2016